COMICS AND THE ORIGINS OF MANGA

COMICS AND THE ORIGINS OF MANGA

A Revisionist History

EIKE EXNER

RUTGERS UNIVERSITY PRESS
NEW BRUNSWICK, CAMDEN, AND NEWARK, NEW JERSEY,
AND LONDON

Library of Congress Cataloging-in-Publication Data

Names: Exner, Eike, author.
Title: Comics and the origins of manga : a revisionist history / Eike Exner.
Description: First edition. | New Brunswick : Rutgers University Press, [2022] | Includes
    bibliographical references and index.
Identifiers: LCCN 2021009090 | ISBN 9781978827226 (paperback) | ISBN
    9781978827769 (cloth) | ISBN 9781978827233 (epub) | ISBN 9781978827240 (mobi)
    | ISBN 9781978827257 (pdf)
Subjects: LCSH: Comic books, strips, etc.—Japan.
Classification: LCC PN6790.J3 E96 2022 | DDC 741.5/952—dc23
LC record available at https://lccn.loc.gov/2021009090

A British Cataloging-in-Publication record for this book is available from the British
Library.

♾ The paper used in this publication meets the requirements of the American National
Standard for Information Sciences—Permanence of Paper for Printed Library Materials, ANSI Z39.48-1992.

www.rutgersuniversitypress.org

Manufactured in the United States of America

CONTENTS

ILLUSTRATIONS

PREFACE

When I started studying the history of comics and manga, I found it odd how two things so similar could have developed independently of each other. Reading my first book on the history of manga, Kure Tomofusa's "The Overall Picture of Modern Manga" (*Gendai manga no zentaizō*), I was strangely comforted to learn about the introduction of European caricature to Japan in the 1860s by Charles Wirgman, Japan correspondent for the *Illustrated London News*. *There* was a link between Euro-American comics and Japanese manga that seemed to explain their uncanny similarity. On second thought, however, this link did not explain why both had independently embraced speech balloons and rejected external narrative text in their respective developments. It was difficult to see how Wirgman's single-panel cartoons, which didn't much resemble a modern comic book, could have caused such a change. Were the similarities in form and function between comics and manga a coincidence after all?

I first learned about the existence of American comics translated into Japanese before World War II from Frederik L. Schodt's *Manga! Manga!* Most Japanese historiographies of manga, too, mentioned the translation of George McManus's *Bringing Up Father*, albeit usually in passing. I was—and still am—surprised that so little research has been undertaken regarding these translated comics. After all, it sounded as though these translations could have been an important factor in the resemblance between present-day American and Japanese comics. The fact that the appearance of Japanese manga in the United States and elsewhere is a comparatively recent phenomenon made the idea that hundreds of thousands of Japanese newspaper readers had been consuming American comic strips back in the 1920s even more intriguing.

Curious to find out more, I looked for additional early translated comic strips at the National Diet Library in Tokyo. I was astonished to discover that the American strips I found in Japanese prewar publications looked far more similar to today's Japanese comics than many of the works written and drawn by Japanese authors concurrently printed in the same publications. Despite this, and in stark contrast to the universally acknowledged influence of Charles Wirgman's caricatures on Japanese cartooning, no manga historiography has focused in depth on the influence of American newspaper strips on narrative manga.

In order to be able to survey more Japanese prewar publications, I took on a visiting faculty position at Josai International University and moved to Tokyo for two years, conducting research at the Diet Library and other Tokyo archives, the Kyoto International Manga Museum, and the Kawasaki City Museum. Since no comprehensive list of translated comics and their dates and places of publication existed, this research required examining more than a decade of content in microfilm reels for each of the most relevant and several minor Japanese publications from the 1920s and 1930s. As was to be expected given that not every publication featured American comics and that those which did publish them did not do so for the entire time period surveyed, much of this research turned out to be futile, but the laborious microfilm perusal provided such serendipitous finds as the numerous advertisements starring comics characters and the left-to-right manga discussed in this book. It is unlikely that my list of translated comic strips contains every single one published in prewar Japan, but readers will hopefully be as amazed by the number of entries as I was. I would be exceedingly happy if others were to build upon and expand this list in the future.

Just when I was glad to have solved one riddle that had puzzled me for years, I was confronted with another: that Japanese comics had come to resemble American ones because of the popularity of translations of the latter did not explain why no Japanese author had "figured out" on his own that you could make characters talk to each other on the page by using speech balloons. In order to find an answer to this question, I began to look more closely at the process by which American comics had come to incorporate speech balloons. Though most scholars agreed that Richard Felton Outcault started a trend of speech balloons with his famous *Yellow Kid* cartoon about the phonograph, there was almost no research on the time *between* this cartoon and the first comic strips that look recognizably like contemporary comics.

Scrolling through newspaper microfilm reels once more, I was surprised to find that it had taken more than two years after Outcault's cartoon for someone (Rudolph Dirks) to draw the first comic strip in which characters actually talk to each other. Rather than being the result of a single ingenious idea, sound-filled "audiovisual" comics turned out to be the product of a long and complex development during which cartoonists in the late nineteenth century processed the experience of seeing motion and hearing sound recorded and reproduced for the first time in history. The speech balloon seems like a deceptively simple device to us now, but this is merely because, having grown up with recording technology, we tend to underestimate the impact that it has had on society. As Kerim Yasar points out in *Electrified Voices* about the development and spread of sound-recording technology, "For the first time, sound recording and transmission allowed human beings to capture sound, reproduce it, replay it, and archive it. This was a transformative cultural and technological innovation of modernity, one whose importance has until recently been overlooked or downplayed, even by scholars of sound."[1] Prior to such technology, the idea of seeing and hearing characters move around and speak to each other on a page (even if—or perhaps precisely because—they do both only in our heads) must have been literally unthinkable. The radical newness of being able to reproduce human voices explains why even after American cartoonists began to use "sound images" (visual representations of sound) to make fun of the phonograph, it still took them several years to create the first audiovisual comics in which sound images were used to depict regular conversations. This is also why it took the success of American comics in Japan for Japanese artists to adopt this audiovisual form of storytelling: comics and manga as we know them today were the result of a revolution of the imagination that was so fundamental that it is hard for us to imagine a state of mind prior to it.

A NOTE ON IMAGES

Since the agreed-upon number of images for this book was sixty (fifty in grayscale, ten in color), I was unable to include images for all works referenced. Whenever possible, I have tried to provide links to additional images available online to which interested viewers can refer. Many early comic strips, both in the United States and in Japan, were partially colorized with red, yellow, and/or blue ink. These colorations are unfortunately lost in grayscale, but I have chosen to use the limited color slots mostly on images that cannot be found anywhere else, since many of the early American audiovisual comics I discuss can be viewed in their original coloration online in the image database of the Billy Ireland Cartoon Library and Museum, in my article "The Creation of the Comic Strip as an Audiovisual Stage in the *New York Journal* 1896–1900" (available at http://imagetext.english.ufl.edu/archives/v10_1/exner/), or using the website of the Library of Congress to access digitized copies of the *New York Journal*. Additional images supplementing *Comics and the Origins of Manga* can be found at the Instagram account @prewar_manga.

The images printed in the book sometimes vary greatly in quality due to the original material's state of preservation and the fact that many libraries and organizations that own paper copies of old newspapers and magazines in Japan restrict access to these materials, have either not digitized them at all or only monochromatically and at low resolutions, and do not offer image services. The National Diet Library, for example, allows patrons only to make physical printouts of digital images taken from microfilm reels, which one then has to redigitize, and this was the only way of procuring several of the images in this book. Much research on early graphic narrative would be immensely facilitated if more material in the public domain were digitized properly and made available to the public.

COMICS AND THE ORIGINS OF MANGA

INTRODUCTION

In and outside of Japan, "manga" is often discussed in opposition to "comics," as if the two were completely unrelated media. As Osvaldo Oyola points out as part of his report on the 2016 International Comics Arts Forum and my research presentation there, "Since Japanese translations of comics like *Bringing Up Father* and *Felix the Cat* were common and popular in Japan in the 20s and 30s, I am struck by those Western comics scholars who think of Japanese manga as emerging from some unknowable culture, like you need to be Doctor Strange to truly learn its mystic ways."[1] Unfortunately, it is not only Western comics scholars who think that Japanese comics are fundamentally different from "Western" ones, but there certainly exists a strong Orientalist bent to many discussions of manga, from some comics scholars' assertions that they "just don't get manga" to Scott McCloud's hypothesis that manga may be the product of meandering Eastern philosophy, in contrast to "our" "goal-oriented culture."[2] In McCloud's view, "The Japanese offer a vision of comics very different from our own."

In foreign countries, Japanese manga are commonly marketed to different audiences and sometimes even sold in different venues from American and other "Western" comics. Their otherness and Japaneseness are often emphasized, such as in the American translation of Ōtomo Katsuhiro's *Akira*, whose original title is written in the Roman alphabet, but whose U.S. edition additionally transliterated it into Japanese katakana. In *Akira*'s German translation, the protagonist in one scene even uses the word *sayonara* despite its absence from the original dialogue. It is as if the reader should be reminded that she is reading not just a comic but a *Japanese* comic—or perhaps not even a comic but a *manga*. Many Japanese critics have embraced this view of fundamental difference rather than deconstructed it. It has even been endorsed by the Japanese government via curricular guidelines that teach the connections between medieval picture scrolls and modern manga.

Across the rest of the world, *manga* has also become synonymous with the mainstream style of drawing seen in narrative comics in contemporary Japan. Books on *How to Draw Manga* are not designed to teach the reader how to create comics for the Japanese market but meant to teach a particular drawing *style* that has come to be identified with Japanese comics and anime. The extent to which a single drawing style has come to represent the majority of Japanese comics and animated films is itself a fascinating phenomenon deserving of critical inquiry,[3] but there is no intrinsic link between this particular drawing style (which has a history of its own) and the form of Japanese comics. It may be tempting to see in *the* "manga" drawing style an expression of some kind of unique Japanese essence, and it is perhaps one reason the view of manga as comics' other has become as common as it has. But as we will see, drawing styles in early audiovisual manga were diverse and show that the medium is not defined by the style in which it is drawn.

Because the word *manga* has come to mean different things to different people in different times, it's necessary to specify what denotation of *manga* is intended when discussing the subject. This book's central argument regarding manga is not about drawing styles, publishing formats, or content. It is also not about political cartoons or Hokusai's sketches but about *narrative* manga as a storytelling medium that depicts a story unfolding over multiple panels, generally without external narrative text and relying on transdiegetic content instead. What I mean by *transdiegetic* content is visual representations of phenomena that are themselves nonvisual—the most common being sound, usually represented by the aforementioned speech balloon. Film studies distinguishes between intradiegetic (*intra*, "inside"; *diegesis*, "the story world") content, which is perceptible to characters inside the story, and extradiegetic ("outside the story world") content, which is perceptible only to the audience. Transdiegetic ("crossing the story world") content depicts intradiegetic elements like sound and movement but does so in extradiegetic form, such as through speech balloons and motion lines. These devices represent sound and movement perceptible to story characters but do so in ways that are perceptible only to the reader (since characters cannot see the balloons or lines themselves). Figure I.1 shows a four-panel *Bringing Up Father* episode, colored to provide an illustration of the three different types.

Intradiegetic content has been left in black and white, whereas extradiegetic content has been shaded in blue and transdiegetic content in red. In order to demonstrate the profound difference between such an audiovisual comic and a picture story, figure I.2 shows the episode from figure I.1 turned into a picture story by deleting transdiegetic content and adding extradiegetic narration.

Note how static and lifeless the images appear in the picture-story version. Most importantly, in the picture story, the narrative text provides all the information necessary to understand the story, even without looking at the images, while the reverse is not true. The humor of the audiovisual version is furthermore largely derived from the contrast of the abundant sound in the first two panels with the sudden emptiness of the third and the reappearance of both sound and the protagonist at a completely different location in the last, which cannot be replicated in a classical picture story.

Figure I.1. Episode of George McManus's *Bringing Up Father*, colored here to illustrate the different types of content: intradiegetic (black and white), extradiegetic (blue), and transdiegetic (red).

This book seeks to explain how Japanese and American comics came to rely on transdiegetic content like speech balloons instead of external narration to tell stories. Such audiovisual comics first developed in the United States and from there moved to Japan. By the 1920s and 1930s, many now-canonical American comics characters were conversing in Japanese: newspaper and magazine readers in Japan were well-acquainted with Jiggs and

Figure I.2. Audiovisual comic strip from figure I.1, re-created as a picture story.

Maggie, Mutt and Jeff, Happy Hooligan, Felix the Cat, the Katzenjammer Kids, the Gumps, and dozens more. Jiggs and Maggie, who were introduced by a Japanese translation of George McManus's *Bringing Up Father* in 1923 and continued appearing in Japanese until 1940, were a veritable pop culture sensation, recognizable to newspaper readers all over Japan. The fact that even comic strips like E. C. Segar's *Thimble Theatre* (starring Popeye) and George Herriman's *Krazy Kat*, which in light of their nonstandard language and often absurdist humor must have been most difficult to translate, made it across the Pacific demonstrates both to what immense extent American comics were appearing in Japanese translation in the twenties and thirties and Japanese readers' voracious appetite for American comics at the time. However, as is true for most of the American characters that were appearing in Japan in the 1920s and 1930s, that Popeye and Krazy Kat had ever spoken Japanese was eventually forgotten.

Though the body of English- and Japanese-language scholarship on manga has previously documented only a small number of foreign comic strips in prewar Japan, the actual number of such strips should not be all that surprising when one takes into consideration the historical circumstances of their translation. With the Meiji period (1868–1912), Japan had embarked on a national project of rapid industrialization and modernization to catch up to the European powers and the United States. Though

Japan joined the ranks of the major world powers as early as 1905 with its military performance in the Russo-Japanese War, the Japanese culture industry continued to show great interest in Euro-American culture, both classical and contemporaneous. To Japanese elites, *modernization* was not entirely synonymous with *industrialization*, but went beyond it and included the importation of cultural techniques and artifacts from Western Europe and the United States. Japan's modernization was hence a process with both technological and cultural dimensions, and it was often difficult to distinguish between the two. Albert Memmi points out in *The Colonizer and the Colonized* that "science is neither Western nor Eastern, any more than it is bourgeois or proletarian. There are only two ways of pouring concrete—the right way and the wrong way."[4] But in practice, it can be hard to decide which aspects of pouring concrete are cultural and specific and which are essential and universal—if such a thing as technology entirely independent of culture can be said to exist in the first place. This difficulty of separating the essential parts of a technology from the culturally specific is perfectly illustrated by the way Japanese creators of early domestically produced audiovisual manga would often adopt not only the technical conventions of the universal medium imported from abroad but also American comic strips' foreign reading direction.

Japan's importation of Euro-American technology thus went hand in hand with its importation of Euro-American culture, including in the field of visual arts and visual culture. The country's newspaper, publishing, and advertising industries all emulated their "Western" counterparts, adopting what the latter (and by extension the former) considered the "right way," which naturally was closely intertwined with French, German, American, and other culturally specific ways of doing things. In discussing Japan's advertising industry in the 1930s, Gennifer Weisenfeld explains that "modernist styles were popular among advertising executives and designers precisely because of their close associations with the modern, the new, the scientific, and the machine aesthetic. Not coincidentally the companies who employed modernist aesthetics were largely (although not exclusively) companies marketing new types of modern consumer products like Western-style foodstuffs and new technologies—all goods that intrinsically reflected the rapidly changing nature of daily life in twentieth-century Japan."[5] Weisenfeld's case study of the advertising industry exemplifies the broad link among "the modern," new technologies, "Western" aesthetics like modernism, and "Western" products in Taishō (1912–1926) and early (1926–1940) Shōwa period Japan, and how all the above were associated with notions of progress and improvement.

Although Japan's first domestic daily newspaper, the *Yokohama Mainichi Shinbun* (Yokohama daily newspaper), had been founded comparatively late, on January 28, 1871,[6] by 1924 the total daily newspaper circulation had already risen to 6.25 million.[7] A population of nearly 59 million and an average household size of close to five meant that roughly half of Japanese households were reading a newspaper at the time.[8] Between 1900 and 1919, a new middle class had replaced the nobility as the main class of newspaper readers, and formerly separate political and entertainment papers fused, now featuring both news *and* entertainment.[9] In addition, during the early 1920s, an audience of middle-class "popular readers" emerged that turned to newspapers more for entertainment than news and opinion, increasing newspapers' incentive to provide humorous content.[10] Given their readership and the well-developed state of the Japanese press and publishing industry by the 1920s, it is unsurprising that in 1923, publications began to import comic strips, which had begun to dominate American newspapers around 1900.

By 1923, Japan had also become extremely receptive to "Western" imagery. Gennifer Weisenfeld elsewhere points out that in the world of "high art," Euro-American painting had by the 1920s "become a domesticated and legitimate mode of native self-expression by Japanese artists, no longer perceived as problematic or foreign."[11] In the world of cinema, Japanese narrative film production began to flourish around 1908, and movie theater construction picked up in the 1910s.[12] The cinematoscope and cinematograph had first come to Japan in 1896 and 1897, respectively, and the first dedicated movie theater had been established in 1903.[13] Japanese film scholar Yomota Inuhiko writes that cinema came to Japan as "cutting-edge Western technology" and considers it no accident that the early introduction of cinema coincided with Japan's earlier "modernization" compared to other Asian countries. Yomota furthermore describes a conscious effort in the 1910s to "raise Japanese cinema to the level of Europe and the US."[14] Numerous Japanese newspaper advertisements for foreign films in the 1920s and 1930s (such as *The Cabinet of Dr. Caligari* and *King Kong*) demonstrate the popularity of visual culture imported from Europe and the United States. Given the rapid importation and assimilation of Euro-American painting and film over the early decades of the twentieth century, it appears only logical that "Western" comics would similarly become a part of Japanese culture. In fact, there is significant overlap between those newspapers that advertised foreign-made motion pictures and those that featured foreign-made comic strips.

Unlike in painting or film, however, this foreign influence on manga has been obscured by a tradition of historiography that for nearly a century has sought to establish a continuity between present-day narrative Japanese comics and centuries of domestic visual art preceding them. The impact of foreign, primarily American comics on graphic narrative in Japan and the resulting paradigm shift from picture story to audiovisual comic strip complicates the popular account of contemporary manga as the culmination of centuries of domestic popular art, which may explain why few have been interested in the recovery of this foreign influence.

Another reason the narrative of a centuries-old continuous tradition of manga has been unchallenged for so long is that historical research on "comics" and "manga" generally has suffered from a reluctance to clearly define its object of study, sometimes coupled with an eagerness to expand the meaning of the above two terms. *Manga* has meant everything from scribblings on temple walls to animated film, from picture scrolls to political caricatures. *Comics* has been used similarly inflationarily.[15] These umbrella terms often lump together distinct, historically specific forms, so it is important to stress that audiovisual, transdiegetic manga/comics function differently from other, older forms of graphic narrative that have also been referred to as *comics* or *manga* (see the difference between figs. I.1 and I.2, for example) and that this book is specifically concerned with the former. The terms *comics* and *manga* are largely arbitrary, and I do not mean to argue what constitutes "true" comics or "real" manga. Instead, I am interested in tracing the origins and development of a specific historical form of graphic narrative that overlaps with what most people today think of when they hear the word *comics* or *manga*.

Multipanel narratives using "sound images" to make possible conversations between characters across successive images were unheard of prior to the first audiovisual comic strips in the *New York Journal* in 1899 and are thus younger than other forms of graphic narrative like the picture story, which can be traced back to the works of Rodolphe Töpffer (1799–1846).[16] Understanding why early twentieth-century American audiovisual comics had such an enormous influence on the trajectory of Japanese graphic narrative requires appreciating that these audiovisual comics represented not a stylistic change but an entirely new medium—the first mass medium in history that told stories audiovisually, by mimetically and synchronously reproducing sound and motion.

Chapter 2 demonstrates the complexity of the development of this mimetic, audiovisual form of graphic narrative that uses transdiegetic elements to relate a story without the mediation of a narrator. Transdiegetic, audiovisual comics did not result from an arbitrary decision to "start using speech balloons" but were the indirect result of a monumental shift in Euro-American conceptions of motion and sound over the nineteenth century. Such comics were in large part brought about by the appearance and spread of devices that for the first time in history enabled the recording and reproduction of motion and sound and led artists to develop ways of representing both in still images on the page.

The complex origins of transdiegetic comics, born in a society in which the experience of sound-recording and motion-recording technologies had already become widespread, explain why these comics first appeared in the then technologically and economically more advanced United States and only later spread to Japan as the same technologies of aural and visual entertainment became more commonplace there as well. Transdiegetic comics' revolutionary nature not only shows that the American comic strips that were suddenly appearing in Japan represented far more than a stylistic difference. It also explains why these comics were so eagerly published, consumed, and assimilated by Japanese editors, readers, and artists. Transdiegetic comics were not only popular because they were "Western." Unlike other, earlier forms of manga, they also functioned much like the phonograph records and motion pictures now popular in Japan: as mimetic forms of mass entertainment. The Japanese public's embrace of transdiegetic American comics in turn led Japanese editors and artists to adapt accordingly, bringing about the same paradigm shift from illustrated story to transdiegetic comic strip in Japan over the course of the 1920s and 1930s that had happened in the United States around the turn of the century.

The evidence presented in the following chapters shows that the history of contemporary Euro-American comics and that of contemporary narrative manga, which both predominantly use the same audiovisual form, are inextricably linked. I do not mean to deny other foreign influences like the works of Charles Wirgman, George Bigot, or Wilhelm Busch (whose work was available in Japanese translation as early as 1887, though its influence has received little scholarly attention) or the legacy of a rich, long, and variegated tradition of Japanese visual culture preceding these influences. The influence of Japanese *ukiyo-e* prints on George McManus, whose *Bringing Up Father* in turn became the most influential and longest-running graphic narrative in prewar Japan, exemplifies the complexity of transnational cultural influence. It would be simplistic to say that modern comics were "invented" in America and "copied" by the Japanese. Their shared origins do not mean that audiovisual comics/manga are "all the same" and that there are no meaningful differences between regions, nations, periods, and so on. There are even elements that could be argued to constitute distinct "national cultures" in comics, such as the dominance (and influence on other types of American comics) of the superhero genre in the United States and the standardized "manga" drawing style and unique visual elements (such as a new type of motion lines or use of snot bubbles to indicate sleeping) in Japan.

I do hope, however, that this book demonstrates that today's narrative "manga" and "comics" are far more similar than they are different from each other and that their similarities are fundamental to the nature of the medium, while their differences are not. What the link between American and Japanese comics discussed in this book shows is that claims to "not get" or not be interested in manga on the one hand or *amekomi* (American comics) on the other result primarily from insufficient awareness of the great variety of comics available. To many Japanese readers, American comics equals Marvel, while manga to many Americans is *Dragon Ball* and *Sailor Moon*—that is, the mass culture successes—with more critically acclaimed works often being little known across the Pacific. It would hardly be a negative consequence if knowledge of the shared past of American and Japanese comics led to a greater interest in supposedly "foreign" works. After all, you *don't* need to be Doctor Strange to truly learn their mystic ways.

PROLOGUE

THE HISTORICAL ORIGINS AND CHANGING MEANING OF "MANGA" UP TO 1923

The aesthetics and techniques of Japanese manga and animation came into being during the fifteen years under the fascist regime from 1931 to 1945.
—Ōtsuka Eiji, *Mikkī no shoshiki* (2013)

The genesis of manga derives directly from the storytelling tradition through the performance of the kami-shibai *[paper plays].*
—Robert S. Petersen, "The Acoustics of Manga" (2009)

An Englishman invented contemporary manga. Don't let anybody tell you anything different.
—Helen McCarthy, "A History of Manga" (2012)

Hokusai manga: The starting point of Japanese manga
—Shimizu Isao, *Hokusai manga* (2014)

One can trace manga back to the "Scrolls of Frolicking Animals and Humans."
—Matsumoto Reiji and Hidaka Bin, *Manga daihakubutsukan* (1980)

The origin of manga was probably graffiti.
—Ishiko Junzō, *Sengo mangashi nōto* (1975)

As evidenced by the above quotations, claims made about the origins of manga vary widely and include graffiti by construction workers at the Hōryūji and Tōshōdaiji temples, medieval picture scrolls, sketches by Katsushika Hokusai, the introduction of European cartooning through newspaper correspondent Charles Wirgman and his satire magazine *Japan Punch*, the work of Japanese cartoonists Kitazawa Rakuten and/ or Okamoto Ippei, and the influx of Disney animation.[1] Most of these claims attempt to tie contemporary manga to other, older artistic or narrative Japanese traditions. This diversity of asserted origin points is made possible by the general absence of a precise, universally accepted definition—or often any definition at all—of the term *manga* itself from historical accounts of "manga's" origins. Because manga both in the sense of caricature/cartoons/illustrated stories and as "Japanese audiovisual comics" has its primary roots in traditions imported from European and American sources, accounts that seek contemporary narrative manga's origins in older Japanese art in fact depend on this conflation of different artistic and narrative forms to be able to ignore fundamental differences between all these forms by grouping them under the overarching label "manga."[2]

Before we delve into the evidence for contemporary narrative manga's evolution out of imported audiovisual comic strips, it will be helpful to first address the pre-1923 history of *manga* and how the meaning of this word has changed over time. The word *manga* originally meant little more than "sketch" until 1891, when it first started to be used to more specifically describe cartooning, caricature, and stories told at least partially via drawings (i.e., silent multipanel cartoons and picture stories). Over the next three decades, between 1891 and 1923, *manga* gradually became the most common term to refer to these three categories of visual art. Later, during the 1920s and 1930s, with an influx of translated audiovisual comics from abroad, *manga* came to also denote such audiovisual comics, which over time largely supplanted picture stories as the dominant form of graphic narrative in Japan.

Though the precise origin of the word is uncertain, the earliest mentions of *manga* in writing occurred in the late eighteenth century, such as in the foreword to Santō Kyōden's 1798 picture book *Shiji no yukikai* (Traffic through the four seasons), in which its Chinese characters are spelled out as *manguwa* via furigana—phonetic characters next to it (see endnote for earlier known uses and hyperlinks to the respective books).³ The images in *Shiji no yukikai* consist of twenty-four scenes showing various people on a busy road, with two scenes for each of the twelve months of the year. The style of the drawings is fairly realistic and few today would refer to them as manga in the post-1891 sense of cartoons or caricature. Since the images do not establish a narrative, they are also not manga in the sense of illustrated stories or audiovisual comics. It is obvious from the way he uses the word that Kyōden did not mean for it to describe a medium or genre. When explaining in the book's introduction that "I have drawn [*manguwa shi*] the high and low, men and women, old and young going back and forth on the road" that he can see from his desk, Kyōden uses *manga* not as a noun but as a verb, in the sense of "to (loosely) draw" or "to sketch." Though Katsushika Hokusai (most famous for his woodblock prints, such as *The Great Wave off Kanagawa*) later popularized the word as a noun by using it to describe his own sketches (the "Hokusai manga"), none of Hokusai's sketches establishes a narrative either, and only some are intended to be humorous. Many are realistic studies of people, animals, plants, buildings, and landscapes, and there is no indication that Hokusai meant for the term *manga* to be associated with narrative or humor, as it later would. Instead, Hokusai used it much like Kyōden: to describe a variety of sketches, primarily observational but occasionally creative in Hokusai's case.

Manga likely never would have acquired additional meanings like "caricature," "cartooning," "comics," or "animated films" had it not been for two aspiring cartoonists by the names of Imaizumi Ippyō and Kitazawa Rakuten, who between 1891 and 1923 dramatically expanded the breadth of what *manga* meant, eventually making it the most common word to refer to anything cartoon- or caricature-related. Imaizumi Ippyō had departed for San Francisco at some point between 1885 and 1888 to study caricature but was unable to find an apprenticeship there as local newspaper artists rejected him for his lack of familiarity with American culture, among other reasons.[4] Upon his return to Japan in the spring of 1890, however, Imaizumi found employment at the newspaper *Jiji Shinpō* (Current affairs news) published by his uncle Fukuzawa Yukichi (see a 10,000 yen banknote for a picture of Fukuzawa).

On July 4, 1890, the newspaper featured its first-ever multipanel cartoon, which Imaizumi likely had brought back with him from the United States, with the order of the panels reversed to fit the traditional Japanese right-to-left reading order (fig. P.1).[5] The cartoon depicts a vaudeville weight lifter raising a large heavy-looking ball with one hand in a supposed show of strength. In the last panel, after the weight lifter has bowed to the audience and is about to exit the stage, a tiny dog is seen carrying the same object in its snout. Although the joke should be obvious from the images alone, the cartoon nonetheless is accompanied by a lengthy Japanese explanation, suggesting that Japanese readers at the time were not yet accustomed to such cartoons.

The next cartoon published in the *Jiji Shinpō* was another foreign (American) cartoon, on June 31, 1890, further supporting the assumption that these cartoons were brought from the United States by Imaizumi. The cartoon, titled "New Questions for the Census-Taker," consisted of a single panel and included all its original English accompanying text. Two months later, on September 27, the *Jiji Shinpō* featured its first Japanese-drawn multipanel cartoon, in which two Japanese men keep bowing toward each other. This cartoon was likely drawn by Imaizumi, given its similarity to the common four-panel pattern in American newspaper cartoons (such as the weight lifter cartoon published previously by the *Jiji Shinpō*) and because it featured an English title, "Perpetual Motion." The "Perpetual Motion" cartoon suggests that Imaizumi was trying to combine the multipanel cartoon form he had studied abroad with localized content (such as the joke about bowing forever).

Figure P.1. Four-panel cartoon in the *Jiji Shinpō*, July 4, 1890. (Image courtesy of Cameron Penwell, Library of Congress.)

The following year, on April 27, 1891, the *Jiji Shinpō* then featured the world's first multipanel cartoon actually labeled a manga, another foreign one likely imported by Imaizumi (fig. P.2).⁶ The cartoon in question is a silent four-panel strip about a Chinese man who ends up catching a fish with his queue, copied from a foreign newspaper, a fact explicitly stated above the cartoon—though the cartoon lacks a caption or title, a header designates it "manga (excerpted from foreign newspaper)." Considering today's emphasis on manga as something specifically Japanese, it may seem ironic that the lineage of the contemporary, post-Kyōden/Hokusai word started with foreign cartoons and was initiated by a cartoonist inspired not by the works of Kyōden and Hokusai (or other Japanese art) but by Euro-American caricature and cartooning.

But Imaizumi, who must have been responsible for the cartoon's publication and its labeling as "manga," never understood *manga* as something uniquely Japanese: for one, in a May 11, 1891, *Jiji Shinpō* autobiographical cartoon, Imaizumi refers to himself as an "American manga artist" (*beikoku mangashi*). In the 1901 book *Ippyō zatsuwa* (Ippyo anecdotes), Imaizumi furthermore defines *manga* universally as "a kind of funny picture [*kokkeiga*], in some cases including a satirical meaning, in others not." Though he asserts that *manga* in this sense have existed in Japan since ancient times, Imaizumi sees the word as little more than a synonym for caricature, flatly stating that "*manga* is called caricature in English."⁷ The expansive concept of manga outlined by Imaizumi includes not

Figure P.2. Four-panel cartoon ("manga") in the *Jiji Shinpō*, April 27, 1891. (Image courtesy of Newspark, the Japan Newspaper Museum.)

only Western caricature but also historically specific Japanese pictorial art forms like *Toba-e* or *Ōzu-e*, marking the first time *manga* was used to describe specific genres of imagery rather than in the technical sense of "sketches" intended by Kyōden and Hokusai.

The inclusion of humor as a defining element makes Imaizumi's *manga* fundamentally different from Kyōden and Hokusai's use of the word, which did not presume a humorous component (only a subset of Hokusai's "manga" sketches were humorous, and those were referred to specifically as *kyōga*, "crazy pictures"). Imaizumi's interest in American cartooning rather than Kyōden's or Hokusai's sketches, and the foreign cartoons published by the *Jiji Shinpō* at the time, indicate how closely intertwined the beginnings of manga as caricature/cartooning—even before the introduction of audiovisual comics in 1923—are with Euro-American cartooning instead of an existing domestic tradition, notwithstanding Imaizumi's own claim that a range of domestic works could be retroactively classified as "manga" under his definition as "a kind of funny picture." Though today's narrative manga no longer have to be funny to qualify as such, Imaizumi's use of the word to describe multipanel cartoons creating brief narratives told via multiple drawings (such as the cartoon about the Chinese man fishing with his queue) also expanded the meaning of *manga* to include "stories told via consecutive drawings" (what Will Eisner has called "sequential art") that would later lead to the word's application to picture stories and audiovisual comics.

At the time, *manga* was still far from being an everyday word. This would change only after 1902, when Imaizumi was succeeded as the *Jiji Shinpō*'s chief cartoonist and manga editor by Kitazawa Rakuten, the second of the two cartoonists responsible for the word's success. Similarly enamored of "Western" cartooning (American in particular), Rakuten had studied it under the Australian artist Frank Arthur Nankivell and had worked for the Yokohama-based English-language publication *Box of Curios*. At the *Jiji Shinpō*, Kitazawa started a regular column called *Jiji Manga*, which later turned into a weekly supplement of several pages.

That *manga* is far from an essential Japanese concept that naturally unites centuries of visual art is illustrated by the amount of time it took until the word repurposed by Imaizumi replaced the existing most common word for caricature and cartooning at the turn of the century. Despite Imaizumi's efforts to popularize *manga* as a synonym for those types of drawings, when Kitazawa succeeded him at the *Jiji Shinpō* in 1902, the most frequent Japanese term for such visual art was still a quite different word that had been coined a few decades earlier: *Ponchi-e*, with *e* meaning "pictures" and *Ponchi* derived from the title of Charles Wirgman's magazine the *Japan Punch*.[8] Wirgman, Japan correspondent for the *Illustrated London News*, had founded the *Japan Punch* (in Yokohama, like *Box of Curios*) in 1862 as a satire magazine based on the British *Punch*. The magazine consisted mostly of single-panel political cartoons and caricatures.[9] Though originally aimed at other Anglophone expatriates, it found favor with Japanese readers as well, introducing the tradition of European caricature to Japan. It also led to the birth of Japanese humor magazines, which were inspired by it, like the *e-shinbun*[10] (picture newspaper) *Nipponchi*, the first such Japanese-published cartoon magazine, whose title was an amalgam fusing the words *Nippon* (Japan) and *Ponchi* (Punch). Its founder, Kanagaki Robun, explicitly references Wirgman in the magazine's introduction, which makes clear the substantial influence Wirgman had on the development of caricature and cartooning in the European tradition in Japan.[11]

The Japanese *Ponchi-e* tradition has led some (especially European and American) manga historians to refer to Wirgman as "manga's British ancestor" and "the forefather of both manga and Western-style Japanese art,"[12] "today considered the patron saint of the modern Japanese cartoon."[13] Wirgman's undeniable impact on caricature in Japan is clear from the term *Ponchi-e*'s prevalence back then. That Japanese readers of the magazine created this neologism instead of simply using the existing word *manga* to describe Wirgman's caricatures also underscores that at the time (the 1860s), the latter still meant something very different to most people (i.e., sketches in general). After all, it was only in the 1890s that Imaizumi Ippyō began using *manga* to refer to caricature and cartoons. It took the success of Kitazawa Rakuten's *Jiji Manga* column/supplement for the word to gradually replace *Ponchi-e* as the most common one to describe cartooning and caricature from 1902 onward.[14]

It was with Kitazawa's work on the *Jiji Manga* supplement between 1902 and 1923 that *manga* also came to be closely associated with picture-story narratives consisting of multiple panels illustrating an external text, in addition to caricature and cartooning (an association initiated by Imaizumi's use of the word to describe the four-panel cartoon about the Chinese man fishing with his queue). Such picture stories were not yet audiovisual, containing little if any transdiegetic content like speech balloons or motion lines, but exhibited a greater level of narrative complexity (including specific, named characters) than the short vignette cartoons published by the *Jiji Shinpō* previously. The earliest picture story with recurring characters (as opposed to a single-issue multipanel cartoon) that Kitazawa wrote and drew for *Jiji Manga* is the 1902 *Kuchi to kokoro* (Mouth and heart), serialized from March 30 to May 11 (see fig. P.3)—and *not* the manga featuring his characters Mokube and Tagosaku (originally titled *Shinpan hizakurige*, though rarely if ever referred to as such) that is usually cited as Kitazawa's first serialized narrative work but didn't appear until October 12, 1902, over half a year after "Mouth and Heart." As can be seen from the cartoon partially visible below "Mouth and Heart" in figure P.3, Kitazawa occasionally experimented with "balloon" shapes to represent captions, a device he had most likely seen in foreign cartoons such as those featured in the *Japan Punch*. As is explained further in chapter 2, such devices function differently from contemporary "sound-image" speech balloons, though it is also conceivable that Kitazawa got the idea to insert dialogue into the image from such speech balloons that he had seen in American audiovisual comic strips, which had begun to proliferate in the United States around 1900. But regardless of what inspired Kitazawa to include dialogue within images, he employed such devices only rarely, and

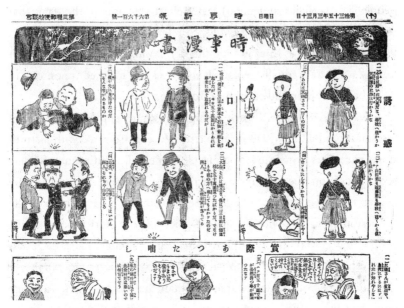

Figure P.3. Kitazawa Rakuten, *Kuchi to kokoro*, *Jiji Shinpō*, March 30, 1902.
(Image courtesy of Yorutori Bunko.)

narrative manga until 1923 continued to consist primarily of silent picture stories narrated by external text.

The close association of *manga* with picture stories until 1923 was cemented by the only cartoonist to eventually rival Kitazawa's popularity between 1910 and 1923, Okamoto Ippei. Okamoto graduated from the Tokyo School of Fine Art's Department of Western Painting in 1910 and originally pursued a career as a classically trained artist. He started out as an illustrator for the newspaper *Asahi Shinbun*, which first published at least nine sketches of outdoor scenes signed by him between April 12 and June 18, 1909, the year before his art school graduation. Though these sketches would have been considered "manga" in Kyōden and Hokusai's time, they were not "manga" in the sense of caricature or cartooning established by Imaizumi and Kitazawa (or in the sense of audiovisual comics today).[15] Okamoto soon abandoned his pursuit of "serious" art in favor of humor and storytelling, however. From November 30 to December 9, 1912, he published his first illustrated story in the *Asahi Shinbun* in eight installments. In the following years, Okamoto produced both humorous cartoons (including caricatures of parliamentary debates) and other picture stories, a genre he referred to as *manga manbun* (*bun* meaning "text"). At first, his picture stories used only a small number of images (often only one per episode), but around 1920, they began to feature at least one image per scene. Figure P.4 shows the beginning of Okamoto's perhaps most famous picture story, which started on October 17, 1921, in the *Asahi Shinbun* and was later published as a book under the title *Hito no isshō* (The life of a man).[16] The images in all these stories depict occasional moments narrated in the text. While the text can be consumed on its own, the images by themselves do not tell an intelligible story. As in the term *manga manbun* itself, image and text are strictly separated, making these picture stories starkly different from post-1923 audiovisual manga.

Like Imaizumi and Kitazawa, Okamoto drew inspiration primarily from Euro-American sources—not only the European art he had studied formally, but, more importantly, the picture stories of German cartoonist Wilhelm Busch. Okamoto even published an adaptation of Busch's most famous work, *Max und Moritz*, in the magazine *Ryōyū* (Good friend), and at least four additional picture stories by Okamoto are based on Busch's work.[17] Since these adaptations were published after Okamoto's first picture stories, it is uncertain whether his work in narrative manga was inspired by Busch from the start, but excerpts from *Max und Moritz* had been published in Japanese translation as early as 1887, part of the continuing influx of European caricature and cartooning that had begun with Wirgman's *Japan Punch* a quarter century earlier.[18] Meiji-period (1868–1912) "Punch books" (*Ponchi-bon*) preserved in the collection of the Kawasaki City Museum also show scenes copied from *Max und Moritz*, demonstrating the widespread availability and influence of Busch's work in Japan at the time, as do 1890s issues of the *Ponchi-e* publication *Maru Maru Chinbun* and a 1914 issue of the children's magazine *Yōnen Ponchi*.

Figure P.4. Okamoto Ippei, first part of *Hito no isshō*, *Asahi Shinbun*, October 17, 1921.

Okamoto himself later in his career spoke openly about his admiration for Busch's work and even proposed that it should serve as a template to other artists as well.[19]

The popularity of Okamoto's picture stories led others to follow in his footsteps. Disciples such as Miyao Shigeo created similarly popular *manga manbun* of their own and helped establish picture stories as a common narrative art form by the 1920s. Between 1891 and 1923, creating a manga hence meant creating a caricature, a political cartoon, a short single- or multipanel gag cartoon, or a picture story. *Narrative* manga that told stories with identifiable, named protagonists were virtually synonymous with picture stories. In 1923, however, this state of affairs was dramatically upended by one Japanese editor's fateful decision to try to boost the sales of his newspaper by ordering the translation of an American comic strip he liked.

CHAPTER 1

"POPULAR IN SOCIETY AT LARGE"

THE FIRST TALKING MANGA

Having already transitioned from being a synonym for "sketches" between 1798 and 1891 to describing caricature, cartooning, and illustrated stories from 1891 onward, *manga* would change once more, this time to include (and eventually primarily describe) audiovisual comics. This second shift began in 1923, was largely complete by the end of the 1930s, and is the reason *manga* today to people around the world refers to Japanese audiovisual comics rather than single-panel cartoons or picture stories. Though many historical accounts portray narrative manga's shift from text-based picture stories to audiovisual comics as the more or less natural evolution of a continuous domestic tradition, in reality, the transition was sparked by the sudden influx of a large number of audiovisual comics from abroad. The first major one of these was George McManus's *Bringing Up Father*, whose translation occupies a singular position in the history of manga as the first successful audiovisual Japanese-language comic and the most popular manga up to that point in history.

As is true for manga between 1891 and 1923 as well, foreign influence on the birth of contemporary Japanese comics has generally been downplayed. Few histories of manga address at all the question of why the majority of narrative works published and consumed under the label of "manga" shifted in the 1920s and 1930s from picture stories narrated by external text in the vein of Okamoto's *manga manbun* to audiovisual comics mimetically relating a story through images alone. The prevalent explanation in those histories that do is that in 1923, the manga *Shō-chan no bōken* (The adventures of little Sho) introduced speech balloons alongside narrative text and Asō Yutaka's *Nonki na tōsan* (Easygoing daddy) soon after dropped external narration, but this development is never examined closely.

Such accounts fail to explain *how and why* manga suddenly underwent such a drastic transformation. Ōtsuka Eiji's book *Mikkī no shoshiki* (The Mickey format) represents a rare attempt to explain this shift, ascribing it to the influx of American animated films, but such films became broadly available only in the 1930s, when audiovisual comic strips had already come to constitute the majority of narrative manga. Overall, the crucial period of the 1920s and 1930s remains vastly underappreciated in manga historiography.[1] The dearth of research on manga that were published in these two decades has meant that the large-scale importation of translated foreign comic strips by Japanese publications between 1923 and 1940—without which the shift to the audiovisual, transdiegetic model of comics in Japan cannot be fully understood—has remained invisible.

That manga did not turn audiovisual before 1923 seems at first perplexing, given that Kitazawa Rakuten was already familiar with this form over a decade earlier. After founding his satire and cartoon magazine *Tōkyō Puck*, Kitazawa included an episode of Jimmy Swinnerton's comic strip *Mr. Jack* in the magazine's November 10, 1908, issue—the first known instance of a Japanese translation of a foreign comic strip (fig. 1.1).[2] The strip's eponymous antihero, Mr. Jack, is a philandering anthropomorphic tiger and had emerged out of Swinnerton's earlier cartoons about anthropomorphic tigers in the *New York Journal*.[3] Kitazawa probably had to copy *Mr. Jack* by hand from an imported issue of the newspaper, and the episode shows how

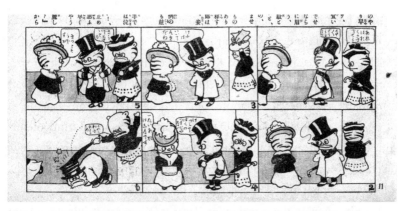

Figure 1.1. Translation of Jimmy Swinnerton's *Mr. Jack* in *Tokyo Puck*, November 10, 1908. (Image courtesy of Yorutori Bunko.)

difficult it was to translate an American audiovisual comic strip, due to the significant editing required. Whereas Euro-American comics and picture stories were read from left to right (by word), then top to bottom (by line), the standard reading direction in Japanese was top to bottom, then right to left. Although Kitazawa reordered the *Mr. Jack* episode's panels to fit the Japanese top-to-bottom, right-to-left reading order, he avoided the laborious process of "flipping" them (i.e., mirroring the panels along the *y* axis), which resulted in panels that need to be viewed top right to bottom left (note the numbering in the lower right corners), but speech balloons within them that still have to be read left to right (with the text contained inside them again top right to bottom left!) in order to make sense. The problem of how to deal with different reading orders between Japanese and English was left for other editors to resolve years later.[4]

Whether due to the difficulty of adapting foreign comics to the traditional Japanese reading order or because Kitazawa only possessed a single issue of the strip, *Mr. Jack* did not become a regular feature of the magazine. If Kitazawa had decided to adopt *Mr. Jack*'s audiovisual form for his own work, the historical trajectory of manga might have taken a different turn, but due to Kitazawa's lack of interest in the form prior to the Japanese publication of *Bringing Up Father*, fully audiovisual comics remained virtually absent from Japanese publications until 1923 and from Kitazawa's own work until 1924, another year later.[5]

The curious combination of Kitazawa's early familiarity with American comics and his simultaneous reluctance to adopt their narrative form until many years later is even more concretely illustrated by an earlier issue of *Tōkyō Puck* (July 1, 1907), for which Kitazawa borrowed from an episode of R. F. Outcault's audiovisual comic strip *Buster Brown*, in which its juvenile protagonist plays a prank on an unsuspecting man by placing the adult's bowler hat over a chicken (figs. 1.2 and 1.3).[6]

Despite copying the central plot element, Kitazawa strikingly did not adopt *Buster Brown*'s audiovisual form and instead rewrote the plot as a picture story reliant on external narration. Kitazawa's version, part of the series "Chame's Tricks" (*Chame no itazura*), consists of four panels with narrative text in Japanese to the right of (and in English below) each panel. The images are read top to bottom, right to left (top right, bottom right, top left, bottom left), and the English text, an apparent translation from the Japanese, reads,

1. Chamé's Dad: "People may laugh at my old-fashioned belief in ghost story. But, I say, even in this bright 20th century, the ghost is a solid fact."

2. While Dad and Highcollar Kidoro were engaged in hot discussion on ghost, Chamé stole in, and putting a cock into Kidoro's hat: "Hurrah! Mr. Kidoro's hat's flying!"

3. Highcollar: "What! that's my hat only bought yesterday." Dad: "That's the evil inflicted by the Ghost." Highcollar rushes on running.

4. Chamé: "What a joy! See, Mr. Highcollar is without shoes!" Dad: "Chamé, you nice goin' fellow, I am really delighted at your trick. I give you ten sen as prize." Chamé: "Thank you."

The main joke is of course that Chame's prank has made it seem to Highcollar Kidoro, who is unaware of the true reason his hat is rapidly moving away from him, as if there really are supernatural forces in the

Figure 1.2. Kitazawa Rakuten, *Chame no itazura*, 1985 reprint, originally published in *Tokyo Puck*, July 1, 1907. (Image courtesy of the Ohio State University, Billy Ireland Cartoon Library and Museum.)

world. This then explains why Chame's father does not reproach his son for playing a prank on his guest but instead rewards him for it. The visuals leave out this crucial plot element of the argument about the existence of ghosts, which is related exclusively through the outside text. Typically for much of Kitazawa's work, the images in "Chame's Tricks" illustrate more of the narrative than they do in most of Okamoto Ippei's *manga manbun*, but in Kitazawa's pre-1924 work, too, the external narrative text remains crucial to a complete understanding of the story.

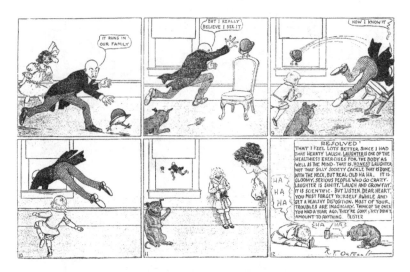

Figure 1.3. R. F. Outcault, second half of the *Buster Brown* episode "Getting an Education," 1977 reprint, originally published 1906.

Even the first Japanese-drawn manga to regularly feature dialogue within the image remained primarily an illustrated story. Published from January 25, 1923, in Japan's first tabloid newspaper, the *Asahi Graph*, this manga, called *Shō-chan no bōken* (The adventures of little Sho), combined an externally narrated story with images that included speech balloons (fig. 1.4).[7] Like so many significant works in the early history of manga, *Shō-chan no bōken* was strongly influenced by a foreign model: devised for the *Asahi Graph*'s first issue by editor in chief Suzuki Bunshirō, it was inspired by the London *Daily Mirror*'s feature *Pip, Squeak and Wilfred*, a graphic narrative that used the same combination of speech balloons and external narration.[8] According to Suzuki, he wrote the first Little Sho scripts himself, having them illustrated by artist Kabashima Katsuichi, with Oda Nobutsune later taking over as writer for Suzuki.[9] The new strip, which chronicled the adventures of a boy called Sho and his squirrel companion, was an immediate success. It became so popular that after the protagonist's original school uniform cap was replaced with a knit hat with a pom-pom (for a ski trip on February 13, 1923, but the change

Figure 1.4. First *Shō-chan no bōken, Asahi Graph,* January 25, 1923.

became permanent), Sho's style of headwear even rose to national fame as a *Shō-chan bō* (Little Sho hat), generating a corresponding fashion trend among Japanese children.[10] There was something about *Shō-chan* that distinguished it from other picture stories and made it more popular than the rest, and that something may well have been the more immediate way it told stories by using speech balloons.

Its combination of speech balloons and external narration has led some manga historians to consider *Shō-chan no bōken* a kind of "missing link": a "transitional" form in the shift from extradiegetic narration to transdiegetic speech balloons,[11] an "intermediary" between the illustrated picture story and audiovisual comic strip,[12] with visuals and speech balloons that simply duplicate the narration.[13] A careful examination of *Shō-chan,* however, reveals that although some episodes can be understood without consulting the external narration, others demonstrate that intradiegetic images and transdiegetic content (speech balloons) on the one hand and extradiegetic narration on the other are not mutually redundant and that the extradiegetic narration retains its primacy. This is especially obvious from episodes in which one of the four panels features no visuals at all, consisting entirely of Oda's narration, which fills the panel instead of being written next to it (such as in fig. 1.5).[14] Such episodes perhaps occurred whenever illustrator Kabashima considered the narrative content of writer Oda's scripts too complex to depict in a single panel.

It is understandably tempting to view *Shō-chan no bōken* as an intermediary step in a gradual transition from *manga manbun* picture story

Figure 1.5. *Shō-chan no bōken, Ōsaka Asahi Shinbun*, March 4, 1924.

to audiovisual comic strip because of its use of balloons to render dialogue. But this characterization is undermined not only by the existence
of episodes like fig. 1.5 but also by the fact that many if not most *Shō-
chan* episodes are difficult or impossible to follow without consulting the
external narration. Additionally, the images never supply crucial information omitted from the narration—unsurprising given its creation process,
in which the written text establishing the plot always came first. Thus
Shō-chan no bōken at its core remains a *manga manbun*–style picture
story in which Oda's narration is primary and Kabashima's visuals serve to
illustrate a plot already established by this extradiegetic narration. More
importantly, regardless of how one classifies *Shō-chan no bōken*, it did not
exert substantial influence on other manga or initiate the proliferation
of audiovisual comics in Japan: no manga started using speech balloons
in response to it.

On April 1, 1923, the history of contemporary narrative manga began in
earnest when the *Asahi Graph* commenced publishing its first fully audiovisual comic strip, George McManus's *Bringing Up Father*, in Japanese
translation under the title *Oyaji kyōiku* (fig. 1.6). Started by McManus
in 1913, the strip revolved around the misadventures of Jiggs, a formerly
working-class Irish American nouveau riche who still wants nothing more
than to keep eating corned beef and playing cards with his old friends,
much to the chagrin of his wife, Maggie, who is eager to be a respectable
member of high society. Many of *Bringing Up Father*'s jokes derive from
this basic conflict between the two protagonists. That Japanese readers
in the 1920s were well-acquainted with the concepts of fortuitous nou-
veaux riches and more assertive women may explain part of its attraction,[15] but *Bringing Up Father* appealed to its new audience to a degree
never seen before in a manga. Its Japanese translation, *Oyaji kyōiku*, would
not only become the most successful and longest-running Japanese-
language manga of its time but through its enormous popularity lead
Japanese manga creators to adopt the audiovisual comics model as the
primary way to tell visual stories on the page.

Figure 1.6. First four-panel *Bringing Up Father* in the daily *Asahi Graph*, April 1, 1923.

Jiggs and Maggie's longtime success in Japan was made possible by both an active effort by its American distributor to sell comic strips overseas and the fandom of a discerning editor: *Asahi Graph* editor in chief Suzuki Bunshirō, who had been following *Bringing Up Father* in an American newspaper for several years before he decided to license it from a Tokyo representative of International Feature Service, the Hearst company holding the distribution rights to it.[16] The Asahi publishing conglomerate seems to have known that it had secured something big, as it considered

the occasion momentous enough to publish an advertisement in its flagship newspaper, the *Tōkyō Asahi Shinbun*, on the day of *Bringing Up
Father*'s first appearance in the *Asahi Graph* in order to announce the strip's
arrival.

Oyaji kyōiku at first consisted of episodes of *Bringing Up Father*'s weekday edition (four panels long) in the daily *Asahi Graph* but was interrupted
when the September 1, 1923, Great Kantō Earthquake and fires resulting
from it devastated Tokyo and the surrounding area, destroying the majority
of buildings and killing over one hundred thousand (including massacres of
mostly Korean immigrants by police and vigilantes[17]). After the quake, the
Asahi Graph appeared only intermittently and without comics for two and a
half months but resumed regular, now weekly publication on November 14.
Despite the havoc wreaked by the earthquake, the *Asahi Graph* did not abandon its promising new feature. The tabloid instead switched from the four-
panel weekday edition of McManus's strip to the longer Sunday version
(around twelve panels), and published it continuously for nearly *seventeen
years*, until July 31, 1940 (fig. 1.7 shows the first twelve-panel episode from
November 14).[18] This made *Bringing Up Father* the (by far) longest-running
serialized manga in Japanese history at the time; it was surpassed only in
the postwar era. It appears that Asahi would have preferred to publish its
most famous regular feature even longer, for after *Bringing Up Father* disappeared from the *Asahi Graph* in July 1940, it was followed on October 30 by
a strip called *Oyaji soku-kyōiku* (Bringing up father right away) by Matsu-
shita Ichio. As if the reference to *Bringing Up Father* had not been obvious
enough, the strip was renamed *Kokusan oyaji kyōiku* (Bringing up father,
made in Japan) beginning with its second issue on November 6. This brand-
ing suggests that the *Asahi Graph* did not cease publication of McManus's
strip due to diminished interest in it on the part of its readership, but rather
because of the changed political climate, in which publication of American
material was now frowned upon by the nationalist military government.

Bringing Up Father remained audiovisual in translation for the entirety
of its long run; as in the translation of *Mr. Jack* fifteen years earlier, no

Figure 1.7. First twelve-panel *Bringing Up Father* in the weekly *Asahi Graph*, November 14, 1923.

explanation or external narration was added. The first episode in the *Asahi Graph* on April 1, 1923 (fig. 1.6), shows Jiggs returning home and running into a man carrying Jiggs's clothes out of his house; the man claims to be a local tailor, leading Jiggs to hand over the coat he is wearing for alterations as well, but the man turns out to have been a burglar. All of this brief narrative is mimetically acted out on the page without the need for a narrator; dialogue is rendered as sound images inside speech balloons, synchronous with the depicted action. Other transdiegetic content besides sound, such as pain stars and an exclamation point emanating from Jiggs's head in the final panel to underscore his painful realization that he gave his coat to a burglar, was preserved as well, making McManus's strip the first fully audiovisual, transdiegetic manga to capture the attention of the Japanese public.

Like Kitazawa Rakuten when he translated the episode of *Mr. Jack* (fig. 1.1), the *Asahi Graph*, too, struggled with the problem that Japanese text (and images) were read top to bottom, then right to left, but American material left to right, then top to bottom. The simple plot of the first episode was made more difficult to follow due to the *Asahi Graph*'s failure to bridge this gap between the conflicting American and Japanese reading orders: while the translation preserved the original American panel and speech balloon orders (read horizontally from left to right, then proceeding to the next line from top to bottom), it changed the transdiegetic writing inside the balloons to the traditional Japanese reading order (read vertically from top to bottom, then proceeding to the next column from right to left), which caused the reading order for text to conflict with that for panels and balloons. In order to clarify the panel order, the translation added extradiegetic Arabic numbers in parentheses to the panels—a common feature in most other translations *and* later Japanese-drawn audiovisual comics as well, necessitated by the newly introduced foreign reading order—but the reading order for the speech balloons can only be discerned from context, since it is not obvious whether or not the panels have been mirrored ("flipped").

It would take the *Asahi Graph* over a month and more than forty episodes to figure out a permanent solution to the reading order problem, after experimenting with various attempted solutions to address the issue.[19] Perhaps inspired by the second foreign comic strip to be regularly published in Japan—Jimmy Swinnerton's *Little Jimmy*—which preserved all American reading directions from its very first episode on April 16, 1923, *Oyaji kyōiku* on May 16, 1923, likewise finally resolved the reading order problem by rendering all text in the same reading direction as the American original: left to right, top to bottom.[20] This solution, though still an unconventional way to read Japanese at the time, turned out to be ingeniously simple and was adopted by nearly all translations of European and American comic strips afterward. In fact, as we will see in chapter 4, many of the first Japanese-drawn audiovisual manga would follow this example and normalize the unconventional practice, making left-to-right writing one of the most obvious signs of the impact of foreign comics on manga.

According to Yanaike Makoto's *Yokogaki tōjō* (The appearance of horizontal writing), the history of left-to-right horizontal Japanese writing actually goes back to at least September 22, 1875, when a *Yomiuri Shinbun* article mentioned a police sign written this way. The highly unusual nature of such writing at the time is evinced by the confusion it created among citizens.[21] During the Meiji period (1868–1912), left-to-right writing was mostly limited to imported Euro-American texts and products and hence confined to political, cultural, and economic elites until more people became exposed to such writing during the Taishō period (1912–1926) due to expanded education and the spread of foreign inventions like phonograph records and films, which often featured writing in European languages. Left-to-right writing's connection to science, technology, and "Western modernity" led more of the new Japanese urban middle class to embrace it (likely as a class marker, though Yanaike does not say so directly). Train tickets were first printed with left-to-right writing in 1920, though the earliest example of left-to-right newspaper content is a sports column from February 12, 1923, preceding the translations of

Bringing Up Father and *Little Jimmy* by a mere two months. Most such left-to-right columns appeared in major city newspapers for educated middle-class readers, though some children's columns were written the same way.[22] Newspapers targeting the lower classes like the *Yorozu Chōhō* and the *Miyako, Mainichi,* and *Niroku Shinbun* did not feature left-to-right columns, whereas middle-class papers like the *Jiji Shinpō* and the *Hōchi, Yomiuri, Kokumin,* and *Asahi Shinbun* did.[23] The former category of newspapers also featured very few audiovisual comics, which were concentrated in the latter. The presence of left-to-right columns thus strongly correlated with the presence of translated American comics and the Japanese ones emulating them, which not only confirms that an important part of these comics' attraction was their "modernist" appeal but also means that their primary audience consisted of educated middle-class readers. Their consumption by these readers possibly helped establish audiovisual comics as a culturally "legitimate" medium, contributing to their successful integration into Japanese society.

Though Japanese is much more flexible with its reading order than English, left-to-right horizontal writing thus was still quite unusual in the 1920s, making its adoption for comic strip translations a surprising choice, most likely motivated by the fact that it was the simplest solution but also by connotations of "Western" and "modern," given that the frequency of such writing in advertisements also increased in the mid- and late 1920s. Although reading Japanese that way in 1923 no doubt took readers time to get used to (!this like text lish-Eng all read to ing-hav ly-den-sud gine-ma-I), it may have been less jarring than reading top to bottom, left to right, since many educated Japanese in the 1920s were used to reading European languages.

That its exotic nature was a significant factor in *Bringing Up Father*'s appeal is also suggested by the *Asahi Graph*'s earlier decision to add the labels "American manga" (*beikoku manga,* from April 6 onward) and "company exclusive" (*honsha tokuyaku,* from April 13 onward) to the strip's header. This move to advertise both a strip's American origins and its exclusivity would later be imitated by many other publications publishing American comic strips in the wake of *Bringing Up Father*'s success. The sheer number of publications that did so shows that featuring an American comic strip that readers would be unable to find anywhere else was expected to boost sales.[24] Of course, "American" can also be understood as a stand-in for "audiovisual" at this point, and it is plausible that readers were more attracted to comic strips' audiovisual nature rather than their American origin—a theory supported by the fact that American comics translations eventually decreased in number once Japanese-drawn audiovisual comic strips began to proliferate.

Bringing Up Father turned out to be such a success for Asahi that the publisher ran the strip's weekday edition also in the *Tōkyō Asahi Shinbun* (October 1923 to November 1925), the *Ōsaka Asahi Shinbun* (February 1924 to April 1925), and the women's periodical *Zen-Kansai Fujin Rengōkai* (December 1925 to March 1928), drastically expanding Jiggs and Maggie's readership. The English-language *Japan Times*, which also published Sidney Smith's comic strip *The Gumps* (in English, from December 1923 to July 1928), additionally began publishing *Bringing Up Father* in February 1924 (in English, until October 1931).[25] In 1924 and 1925, respectively, two book volumes of translated *Bringing Up Father* strips were published as well. A February 20, 1928, article in the *Japan Times* about a reporter's interview with McManus also mentions that "he showed me a book *which has just been issued* by a Japanese publisher containing a series of 'Bringing Up Father.' All the words are written in the Japanese language," which would hint at the existence of a third Japanese anthology.[26]

In 1924, McManus's *Bringing Up Father* comic strip also appeared in an ostensibly unlicensed volume called *Eigo manbun manga no kenkyū* (English *manbun manga* studies; it's unclear why the title sported the word *manbun*, especially in front of *manga*, rather than following it). The book featured English-language *Bringing Up Father* strips taken from a Chinese newspaper and supplemented with Japanese translations underneath. The volume also included episodes of Asō Yutaka's "Easygoing Daddy" (*Nonki na tōsan*) and Kitazawa Rakuten and Nagasaki Batten's "Hineko the Only Daughter" (*Hitorimusume no Hineko-san*), two audiovisual comic strips created by Japanese authors in response to *Bringing Up Father*'s success. The two Japanese strips (whose original authors had supposedly agreed to their being reprinted) featured English-language translations. Of the entire book, 17 pages consist of Asō's strip, 37 of Kitazawa and Nagasaki's, and a full 201 of McManus's. The professed purpose of the text was to serve as English-language study material, to teach learners a more natural English than that which they would learn from regular textbooks, but it appears that the author and publisher were also trying to profit from *Bringing Up Father*'s popularity, given that McManus's strip makes up nearly 80 percent of the book's content.

In stark contrast to most picture-story narrative manga preceding it (such as many of Okamoto's *manga manbun* or *Shō-chan no bōken*), the target audience of the Japanese translation of *Bringing Up Father* (*Oyaji kyōiku*) was adults rather than children, which likely increased its influence. That *Oyaji kyōiku* was aimed at adults is obvious from the prevalence of kanji (Chinese characters) in its dialogue without furigana (small hiragana or katakana Japanese phonetic characters to clarify the Chinese characters' Japanese pronunciation). While the kanji in the strip title and episode name were adorned by such furigana, kanji in the dialogue text were not. This indicates that the comic strip's translation was meant for the same educated adult readership for whom the overall newspaper was intended, not a supplement to be handed over to the children, who would not have been able to read the strip without the assistance of furigana. In contrast, *Shō-chan no bōken* was written entirely in katakana—apart from Sho's name and the strip's title, which included kanji with furigana. Of course, *Bringing Up Father* was not alone in its focus on adult readers: many of the other American comic strips published in Japan in the 1920s and 1930s were aimed at a mature readership (both in their homeland and in Japan) and frequently featured rowdy adult humor. Furigana were thus absent not only from *Oyaji kyōiku* but from the majority of translated strips published in Japanese newspapers. The ubiquity of *Bringing Up Father* in the 1920s also meant that the vast majority of Japanese adults were familiar with it, even if they weren't reading the strip themselves. Advertisements for the first *Bringing Up Father* anthology, for example, can be found not only in Asahi publications but also in competing newspapers such as the *Tōkyō Nichi Nichi Shinbun* and the *Hōchi Shinbun*, showing that the publisher presumed even readers of newspapers outside the Asahi group knew Jiggs and Maggie and would potentially be interested in their stories.[27]

George McManus was highly aware of Jiggs and Maggie's overseas success. The ads for the first *Bringing Up Father* volume, for example, emphasize its exclusive cover art and a letter "To Japanese Readers," both created especially for the Japanese edition by McManus himself (figs. 1.8 and 1.9; based on other photographs of him, it appears that McManus tried to look as 1920s Japanese as possible for this one, including by sporting a likely fake mustache).

The author's personal involvement is unsurprising given how happy he was about his creation's success in Japan. In the anthology's letter/foreword, McManus expresses that he is "extremely proud that any work of mine has found favor in a land so far from the United States as the land of the Rising Sun." According to *Asahi Graph* editor Suzuki Bunshirō, McManus was so pleased to see Jiggs and Maggie speak Japanese that he published an article or cartoon about this development in the magazine *Editor & Publisher*.[28] The February 20, 1928, *Japan Times* article about McManus similarly mentions his fascination with the Japanese translation of his work: "'Look how they snore over there,' McManus exclaimed, pointing to a strip in which a number of queer figures were issuing from the mouth of Jiggs. Like a child with a new toy he turned the pages. The compliment of the thing which had been done was not half as important to him as was the way the editor had translated the words with the topsy-turvey Japanese symbols." On November 16, 1938, the *Asahi Graph* even featured a telegram by McManus commemorating his strip's fifteen-year anniversary in the publication:

Figure 1.8. Cover of the first Japanese *Bringing Up Father* anthology. (Image courtesy of Yorutori Bunko.)

To Japanese Readers

First of all I want to say that I am extremely proud that any work of mine has found favor in a land so far from the United States as the land of the Rising Sun.

I have always tried to put into my pictures the humor that appeals to human natures. The fact that a Japanese publisher has been interested enough——and brave enough——to put out an edition of these pictures, proves, that my effort was successful with at least one reader.

Human nature, after all, is pretty much the same in Japan as it is in the United States. Or in Egypt or Czeckoslovakia.

There are certain feelings in the men and women and children of all countries and all races of God's creation, that are never influenced or affected by wars or politics or rivalry of any kind.

Love is the same everywhere. Kindness is the same everywhere. Charity is the same everywhere. And, above all, humor appeals to all the world alike.

I sincerely hope that you will like Maggie and Jiggs. You must always bear in mind that no matter how much they quarrel, they are extremely fond of each other. Jiggs would never dream of running away from any other woman but his wife. And Maggie would absolutely refuse to hit any other man with a rolling-pin, excepting her own, dear husband,

People who are in love are always peculiar.

GEO McMANUS

Oct. 1924, New York,

日 本 の 讀 者 諸 君 に

先づ第一に、『日いづる國』のやうな、米國からさほく離れた國で私の作品が、歡迎をうけてゐることに就いて、私は非常に誇りを感じてゐることを云ふことを申し上げたいのであります。

私はこれまでしよつちう自分の畫に人間性に訴へる讚護味を入れることに骨折つて來て居ります。日本の一出版會社がかうした畫を出版しようさ云ふ意氣込さ勇氣さは、私の努力が、尠くさも一人の讀者に對しては効果を收めた證據であるさ云ひ得るのであります。要するにです、人情さいふものはこの國もたいがい同じものであります――日本も**アメリカ**も、或は**エヂプト**も、**チエツクスロヴキヤ**も。苟くも神様の創造になるこころの總ゆる國、あらゆる人種に屬する男、女、子供の間には、一つの共通の感情があつて、戰爭の爲にも、政治の爲にも其他如何なる競爭の爲にも、決して影響、打撃をうけないのであります。

愛はいづくも同じ。親切はいづくも同じ。慈善はいづくも同じ。だが、更に、讚護味は全世界にわたつて同じくうけいれられるものであります。皆さんが、**マギイ**さ**ジグス**を、さうぞお好き下さることを私は衷心から希望いたします。この二人は、いくら喧嘩をしても、實際はお互に、非常に愛し合つてゐるのださいふことをお忘れないやうに頼ひます。**ジグス**は、**マギイ**以外の女から夢にも逃けようなんて思はないのであります。又**マギイ**も、例のパン棒で、他の男を毆ることは絶對に拒絶します。――毆られるのは、親愛なる彼女の御亭主さんだけであります。

相惚れ仲間は一風變つてゐますよ。

一九二四年十月

紐育にて、　**ジヨージ マクマナス**

Figure 1.9. Bilingual foreword by McManus. (Image courtesy of Yorutori Bunko.)

> I am honored and pleased to learn that jiggs and his family and friends have been entertaining the readers of asahigraph for fifteen years stop
>
> My heartiest congratulations and best wishes for a continuance of our relationship banzai[29]

McManus may have considered his work's enormous success in Japan particularly amusing in light of a prescient joke he made in the foreword to a collected volume of *Bringing Up Father* strips published in the United States in 1919, four years before Jiggs and Maggie spoke Japanese for the first time:

> I could easily tell you how good this book is, how clever and artistic the drawings, how humorous the jokes, what a really fine job I made of the whole business and how it is easily worth ten times the ridiculous price it is sold for. But modesty forbids. The greatest rooter for this series is the Mikado of Japan who, in his annual message to the Japanese parliament, made the flat-footed statement:
>
> "[illegible] BRINGING UP FATHERニュウ, ニフの假名遣に属するもののみを"
>
> The italics are all his own.[30]

Whether the Japanese emperor later actually became a fan remains unknown, but the immense popularity of *Bringing Up Father* jokingly predicted by McManus is beyond doubt and illustrates why Japanese manga artists became eager to adopt its form.

Just how big a cultural phenomenon *Bringing Up Father* was in 1920s Japan is made clear by Jiggs and Maggie's appearances in a variety of product advertisements in Japanese newspapers and magazines. Between 1923 and 1932, a vast number of copies of more than two dozen different original ads was published in which McManus's characters endorse goods as diverse as insurance, beauty products, stoves, alcoholic beverages (fig. 1.10), nutritional supplements, bicycle parts, shaving cream, soap,

Figure 1.10. Daikoku wine advertisement. (Image courtesy of Yorutori Bunko.)

frozen fish, medication, and most appropriately, corned beef, Jiggs's favorite foodstuff.[31] According to an October 31, 1926, *Japan Times & Mail* article on *Bringing Up Father*, "The Laugh that Circles the Globe," the food at first was actually not associated with Jiggs in Japan: "It literally required an earthquake to make corned beef and cabbage universal. When Jiggs and Maggie first went to Japan, it was necessary for that delectable dish to be changed to gemai [*sic*; perhaps *genmai*, brown rice]. Then came the earthquake. American food was rushed to Japan, and among the American foodstuffs was corned beef. Now Jiggs sneaks down to Dinty Moore's for corned beef and cabbage in Tokyo just as he does in Chicago."[32]

During the 1920s, advertisements featuring Jiggs and/or Maggie far exceeded in number all ads featuring characters from other comics or picture stories *combined*, though Jiggs and Maggie were eventually overtaken in terms of advertisement appearances during the 1930s by Popeye, Betty Boop, Mickey Mouse, and the Japanese character Norakuro. Three crossover advertisements with other comics characters also exist[33] and some advertisements are even written as comic strips.[34] The high concentration of advertisements featuring Jiggs and/or Maggie between 1923 and 1925 suggests that these years represent the peak of their popularity, when *Bringing Up Father* was still relatively new. On the other hand, an advertisement from 1932 shows that although their popularity waned somewhat after 1925, Jiggs and Maggie were far from forgotten.

The remarkably large number of advertisements based on *Bringing Up Father* not only constitutes strong evidence that McManus's strip was the most popular work of graphic narrative in Japan during the 1920s but further illustrates that its characters were famous enough to be recognized also by readers of newspapers other than the Asahi publications in which Jiggs and Maggie's stories were printed.[35] Even newspapers such as the *Miyako Shinbun*, for example, which published almost no picture stories or comic strips of any nature during the 1920s and 1930s, featured ads based on *Bringing Up Father*, showing that the agencies or companies paying for the advertisements assumed a general familiarity with Jiggs and Maggie among a significant share of *all* Japanese newspaper readers. The extent to which their likenesses were used in advertising also exceeds that preserved in the surviving copies of newspapers and magazines. For example, the Tokkapin brand of nutritional and medical products (still sold today as a nutritional supplement drink) used Jiggs not only to recommend a nutritional supplement as "Jiggs's best friend" in a newspaper advertisement but also to advertise their "Tokkapin Hit" series of products on a flyer addressed to retailers (fig. 1.11; though the flyer is undated, it was likely printed between 1923 and 1925, when Jiggs and Maggie starred most frequently in advertisements). Given that the product featured most

prominently on the flyer is targeted toward women (a vaginal supposi-
tory, upper left of fig. 1.11), one might wonder why only Jiggs was included
and not Maggie, but rather than vouching for the products' efficacy, Jiggs
here is providing business advice to retailers (e.g., to order and stock good
products quickly). His use in such a flyer implies that at one point, Jiggs
was a universally recognized character in Japan and sufficiently beloved
that a company could safely assume that being associated with him would
be to its advantage.

   An article on *Bringing Up Father* published in the May 22, 1924, morning edition of the *Tōkyō Asahi Shinbun* supports this conclusion by stating that Jiggs "has surpassed being a popular character on paper and has
become a popular character widespread *in society at large*."[36] This popularity is also reflected in letters to the editor that the *Asahi Shinbun* received
about Jiggs and Maggie. A month before the article extolling Jiggs's
popularity, for example, the paper published a letter from a reader in its
"voices from the street" column (*chimata no koe*; April 19, evening edition) inquiring about a planned publication of a stand-alone volume of
Bringing Up Father strips that the reader had heard about. The newspaper's response was that a book would be published soon. On the same day,
the manga-related letter-to-the-editor "Memo" column also published a
letter signed "Jiggs's best friend" (no relation to the Tokkapin brand, presumably) inviting Jiggs to go see the cherry blossoms together, promising
him corned beef and cabbage. On May 28, the *Tōkyō Asahi Shinbun* even
announced the winners of a *Bringing Up Father*–related contest. One week
later, the June 6 evening edition featured a reader-submitted *Bringing Up
Father* strip (guest-starring Sho-chan from *Shō-chan no bōken*; fig. 1.12),
which apparently had been the winner of the earlier contest. On May 29,
the newspaper in its "Memo" column had also printed another letter from
a reader asking if a *Bringing Up Father* book had already been published
and, if so, where it could be bought. The response this time informed the
questioner that he must be mistaken; the book had not yet been published. The book was finally formally announced in the newspaper on

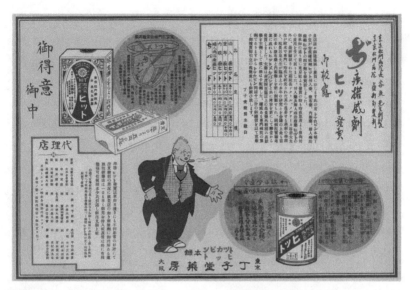

Figure 1.11. Tokkapin flyer featuring Jiggs. (Image courtesy of Yorutori Bunko.)

Figure 1.12. Reader-drawn strip using *Bringing Up Father* characters, *Tōkyō Asahi Shinbun*, June 6, 1924.

November 10, purportedly in response to reader demand. Readers apparently even cared so much about the strip that when it was moved from the front to the second page on June 3, 1924, the *Tōkyō Asahi Shinbun* added a note to the front page assuring readers that they would find it on page 2.

The *Asahi Shinbun* was correct that Jiggs and Maggie were so well-liked in Japan that the characters had moved beyond the printed page: A *Bringing Up Father* stage play was performed beginning June 24, 1924, at the Ushigome Kaikan at Kagurazaka, with related coverage in the *Tōkyō Asahi Shinbun* on June 16, 23, and 24.[37] According to the June 24 article on the play, a Tokyo representative of International Feature Service named Perry attended the rehearsal and was sufficiently impressed to proclaim that he would send a telegram about the play back to the United States. This Perry may have been the same person as the representative from whom Suzuki Bunshirō originally purchased the translation rights. On September 13, the Tokyo Asahi newspaper announced in its music column the sale of a record based on *Bringing Up Father*, written by Machida Ōen and performed by the Tsurumi Kagetsuen Shōjo Kagekidan (Tsurumi Kagetsuen Girls' Musical Revue; it is unclear whether there was any connection to the stage play). The 1925 New Year's issue of the *Asahi Graph* even included a *sugoroku* game board featuring Jiggs and Maggie, Bud Fisher's characters Mutt and Jeff (who by then were appearing in the *Asahi Shinbun*'s Osaka edition), and Sho-chan and his squirrel (fig. 1.13), and when an American live-action *Bringing Up Father* movie by Metro Goldwyn Meyer was confirmed in 1927, the *Tōkyō Asahi Shinbun* reported on it on December 9 of that year.

The number of advertisements featuring Jiggs and Maggie, the letters from readers, newspaper articles, merchandise like the *sugoroku* board, the stage play, and the extent to which the strip was featured in various publications all suggest that in 1920s Japan, *Bringing Up Father* was both the most popular work of graphic narrative as well as a genuine popular culture phenomenon. A January 1928 article in the *Zen-Kansai Fujin Rengōkai* on the effects of (theoretically) switching one's sex/gender even featured Jiggs and Maggie's faces as part of its headline, indicating that at this point

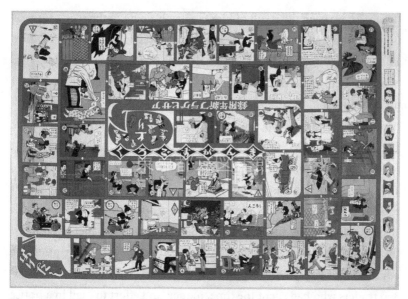

Figure 1.13. Manga *sugoroku* board, *Asahi Graph*, January 1925.

the couple was seen as representative of the relationship between men and women generally. An editorial in the August 1937 issue of *Manga no Kuni* (Land of manga) referred to Jiggs and Maggie's strip as popular all over the world, and as "unexpectedly popular even in our country,"[38] but Japanese readers' embrace of Jiggs and Maggie was more than one facet of a global trend: though *Bringing Up Father* was indeed popular in other countries at the time as well, there are none in which it occupied a similarly preeminent position as it did in Japan.

It is difficult to ascertain what precisely made *Bringing Up Father* so much more popular than other audiovisual comics. The May 22, 1924, article in the *Tōkyō Asahi Shinbun* cited earlier claimed that the popularity of *Bringing Up Father* showed how Americanized the Japanese had become, but this does not explain why it was more popular than other American strips. After all, despite the multitude of other foreign strips published in prewar Japan, none came close to *Bringing Up Father*'s seventeen years of continuous publication. *Asahi Graph* editor Suzuki Bunshirō hints that this may have been the result of his own involvement in the strip's translation and publication. In Suzuki's opinion, a successful comic strip requires a discerning editor, because it is often the case that newspaper staff will tire of a strip before the readership and become overly critical of it and end up canceling it.[39] According to the article accompanying McManus's 1938 telegram, the *Asahi Graph*, too, at one point considered dropping *Bringing Up Father* but decided against it because of readers' overwhelming support for its continuation. Suzuki and this article are likely referring to August 14 and 21, 1935, when the *Asahi Graph*, under its respective *Bringing Up Father* episodes, urged its readers to weigh in by postcard as to whether the comic strip should be continued or not. On September 4, the paper announced the results: approximately 7,300 readers had voted to keep printing the adventures of Jiggs and Maggie, with roughly 2,900 opposed (plus about 800 readers who had spent the time, money, and effort to mail in a notice saying that they did not feel strongly enough one way or the other). Suzuki may have been partly responsible for this solid support: although he declares that the other American comics published in Japan were simply "not funny," it is more probable that Jiggs and Maggie's outstanding popularity was due rather to Suzuki's practice of discarding issues whose jokes did not translate well into Japanese and only publishing those that he personally deemed able to preserve their humor in translation.[40]

The *Asahi Graph* also seems to have taken more care in translating its flagship manga than other publications did. The paper's vice editor in chief Hata Sankichi told the *Japan Times* for an October 17, 1932, article that translating the dialogue proved rather difficult but that the attention to detail paid off: "We suffered bitter experiences in translating the 'patter' in this cartoon. Mr. Nakazato, the translator, sometimes corrected his words more than ten times. This scheme met with great success. The public were convulsed with laughter over Jiggs and Maggie."[41] The article on the global success of *Bringing Up Father* in the October 31, 1926, *Japan Times & Mail* ("The Laugh That Circles the Globe") suggests that supply-side awareness of translation issues may have benefitted Nakazato in his work:

It is the tendency of Jiggs and Maggie to travel further afield each year, which causes Mr. McManus most of his troubles. "Hey!" yelled his syndicate editor only the other day, "don't crack any more Fourth of July jokes. We are sending 'Bringing Up Father' to the Chinese papers now, and your Chinese readers will think the firecrackers mean 'Happy New Year.'" As the reading public of each additional nation is introduced to Jiggs and Maggie, Mr. McManus must make pictures more universal in their appeal. Gone are the days when a comic character could celebrate Christmas, St. Patrick's Day, and Washington's Birthday just like any other person. *A Christmas joke does not mean a great deal in Japan* [emphasis added], the German reading public is not keenly interested in March 17th, and Washington's Birthday is not yet a public holiday in Buenos Aires.

Certainly, a combination of factors contributed to making *Bringing Up Father* both more popular in Japan than in other countries and more popular there than other foreign strips and domestic picture-story manga: International Feature Service's and McManus's efforts to make the strip as universal as possible on the one hand, and Suzuki's vigilant editing and Nakazato's careful translations (to ensure that each episode would be funny to the Japanese readership) on the other. Through the resulting success, these factors then also contributed to the rush among competing publications to secure their own foreign audiovisual comic strips—as well as to the eventual adoption of these strips' underlying form by Japanese artists.

CHAPTER 2

"LISTEN VUNCE!"

THE AUDIOVISUAL REVOLUTION IN GRAPHIC NARRATIVE

The unique factors that made *Bringing Up Father* the *most* popular manga of the 1920s do not explain why so many other foreign comic strips were also successful—often more so than Japanese-drawn works. Refined drawing and funny writing surely played a role in the general success of American and other foreign comics in Japan, but the central factor was likely that these comics were an entirely new medium, one most suited to the audiovisual age of phono-, photo-, and cinematographs that Japan had entered.

As is evident from the many translations that kept the comic strips' original reading order and were advertised as "American manga," a significant part of foreign comics' popularity was their status as "Western," which in Taishō-period Japan translated to "modern." What made these translated comic strips so modern and different from existing manga was not their place of origin, however, but their audiovisual nature: the "talking" and "moving" nature of audiovisual comics represented a revolutionary break with previous forms of storytelling on the page. Prior to the influx of American comics, Japanese manga characters didn't speak to each other. Their stories were for the most part relayed by narrative text, with static images serving as illustrations (see figs. P.3, P.4, or 1.2, for example). Jiggs and Maggie and the other comics characters that would follow them, on the other hand, seemed to move around on the page, thanks to motion lines and similar devices, and to actually, almost audibly (in the reader's head) speak to each other. Sound images, as well as devices introducing motion and sensation (pain, primarily) to graphic narrative, are fundamentally modern in that they developed in response to new nineteenth-century scientific and technological advances, with sound being the final component to complete the basic model of contemporary comics as an audiovisual medium relaying stories mimetically through the pretense of recording events "mechanically," without the need for narratorial mediation.

It is difficult to understand in retrospect how different *Bringing Up Father* and other American comic strips must have appeared to their Japanese audience in 1923 and to appreciate how radically different these comic strips were from previous forms of storytelling as opposed to simply being picture stories that "happened to use speech balloons." The first transdiegetic, audiovisual comics, however, represented not merely a shift from "no balloons" to "balloons," but from still images to motion and from silence to sound. The emergence of visual representations of phenomena like sound and motion, and their use to create what comics historian Thierry Smolderen has called "an audiovisual stage on the page," were nothing less than the result of a philosophical and technological revolution in seeing and hearing. The ability to "hear" a speech balloon is not an ahistorical, universal one that has existed throughout human history. Instead, being able to hear characters on a page actually speak to one another required a transformation of people's imagination, jump-started by the technology to record and play back sound.

This transformation of the imagination occurred first in the United States and made audiovisual comics not only possible but one of the most popular forms of entertainment in the country. Once devices like the phonograph had also sufficiently permeated Japanese society and transformed it in similar ways, those same audiovisual comics fell on fertile ground across the Pacific as well. Suzuki Bunshirō's introduction of *Bringing Up Father* spearheaded this massive importation of such comics from overseas.

Though the contemporary speech balloon as a sound image developed only between 1896 and 1899, shapes resembling balloons or scrolls that encapsulate text inserted into images could be found as early as the 1670s, in British prints like Francis Barlow's 1673 *The Egg of Dutch Rebellion*. These prephonographic word balloons were usually referred to as "loops" or "labels." Their superficial resemblance to the modern speech balloon has made possible the ahistorical narrative that contemporary comics have existed in more or less the same form for centuries (which of course parallels a similar ahistorical narrative for manga), but as Smolderen puts it, "The speech balloon couldn't have been more remote from its precursor, the label."[1] The primary purpose of loop/label word balloons was to provide information to help readers decipher the visual composition, not to render spoken dialogue. This is quickly demonstrated by the many prephonographic cartoons included in newspaper editor and writer Joseph Bucklin Bishop's 1892 article "Early Political Caricature in America," for example (freely accessible at www.archive.org). That it was self-evident for an observer like Bishop, writing before the appearance of the modern speech balloon, that the purpose of loop/label word balloons was "to explain the meaning of the picture" further supports this assumption.[2] Different authors have pointed out that prephonographic word balloons often seem "clumsy" or "awkward" to modern readers,[3] but this is not due to a lack of skill on the part of artists. The appearance of awkwardness when approached as sound images by contemporary readers, who are accustomed to seeing all word balloons as sound images, instead results from the fundamentally different purposes served by these ostensibly similar devices.[4]

The focus on *balloon shapes* (whether representing sound or not) rather than on *sound images* has long obscured the origins of sound in comics and manga. Though the speech balloon has become the primary shorthand for representing sound in comics, sound images do not require balloons and are not limited to them. This should be obvious to the contemporary reader, who is well-acquainted with sound effects like "BANG" and "POW," which are usually not enclosed in balloons. The distinction between "speech" on the one hand and "sound effects" (or "onomatopoeia") on the other, though unfortunately common in comics studies, is arbitrary, given that both are first and foremost representations of sound. The speech balloon is a convenient way of distinguishing speech from writing that is intradiegetic—letters, characters, and symbols existing and visible as such inside (intra) the story world (diegesis)—but a balloon shape is not a necessary condition for the representation of spoken words. Many of the first sound images in fact did not use balloons, and it is possible both to represent "speech" (*linguistic* sound images) without balloons and "sound effects" (*nonlinguistic* sound images) within them. Focusing on a particular graphic shape that came to be used to represent sound, instead of focusing on the representation of sound itself, obfuscates important historical developments and differences between distinct forms of graphic narrative, such as when we apply the term *speech balloon* to label/loop word balloons.

Though it may be impossible to prove beyond all doubt that prephonograph word balloons were never intended as representations of actual sound, there are three major reasons to assume that they were not: First, this older type of word balloon is primarily found in single images with allegorical meaning and functions as a means of decoding what is depicted. Even in the rare instances of groups of two or more images featuring such balloons, these "label" balloons are always deployed to clarify what an image is supposed to depict or the point it is making. Before the 1890s, there is not a single case in which balloons depict an ongoing conversation between characters across multiple images: the entire picture-story genre, first created by the Swiss school teacher Rodolphe Töpffer (1799–1846), which tells a story through narrative text but illustrates it with drawings (represented by figs. I.2, P.3, and P.4), remained devoid of such balloons. The only plausible explanation for why we find pre-1890s word balloons almost exclusively in allegorical images and rarely if ever in picture stories is that because these labels were meant to make comprehensible individual, complete images, and not to record sound audible within the story world, there was simply no way that it could have occurred to an artist to use them for a continuous conversation spanning multiple panels. Since picture stories were almost always narrated, there was no need for word balloons to clarify an image's meaning; the narration already fulfilled this purpose. Had such word balloons been intended as representations of sound in the same way as modern speech balloons, it would be exceedingly strange that over a period of more than two centuries, not a single artist ever decided to use them to represent a conversation over multiple panels.[5]

Second, images featuring prephonograph word balloons never include "sound effects," elements that render *nonlinguistic* sound—that is, any sound other than human language. If artists had understood word balloons as representations of sound even before it became known that sound *could* be recorded and reproduced, we should expect to see visual representations of sound other than word balloons, but such sound images appear only after the invention of sound-recording technology.

Third, the first modern speech balloons do not form a continuous lineage with the older type of word balloon found primarily in political, allegorical single-image cartoons but instead developed in a tradition of mostly wordless multipanel "pantomime" cartoons. Such multipanel cartoons in the late 1890s began featuring sound images (1) in direct response to the spread of the phonograph and (2) at first more commonly using radiating straight lines than balloon shapes. If the word balloons seen in political cartoons had already functioned audiovisually, as depictions of sound, it does not make sense that the first modern speech images would inexplicably abandon the balloon shape for radiating lines and that their immediate origins are so concretely intertwined with the experience of sound-recording technology. Why invent anew something that has already existed for over two centuries?

The answer is that prior to the experience of seeing and hearing actions and sound recorded over a span of time, as made possible by chronophotography (taking multiple photographs of the same object in quick succession) and sound recording, no model existed for the type of storytelling we see in audiovisual comics: one in which sound and motion are stored in a medium that enables them to be replayed at will. The lack of any precedent for the storage and reproduction of sound explains the absence of sound images from earlier graphic narratives (whether European, American, or Japanese). Before the philosophical and technological developments that enabled the recording of sound, the graphic representation of a concrete sound image uttered in a specific space and time, as opposed to the "timeless" representative labels seen in pre-nineteenth-century works, was inconceivable. Of course, writing since its invention has existed as a means of capturing speech, but prior to sound-recording technology, writing was never meant to serve as a *recording* of specific *sound* heard at a specific time, meant to be played back in the reader's head synchronously with an image. Before the nineteenth century, humans could not imagine seeing and hearing characters drawn on a page mimetically act out an unfamiliar story over consecutive images because there was neither a precedent nor a need for it. Stories could be told by narrating them and illustrating certain moments with pictures, such as in the picture stories of Rudolph Töpffer and Wilhelm Busch in Europe or *kibyōshi* (yellow cover) illustrated story booklets in Japan.[6] Before photography and phonography, there was nothing that could have inspired the idea that a story could be recorded visually and aurally in an unmediated, mimetic fashion. The use of speech balloons to represent sound on the page synchronously with the action depicted appears natural and timeless to us today only because we are already intimately familiar with the concept and technology of recording sound and reproducing it at will.

The creation of sound images like speech balloons was part of a broader historical development, an audiovisual revolution in graphic narrative. Though this book focuses heavily on sound images as the "final ingredient," the origins of audiovisual comics go beyond the history of sound images. The development of audiovisual comics in the nineteenth century begins with the appearance of multipanel "pantomime" cartoons, which tell a story by pretending to "mechanically record" events from moment to moment without the mediation of a narrator, and with the creation of forms of "transdiegetic" content preceding sound images: namely, the depiction of motion and pain, in order to facilitate such storytelling.

What do I mean by *transdiegetic*? The terms *intra-* and *extradiegetic* have long been used in film studies, where it is necessary to distinguish for example between music audible only to the spectator (such as the *Jaws* theme, which, fortunately for the shark, is not audible to swimmers) and such music as can be perceived by characters within the diegesis, the fictional world created by the narrative (such as the music coming from John Cusack's character's boombox in *Say Anything*, which, fortunately for him, *is* audible to his love interest). In the former case, the music is extradiegetic; in the latter, intradiegetic. Like films, narrative comics clearly contain intradiegetic elements—such as the characters, objects, and locations depicted—as well as extradiegetic elements, such as titles, panel borders, and authors' signatures. The division between intradiegetic and extradiegetic content is occasionally violated for comedic effect, as done in Winsor McCay's famous 1905 episode of his comic strip *Little Sammy Sneeze*, in which the titular character's sneeze causes the panel borders around him to collapse.[7] Early animated films, too, often contain similar jokes, such as in the 1919 *Feline Follies* when the protagonist, a primitive version of Felix the Cat, builds a vehicle out of music notes he has produced by playing the banjo (though the music itself is obviously intradiegetic, the viewer expects the visible note shapes representing it to be extradiegetic and hence imperceptible to proto-Felix). The existence of such violations does not refute the existence of the intra-extradiegetic boundary but rather confirms it, since such violations would be neither funny nor artistic without it. The more "serious" a comic strives to be, the less likely it will violate said boundary, much like films break the "fourth wall"—the boundary between the intradiegetic world and that of the spectator—primarily for comedic effect.

Comics rely on a third type of content in addition to intra- and extradiegetic, of which the sound-image speech balloon is the most common example and which is simultaneously part intradiegetic and part extradiegetic. In the speech balloon, for example, the balloon and the writing in it are invisible to intradiegetic characters, yet they nonetheless understand its content, by *hearing* it. When Jiggs and the burglar in figure 1.6 are having a conversation via speech balloons, we don't see them as reading each other's balloons, but as hearing each other's spoken words. Their speech balloons merely exist for our sake. In semiotic terms, we can consider the sound-image speech balloon a Saussurean sign consisting of a *signifier* (the convention through which meaning is expressed, e.g., a word) and a *signified* (the concept or meaning expressed by the signifier). The balloon's signifier (i.e., the concrete graphic object on paper) is extradiegetic (perceptible only to the reader), while its signified (i.e., the sound within the story world to which it refers) is intradiegetic (perceptible to characters inside the story world).[8] Devices like the speech balloon thus translate nonvisual intradiegetic content into a visual extradiegetic form, hence my use of the term *transdiegetic*.[9]

Contemporary comics as an audiovisual stage on paper can be understood as the tripartite division of content into intra-, extra-, and transdiegetic. After all, the conceptual division of all narrative content into these three distinct categories, but combined in the same image space, is precisely what distinguishes audiovisual comics from earlier forms of graphic narrative. For example, while picture stories in the European tradition—such as those by Rodolphe Töpffer, Wilhelm Busch, and Okamoto Ippei—establish an intradiegetic world, they spatially separate intradiegetic images and extradiegetic narration and feature little, if any, transdiegetic content. In *kibyōshi* stories, on the other hand, text and images are combined in the same image space, but it is frequently unclear whether text is intended as narrative or dialogue text, there is little to no demarcation between intradiegetic writing and other text, and in one story, a character actually sees and comments on text that is clearly not intradiegetic. Even in R. F. Outcault's 1890s *Yellow Kid* cartoons (see figs. 2.5 and 2.6), which some scholars have claimed "started comics," one cannot say for certain whether the writing on the Yellow Kid's nightshirt is intradiegetic (Can other characters see it?), extradiegetic (Is it written commentary aimed purely at the reader?), or transdiegetic (Is it invisible but signifying spoken words?). But in an audiovisual comic strip like *Bringing Up Father* virtually every element can be understood as clearly intra-, extra-, or transdiegetic.

Transdiegetic content, then consisting primarily of motion images, sound images, and pain images (lines or star shapes indicating pain or confusion), developed over the course of the mid-to-late nineteenth century in response to new technological inventions and a new understanding of sensory perception. As Jonathan Crary explains in *Techniques of the Observer*, the Enlightenment in Europe initiated a shift in philosophical and scientific notions of *seeing* that moved away from understanding vision as a passive reflection of the physical world as it is, and toward understanding vision as images actively created by the human sensory apparatus and brain in response to stimuli. During the nineteenth century, the understanding spread that human vision was rooted in the corporeal observer (i.e., in the concrete bodily functions creating the ability to see) and hence subjective rather than a scientifically precise and objective method of capturing material truth. This change in the conception of vision enabled the development of new technologies of visual perception, culminating both in artistic frameworks like impressionism and cubism, and in devices like the photo camera and kinetograph.

Prior to the nineteenth century, it was inconceivable to depict motion itself, for motion has no material existence that could be accurately captured in a still image, which explains why in pre-nineteenth-century European visual art, moving objects are represented only in their objective state at the precise moment of depiction, which to the contemporary observer used to motion blurs in impressionist paintings and photographs and motion lines in comics, creates the impression of such objects being frozen in time.[10] Though we see early isolated experiments with motion images in the work of Busch ("Ein Abenteuer in der Neujahrsnacht," 1863; "Der Virtuos," 1865) and even Töpffer (*M. Cryptogame*, 1845), they only become more frequent in the late 1880s and early 1890s. Like motion images, pain/ impact images signifying pain or confusion, such as the transdiegetic stars we see in the first Japanese issue of *Bringing Up Father* (fig. 1.6, panel 4), could not have existed prior to the nineteenth-century realization that not everything we see has a material existence. Pain images developed later than motion images, around 1892–1893, but like motion lines and blurs, they became a common element of cartoons by the century's end (and show up in Japan as early as 1902 in Kitazawa's *Jiji Manga*).[11] On May 16, 1897, for example, an episode of the multipanel cartoon series *The Journal Kinetoscope* (published in the *New York Journal*), showed a goat inhaling air from a tire and floating through the air before exhaling and crashing down (fig. 2.1). After the goat exhales, motion lines in the penultimate panel indicate that it is spinning from the sudden movement. The final panel shows the goat on the ground, with several pain stars next to its head.

The Journal Kinetoscope explicitly showcases the link between new nineteenth-century technologies and graphic narrative: featuring the tagline "Taken at the Rate of a Million a Minute," it depicted short humorous vignettes in a manner designed to look like a celluloid film strip. The history of graphic narrative is ripe with such connections between technological devices and formal, artistic, and narrative choices in cartooning.[12] The use of black silhouette figures in graphic narrative in the 1880s and 1890s can be tied to the spread of magic lanterns, for example.[13] And while the magic lantern did not create a moving image, the creation and availability of devices that did, such as phenakistoscopes, zoetropes,

Figure 2.1. *The Journal Kinetoscope*, May 16, 1897. (Image courtesy of San Francisco Academy of Comic Art Collection, Ohio State University, Billy Ireland Cartoon Library and Museum.)

praxinoscopes, zoöpraxiscopes, and kinetoscopes,[14] exerted similar influence, as evidenced, for example, by an 1882 multipanel cartoon called "New Zoöpraxiscopic Views of an Eminent Actor in Action."[15]

So-called pantomime cartoons like *The Journal Kinetoscope* furthermore demonstrated that action could be shown without the crutch of external narration. Several such silent, mimetic multipanel cartoons that no longer required narratorial explication had been created by artists like Busch and others as early as the 1860s but remained rare for the next two decades. It was only after advances in visual technology, such as Eadweard Muybridge's publication of stop-motion photographs of moving objects in the 1870s, that pantomime cartoons surged in popularity and became a common feature of Euro-American humor magazines in the 1880s and newspapers in the 1890s.[16] As Thierry Smolderen points out, what the authors of such mimetic cartoons "tried to emulate (with a grain of salt) was the *mechanical recording of human action* by such processes as chronophotography and Edison's Kinetoscope"[17]—see *The Journal Kinetoscope* and its tagline "Taken at the Rate of a Million a Minute," a direct reference to the process of mechanical recording.

This mechanical recording of events, and the infusion of images with motion, added to graphic narrative a crucial prerequisite for the depiction of sound: the depiction of time, or "chronography." The implied passing of time within and across images makes possible the depiction of sound meant to be replayed simultaneously with the action depicted, since sound itself is a type of movement (sound waves) occurring over time. It would not have made sense to depict a concrete sound within a frozen, "timeless" representation of the physical world or an allegorical image, the only images conceivable to Western artists before the nineteenth century. While this notion may sound abstruse, it helps explain why the modern speech balloon and related sound images evolved in close temporal proximity to other forms of transdiegetic content and in "mechanically recorded" cartoons depicting events unfolding over successive images in relatively small intervals of time, and not in Euro-American prints featuring label-type word balloons or Japanese picture stories with printed lines of dialogue such as *kibyōshi*, which relied on a single image per scene.[18] Though it is theoretically possible to call any combination of image and dialogue text "audiovisual," I would argue that for us to truly read a graphic narrative audiovisually, it must allow us to understand its "sound" as being played back simultaneously and synchronously with depicted events unfolding over time. This is possible only with "chronographic" images and not when text is merely superimposed on a static single-panel composition.

Even more so than other forms of transdiegetic content discussed above, the sound-image speech balloon developed as a direct response to the spread of new technology (i.e., the phonograph) and was understood by the public because of the now-common experience that sound could be stored and played back at will. Like photography, sound-recording technology had been made possible by an underlying shift in Euro-American knowledge about the nature of the human sensory apparatus. In *The Audible Past*, Jonathan Sterne argues convincingly that "sound-reproduction technologies are artifacts of vast transformations in the fundamental nature of sound, the human ear, the faculty of hearing, and practices of listening that occurred over the long nineteenth century."[19] Sterne posits that in the scientific study of sound during that period, attention shifted from the mouth to the ear as the locus of sound—away from the *sources* of those vibrations that the human sensory apparatus perceives and renders as the experience of sound ("the mouth") and to precisely this apparatus ("the ear"). Like Jonathan Crary, Sterne cites the work of biologist Johannes Müller as a factor, which concluded that "sound has no existence but in the excitement of a quality of the auditory nerve."[20] Focusing on the eardrum (tympanum) and how it registered and transmitted vibrations permitted researchers like Alexander Graham Bell to understand that in order to reproduce sound, it was necessary only to replicate the vibrations themselves and not the precise conditions under which they had originally been generated. Other researchers, focusing on the mouth rather than the ear, had tried to create automata that would generate sonic vibrations much like an actual human's vocal apparatus would, but this approach proved ineffective. Seeing the *ear* as the locus of sound production was a prerequisite for making possible the invention of devices such as the phonograph and the telephone, for which the original means by which a sound had been produced were irrelevant.

Sterne's argument has in common with Crary's the proposition that over the course of the nineteenth century in Europe and the United States, the understanding of a sense (sight/sound) shifted away from conceptualizing the sense as a passive reflection of an objective reality that exists outside of the human mind and toward understanding this sense as the active generation of what is seen or heard by nerves and the brain. This explains why we do not see transdiegetic depictions of motion or sound before the mid-to-late nineteenth century. Before, it had been simply impossible to re-create motion and sound on the page, because according to the prevailing knowledge at the time, this would have required reproducing in some form their visible physical reality, which neither possessed. At the time, physical objects and bodies were the only things whose material reality could be reproduced on paper in a similar fashion as it appeared to their observer, if in flattened, simplified, and/or caricatured fashion. It was only with the spreading knowledge that motion and sound were centered in the observer/listener that it became possible to re-create these phenomena on the page, because all that mattered now was to evoke their perception in this observer/listener; their physicality and objective reality had become irrelevant. In other words, it was no longer necessary to reproduce the thing itself; all that was needed was to "excite the right nerves" and trigger a *perception* of movement or sound, which could be achieved via transdiegetic content like motion lines and sound images.

Notwithstanding the speculative nature of this argument, it is indisputable that transdiegetic representations of sound closely followed the emergence of technology that could record it. The development of the speech balloon in response to the phonograph is not the only direct evidence for

this: the earliest definitive representation of sound itself in a graphic narrative that I have been able to find is the 1869 cartoon "The Philosopher's
Revenge" by George du Maurier (figs. 2.2 and 2.3), drawn twelve years after
Édouard-Léon Scott de Martinville's 1857 invention of the phonautograph,
the first machine to record sound, albeit not in reproducible form.[21]

The phonautograph's invention was made possible precisely by the
shift in knowledge described by Sterne: the realization that the key to
understanding sound was not its source but its transmission via the eardrum enabled de Martinville to construct a machine that transmitted
sonic vibrations via a membrane (analogous to the eardrum) to a stylus.
Moved by the vibrations, the stylus would then leave marks on a surface
like glass or paper. Though the bulbs at the end of the sound images in
"The Philosopher's Revenge" are almost certainly derived from the shape
of a music note, when we look at images of phonautograph recordings
such as figure 2.4, it is not difficult to see how news of the phonautograph
and its recording of sound as long jagged lines likely inspired du Maurier
to draw the body of the sound images the way he did (panels 4, 10, and 14).
See how closely the scrawling lines intersected perpendicularly by straight
shorter lines at regular intervals in du Maurier's sound images resemble
the recordings in figure 2.4. Such phonautograph recordings were printed
in European publications as early as 1865, four years before du Maurier
drew "The Philosopher's Revenge."[22] Du Maurier's interest in audiovisual
technology is evident from a cartoon he later drew for *Punch* in 1879, titled
"Edison's Telephonoscope (Transmits Light as Well as Sound)," in which
he imagines a then-futuristic video call.

Note how "The Philosopher's Revenge," despite clearly featuring sound
images, pointedly does not use any word balloons, neither for the singer's
visualized vocals nor for the unvisualized conversation between the philosopher and the street organ player, showing how unnatural an idea it still was to
represent dialogue as transdiegetic sound. It is unsurprising that it took longer
for transdiegetic sound to become a regular element of cartoons than it did for
transdiegetic motion; not only did photography precede phonography, but

Figure 2.2. George du Maurier, "The Philosopher's Revenge," part 1, March 13, 1869.

Figure 2.3. "The Philosopher's Revenge," part 2, March 27, 1869.

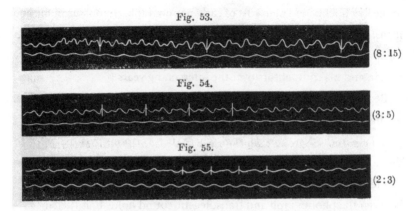

Figure 2.4. Phonautograph recordings depicted in Franz Josef Pisko's 1865 *Die neueren Apparate der Akustik*. (Image courtesy of Library of Congress.)

considering the visual nature of cartooning it must have appeared significantly more obvious to artists to incorporate transdiegetic content related to vision than such content related to sound. Transdiegetic sound images thus remained extremely rare for nearly thirty years after "The Philosopher's Revenge" (mostly confined to cartoons about the telephone in the 1870s and 1880s) and only became a regular part of graphic narrative once the spread of the phonograph across American society made them a necessity.

The phonograph was patented by Thomas Edison in 1877 and used the same "mechanical recording" of sound via a membrane and stylus as the phonautograph. But whereas the phonautograph had turned sonic vibrations into marks on a flat surface, the phonograph carved them into a rotating wax or tinfoil cylinder. When traced again from the beginning with a different type of stylus, this recording could transmit vibrations matching the carved track back to the membrane, generating sound waves similar to the ones that made the recording. It is amazing (to me, at least) that this invention actually worked, but it did (various videos of attempts to replicate the original phonograph to varying degrees of success are available on the internet[23]), becoming the foundation for all sound-reproduction technology that would follow, up to the present. Due to the low fidelity and high cost of early phonographs, it took until the late 1890s, however, for phonographs to become a useful and affordable item for many Americans, after multiple improvements to the technology by Edison and his competitors over the intervening years.[24]

Reproducing human voices had never before in history been possible, so this technology unsurprisingly became a frequent topic of cartoons, especially in the *New York Journal*, where such cartoons eventually led to the normalization of sound images in graphic narrative and the creation of the modern speech balloon.[25] A popular portrayal of the connection between the phonograph and transdiegetic sound holds that Richard Felton Outcault established the contemporary speech balloon in 1896 with a single multipanel cartoon featuring his Yellow Kid character and a phonograph.[26] However, the establishment of sound as a standard feature of graphic narrative was a complex process that took almost three years, demonstrating just how profoundly novel the notion of hearing characters on a page speak truly was.

In Outcault's cartoon, the Yellow Kid responds to—or more accurately, comments on—word balloons coming out of a phonograph advertising the *New York Journal* (fig. 2.5; the Kid's commentary is printed, as was usually the case, on his yellow nightshirt). In the fifth and last panel, a parrot—itself a recurring character in the Yellow Kid cartoons—is revealed to have been inside the phonograph and the true originator of the speech balloons. In this final panel, the Yellow Kid's commentary is suddenly expressed inside a balloon of its own, instead of on his shirt. Rather than the immediate beginning of comics as we know them today, Outcault's cartoon was merely the first of a long sequence of cartoons by various authors processing the astonishing experience of hearing—for the first time in history—voices disconnected from human speakers, what Kerim Yasar has called "the eeriness of hearing voices that can't be traced back to bodies."[27] After the phonograph cartoon, Outcault himself created only sixteen other sequential Yellow Kid cartoons and did not create a sequential narrative work that regularly used speech balloons until years

Figure 2.5. R. F. Outcault, "The Yellow Kid and His New Phonograph," October 25, 1896. (Image courtesy of San Francisco Academy of Comic Art Collection, Ohio State University, Billy Ireland Cartoon Library and Museum.)

later (the comic strip *Buster Brown* in 1902).[28] He largely abandoned sequential narrative after his first ten multipanel narrative cartoons that appeared between October 25, 1896, and February 14, 1897, and during the time that the Yellow Kid was appearing in print, no other artist regularly drew multipanel cartoons featuring sound images either. Uses of sound images in the *New York Journal* were still extremely rare at the time, with only a handful of examples in multipanel cartoons for the entire year of 1897.[29]

The word balloon was somewhat of a trademark for Outcault in the mid-1890s, which explains why he is so readily identified with the modern speech balloon. Word balloons had largely disappeared from American cartooning by the 1870s, when it had become more popular to add captions underneath images or not include text at all (see the numerous examples in William Murrell, *A History of American Graphic Humor [1865–1938]*, and Joseph Bucklin Bishop, "Early Political Caricature in America"),[30] but Outcault made extensive use of the word balloon in his single-panel cartoons featuring the Yellow Kid, repopularizing it. For the most part, Outcault clearly did not intend word balloons to operate as sound images, however. They generally functioned as extradiegetic jokes for the reader rather than as sound images recording intradiegetic sound, as is evident not only from the balloons' general absence in Outcault's "chronographic" multipanel cartoons but also from their near-exclusive use for inanimate objects, animals, and a boy frequently shown falling while calmly commenting on his situation, all situations in which it does not make sense to interpret these balloons as sound images.

It is unclear why Outcault chose to use a balloon for the Yellow Kid's final utterance in the phonograph cartoon instead of the usual writing on his shirt, but it is noteworthy that neither the Kid nor the parrot talks to the other; both address the reader. Outcault uses the balloons primarily as a way to signify that a (seemingly) human voice is coming out of a machine and to make fun of this notion. Out of his seventeen multipanel narratives, several feature no balloons at all (including four narratives out of the last five—indicating a move *away* from an aural component), while the others use balloons exclusively for sound reproduction technology (the phonograph and a talking "phonograph alarm clock," fig. 2.6) and animals, apart from two exceptions (October 25 and December 13, 1896) in which the Yellow Kid himself uses a word balloon (a single one each). In no instance do his characters—human or otherwise—actually converse (i.e., respond to one another's utterances) using speech balloons or another type of sound image. The balloons are used either to address the reader or to make fun of the experience of hearing disembodied human voices, as is the case in the balloons used for phonographic devices and animals. It did not occur to Outcault that these word balloons could be used as sound images to record entire conversations between characters.

Responding to the revolutionary experience of hearing disembodied voices by making it the subject of cartoons, as Outcault did, eventually did lead to the realization that *all* sound could be reproduced on the page, but this process was incremental and most of these early sound images did not

Figure 2.6. "The Yellow Kid's New Phonograph Clock," February 14, 1897. (Image courtesy of San Francisco Academy of Comic Art Collection, Ohio State University, Billy Ireland Cartoon Library and Museum.)

use balloon shapes. Sound images in narrative cartoons during the time between Outcault's phonograph cartoon in 1896 and the first conversation conducted via such sound images, by Rudolph Dirks's *Katzenjammer Kids* in 1899, remained tied to the phenomenon of a "voice-speaker disconnect" that the phonograph had created (Yasar's "eeriness of hearing voices that can't be traced back to bodies") but tended to use straight lines instead of balloons. On January 10, 1897, for example, the *New York Journal* published a six-panel cartoon titled "The Mysterious Trunk—a Story with Words" (fig. 2.7). Its subtitle, "A Story with Words," is a wry comment on the fact that the cartoon, unlike most at the time, does not feature (extradiegetic) narrative text, while it does—again, unlike most cartoons then—feature (transdiegetic) words written directly into the panels—connected to their origin via lines rather than balloons. In the cartoon, a wealthy-looking

Figure 2.7. "The Mysterious Trunk—a Story with Words," January 10, 1897. (Image courtesy of San Francisco Academy of Comic Art Collection, Ohio State University, Billy Ireland Cartoon Library and Museum.)

man is followed by a porter dragging his trunk, out of which cries for help (such as "Police!!" "Let me out . . ." "Murder!!!") can suddenly be *heard*.[31] The surprised porter alerts nearby police, who cut open the trunk to reveal a parrot thanking them for its liberation. What is most striking about the cartoon from a contemporary perspective is the complete silence of the various human actors, especially in contrast with the parrot's loquaciousness in five out of the six panels. As in Outcault's phonograph cartoon, sound images here are used solely for the purpose of representing the shocking experience of hearing a human voice from a nonhuman source.

Since the joke in "The Mysterious Trunk" is this same disconnection of spoken words from a physically present human source, it is not difficult to imagine that the entry of phonographs into American homes at the time was a significant factor both in generating the idea for such a joke and in making the audience receptive to it. The notion that an ordinary (i.e., not supernatural or magical) parrot's voice could be mistaken for that of a human would have been incomprehensible to prephonograph readers, for whom any given human voice (outside of stories of a metaphysical nature) had always been inseparable from its human source. Although parrots are of course known for their ability to imitate human sounds, the parrot in "The Mysterious Trunk," rather than "parroting" individual words, is speaking on its own, much as a phonograph must have appeared to do to the 1897 audience.

At this early stage in their development, "speech images" were used exclusively for this type of joke. Two months after "The Mysterious Trunk," on March 21, 1897, the *Journal* featured a five-panel cartoon called "A Phonographic Proposal," in which a woman's suitor uses a phonograph recording to ask her father's permission to marry her (fig. 2.8). Unfortunately for the suitor, the recording only captures his bad-mouthing the father, which the latter then hears via the phonograph, leading the outraged father to kick the suitor out of the house. All the cartoon's speech is written underneath the panels, disconnected from the images. However, the phonograph's recording alone, when played by the father in the fourth panel, is also represented transdiegetically within the image, with a word balloon coming out of the phonograph. Similarly to "The Mysterious Trunk," the sound image here is used solely to illustrate the phenomenon of human speech originating from a nonhuman source.

Predictably, the next instance of a sound image in the *New York Journal* after "A Phonographic Proposal," too, was in a three-panel cartoon about a parrot (September 26, 1897). Outcault's cartoon about the phonograph had started a trend of cartoons about the voice–human speaker disconnect, which by its nature induced artists to employ early transdiegetic representations of speech—if you want to make a visual joke about someone mistaking a voice for something else, you have to find a way of representing said voice. Considering that in none of the cartoons by Outcault and other artists that employ at least some transdiegetic sound do we see characters interact with one another using transdiegetic speech, fully audiovisual narrative comics did not yet exist in 1897. However, the parrot and phonograph cartoons experimenting with transdiegetic sound laid the

Figure 2.8. "A Phonographic Proposal," March 21, 1897. (Image courtesy of Library of Congress.)

foundation for more complex uses of sound images—and for the speech balloon as we know it today.

The central figure in this development was a young cartoonist by the name of Rudolph Dirks. Though some histories of comics imply that Dirks merely continued Outcault's "invention of the speech balloon,"[32] Dirks's first experiments with transdiegetic linguistic sound used straight lines instead of balloons, and there is no immediate connection between Outcault's 1896 cartoon and the sound images employed by Dirks. Due to their use of straight lines, most of Dirks's early sound images in fact resemble those of "The Mysterious Trunk" more than those of "The Yellow Kid and His New Phonograph."[33] Dirks's *Katzenjammer Kids*, which eventually became the first fully audiovisual comic strip, did make its first appearance on December 12, 1897, a month before Outcault's *Yellow Kid* last appeared on January 23, 1898, but the "Katzies" started out as a silent pantomime strip that occasionally used external narrative text as well. Rather than continuing where Outcault had left off in 1897, Dirks started experimenting with linguistic sound images only in 1899, over a year later, and it was only by building on the voice-speaker disconnect joke that he realized that sound images could be used as a universal means of rendering all sound, including whole conversations.

It is no coincidence that it was Dirks who first discovered the possibility of having characters talk to one another on the page using transdiegetic signs. After all, more so than other cartoonists at the time, Dirks showed great affinity for transdiegetic content and included it liberally in his cartoons, employing motion lines, motion swirls, freestanding exclamation and question marks, hats flying off (i.e., drawn above) characters' heads to indicate surprise, dust clouds to show movement/speed, pain stars and exaggerated bumps as a result of blows to the body, and straight lines and music notes to indicate nonlinguistic sound. All these diverse uses of transdiegetic content happened within just his first year of working on the *Katzenjammer Kids*, which had started out as merely another American newspaper version of Wilhelm Busch's *Max und Moritz* (which, as we saw in the prologue, was popular not only in Busch's native Germany but all over the world, including in the United States and Japan).[34]

Despite Dirks's fluency in transdiegetic content, the discovery that transdiegetic sound could be used to make characters talk to one another took time and gradual experimentation. For over a year after the strip's creation, the *Katzenjammer Kids* used only simple sound images consisting of multiple straight lines (and music notes, in the case of music) to occasionally indicate the presence of sound, but even this use of sound was rare. Even an episode like "Those Artful Katzenjammer Kids and the Telephone" on February 27, 1898, in which sound plays a central role, remained entirely devoid of sound images (fig. 2.9). In this episode, the Katzenjammer Kids drill a hole into the wall that holds the family's telephone and, pretending to be their mother, instruct the maid to serve them pastries. Though characters are clearly shown conversing in panels 1, 2, 4, and 5, the content of their conversations is left for us to imagine. The absence of speech balloons makes the cartoon look antiquated from a contemporary perspective, but its story is perfectly intelligible; Dirks did not include any sound images because there was no need to do so. Still at this point in 1898, the inclusion of sound images was limited to cases where the nature of the events depicted *compelled* artists to use them, as previously seen in "The Philosopher's Revenge" and "The Mysterious Trunk." If the old "label" tradition of word balloons had been understood as a representation of sound all along, it makes little sense that the cartoonists creating these "mechanical recordings of human action" would have been so averse to using them.

The contemporary speech balloon, and with it the idea of capturing an entire conversation in audiovisual form, only came into being the following year, as the culmination of a gradual stretching by Dirks of the voice-speaker-disconnect joke, beginning on March 5, 1899, when the *Katzenjammer Kids* featured its first linguistic sound image (fig. 2.10). In that day's episode, "Those Terrible Katzenjammer Kids and the Toy Balloon," one of the Kids pretends to stab his brother, who screams, "Help!! Murder—Help!" Notably,

Figure 2.9. Rudolph Dirks, "Those Artful Katzenjammer Kids and the Telephone," February 27, 1898. (Image courtesy of San Francisco Academy of Comic Art Collection, Ohio State University, Billy Ireland Cartoon Library and Museum.)

these words are not framed by a balloon, but instead accompanied by several straight lines radiating from the source of the sound,[35] much as was the case with January 10, 1897's "The Mysterious Trunk" and also a July 31, 1898, six-panel cartoon imitative of the *Katzenjammer Kids* called "The Gashouse Twins Nearly Commit Murder," by William Marriner (viewable online via the image database of the Billy Ireland Cartoon Library and Museum or in Exner, "The Creation of the Comic Strip as an Audiovisual Stage in the *New York Journal* 1896–1900" at http://imagetext.english.ufl.edu/archives/v10 _1/exner/, fig. 13). In the latter cartoon, the Gashouse Twins hide a "speaking doll" (a doll featuring a small phonograph) in a well, presumably to prank their parents.[36] The single, repeated sound image is of the doll saying "Mama!!!" over and over again. These are just a few examples of how early cartoons featuring such sound images revolved around the same voice-speaker disconnect brought about by sound-recording technology, which necessitated the use of sound images to be depicted.[37]

Figure 2.10. "Those Terrible Katzenjammer Kids and the Toy Balloon," March 5, 1899. (Image courtesy of San Francisco Academy of Comic Art Collection, Ohio State University, Billy Ireland Cartoon Library and Museum.)

The joke in Dirks's March 5, 1899, "Those Terrible Katzenjammer Kids and the Toy Balloon" is that the Katzenjammer Kid to whom the sound image is attached is using a literal balloon as a fake head above his own (which is hidden inside his coat). The sound image in this case is still linked to the voice-speaker disconnect in that a listener (Mamma Katzenjammer) misattributes the sound to a different source, just as in "The Mysterious Trunk" and "The Gashouse Twins Nearly Commit Murder," in which people mistakenly assume that cries for help are coming from a different source (a human one instead of a parrot or doll). In contrast to "The Mysterious Trunk" and "The Gashouse Twins Nearly Commit Murder," though, the words here are actually spoken by a physically present human speaker. This use of a sound image for a human speaker instead of a parrot or phonograph (and at the same time, unlike in "The Yellow Kid and His New Phonograph," for an utterance clearly audible to other characters) marks an important shift from previous uses.

With "The Katzenjammer Kids Play Mazeppa with Two Dummies" (April 23, 1899; fig. 2.11), Dirks then takes a second major step in liberating the sound image from the voice-speaker disconnect. Again using the

Figure 2.11. "The Katzenjammer Kids Play Mazeppa with Two Dummies," April 23, 1899. (Image courtesy of San Francisco Academy of Comic Art Collection, Ohio State University, Billy Ireland Cartoon Library and Museum.)

"speech lines" type of sound image seen in "The Mysterious Trunk" et al, Dirks depicts the Kids hiding in a haystack and shouting for help (panel 4) in order to play a prank on Mamma. The joke is that the cries for help are misattributed by Mamma Katzenjammer to two dummies of her children, which the Kids have strapped to the back of a mule in order to send their Mamma chasing after it. Like the Gashouse Twins with their speaking doll and the Kids with the toy balloon, the joke remains that of an inanimate object (or a parrot) being mistaken for the source of a human voice. However, in "The Katzenjammer Kids Play Mazeppa with Two Dummies," the sound image is finally emancipated from the voice-speaker disconnect in that the sound images here not only are addressed to another character who reacts to them (Mamma Katzenjammer), as they already were in "Those Terrible Katzenjammer Kids and the Toy Balloon," but are now shown as *directly originating from the Kids themselves* instead of a decoy.

Nevertheless, sound images were still so intertwined with jokes about misattributed voices that Dirks kept drawing the *Katzenjammer Kids* with only occasional sound images for the next four months, such as whistling to attract a dog (June 4 and July 16), a single exclamation by Mamma (July 2), and the cries of a girl whom the Kids have tied to a tree (July 23). In the July 2 episode, "A July Fourth Prank That Didn't Work," Dirks writes the only other line of dialogue as an external caption below the image, as was common practice for dialogue at the time, but puts Mamma Katzenjammer's exclamation "Vat iss!" into a balloon shape.

Dirks had used a single word balloon to emphasize a heavily German-inflected utterance twice before, in two different cartoons on March 19, but due to his intervening expansion of the use of sound images beyond the voice-speaker disconnect Dirks must have realized soon after this—whether consciously or subconsciously—that any dialogue could be rendered as a sound image and that word balloons could be used in the same way as speech lines (which also made it far easier to represent full sentences than when using straight lines). In a historic first, on August 20 in "The Katzenjammer Kids Lose Their Clothes," Mamma Katzenjammer used two speech balloons over two consecutive panels as part of the same ongoing scene, unconnected to the voice-speaker disconnect (fig. 2.12).[38] This use of sound images to "mechanically record" someone speaking continuously over more than a single panel may seem like a rather insignificant innovation, but remember that outside of the context of cartoons about sound-recording technology, it was without precedent. All the previous uses of sound images to show someone (or something) speaking over successive images had been jokes about the voice-speaker disconnect, which made Dirks's cartoon groundbreaking. Note how all the other, silent panels in the episode also depict characters talking or shouting in them, but their words or sounds are not rendered. As seen in all previous multipanel cartoons from the late 1800s, it was far more "natural" for artists to draw stories as pantomimes or supply explanations or captions outside of the images. Sound had only made it into images when it was necessary

Figure 2.12. "The Katzenjammer Kids Lose Their Clothes," August 20, 1899. (Image courtesy of San Francisco Academy of Comic Art Collection, Ohio State University, Billy Ireland Cartoon Library and Museum.)

to get the joke. The plot of "The Katzenjammer Kids Lose Their Clothes," however, would be intelligible even without the two sound images. One could argue that Dirks intended to specify that Mamma Katzenjammer beats the thieves not for their crime but because she confuses them for her children, but in that case, an explanatory external line of dialogue or narration would still have been far more natural at the time, even for Dirks, as demonstrated a month earlier in the *Katzenjammer Kids* episode on July 9, whose plot and dialogue are narrated via text outside the images and which features a sound image (using lines) only for the ticking of a clock. Given his previous uses of balloons to highlight German-accented English, it is more plausible to assume that Dirks found that the addition of Mamma Katzenjammer's scolding in panel 5 ("Don't not make foolishness mit your old ma—you bad boys") and surprised exclamation in panel 6 ("Ach du lieber! Dere iss some more yet") as sound within the image would add to the strip's hilarity, quite possibly due to the specific vocal qualities of Mamma's heavy German accent.

This interpretation appears especially credible in light of the very next *Katzenjammer Kids* episode on August 27, "The Katzenjammer Kids Try to Tell Mamma a Joke" (fig. 2.13), which is based entirely on Mamma's poor English-language proficiency. In the episode, the Kids tell their Mamma the joke "Ven iss a door not a door? Ven it's a jar!" and try to explain it to her in vain (the strip ends with the Kids leaving in frustration while Mamma contemplates a container the Kids pointed to in their attempt, wondering, "Vat should it be, a jug der answer?").[39] This was the first-ever complete transdiegetic conversation on the page. "The Katzenjammer Kids Try to Tell Mamma a Joke" represents the logical conclusion to Dirks's gradual expansion of sound images from a necessary means to joke about the voice-speaker disconnect occasioned by sound reproduction technology to a universal device rendering all sound within a graphic narrative. As the earliest work that "mechanically records" not only individual sounds necessary to understand the plot but all dialogue between characters, it constitutes the oldest definitive common ancestor to all such transdiegetic comics

Figure 2.13. "The Katzenjammer Kids Try to Tell Mamma a Joke," August 27, 1899. (Image courtesy of San Francisco Academy of Comic Art Collection, Ohio State University, Billy Ireland Cartoon Library and Museum.)

that would follow it, including *Bringing Up Father* and all other audiovisual manga, as we will see in chapter 4. We cannot know if this fully audiovisual comic strip would have been intelligible to people before the nineteenth century and the popularization of technology that could record motion and sound. However, it is clear that this fundamentally new form of storytelling came into being only with the newfound knowledge that things *could* be recorded in this manner and with the unprecedented *necessity* to visualize sound itself in order to tell a certain type of story, the experience of hearing disembodied voices generated by the phonograph.

The radical newness of this type of storytelling is underscored by the fact that even after this first transdiegetic conversation in August 1899, sound images were not right away used universally to represent all dialogue, neither by Dirks nor by others, but still primarily for utterances of a particular vocal quality, such as exclamations, singing, recitations, or dialects (for example, in the *Katzenjammer Kids'* September 10 episode, "The Katzenjammer Kids Sing a Few Songs"). This continued limited use of sound images, first and foremost when the narrative required emphasizing certain unique vocal actions, shows the extent to which cartoonists were accustomed to telling stories without the use of sound and to what extent using sound images was *un*natural to them, even after the phonograph had made the representation of sound an occasional necessity.[40]

The above is true even for Frederick Burr Opper's *Happy Hooligan*, the first audiovisual strip to never use narrative commentary or external dialogue and, for this reason, sometimes portrayed as the first "real" comic strip. *Happy Hooligan* would later also become hugely successful in Japan and help establish audiovisual comics there as well, but when it first appeared on March 11, 1900, a few months after Dirks had begun employing the audiovisual form at least occasionally, it was still silent despite the obvious presence of intradiegetic sound like the performer's voice (fig. 2.14). Opper was quick to adopt Dirks's audiovisual form, however, which, considering their close connection, is no coincidence. The *New York Journal*'s Sunday cartoon supplement, in which *The Katzenjammer Kids* was appearing, had been publishing cartoons by Opper since June 4, 1899, and he must have been familiar with Dirks's work at that point. On March 25, 1900, the *Journal* also published a four-panel cartoon signed "F. Opper after sketch by Dirks," evidence of a collaborative relationship between the two cartoonists.

The first use of a (single) speech balloon in *Happy Hooligan* appeared in the same issue, after the strip's first two episodes (March 11 and 18) had been written as pantomime strips. The single speech balloon on March 25 was used to emphasize the act of speaking a foreign language: Happy is speaking German in an attempt to pass as a proper Teutonic member at the "Sangerbundverein's [*sic*] Grand Bierfest" in order to get away with drinking the free beer ("Feller citizens, Hoch der Kaiser! Bully fer de Dutch!"— unsurprisingly, Happy is found out and removed from the premises). It was only from May 6 onward that Opper drew *Happy Hooligan* almost exclusively in audiovisual form, using multiple sound-image balloons. Interestingly, this May 6 issue hearkens back to the voice-speaker disconnect joke begun by Outcault's "The Yellow Kid and His New Phonograph," likewise having its protagonist misled by a parrot's utterances. In contrast to

Figure 2.14. Frederick Burr Opper, *The Doings of Happy Hooligan*, March 11, 1900. (Image courtesy of San Francisco Academy of Comic Art Collection, Ohio State University, Billy Ireland Cartoon Library and Museum.)

the Yellow Kid, however, Happy Hooligan directly (verbally and physically) interacts with the trickster parrot in his strip (fig. 2.15), serving in a way as a culmination of the process begun by the Yellow Kid. That it took three years and a number of incremental steps to get from the Yellow Kid and his parrot to Happy Hooligan and his emphasizes the actual magnitude of this seemingly small change from using word balloons as a means to address the reader, to using them to show characters addressing one another.

As mentioned at the beginning of this chapter, one of the reasons ahistorical claims about prephonographic "speech balloons" are able to persist and why the sudden establishment of the audiovisual form in manga in 1923 has been treated as merely a stylistic change is that it seems such an *obvious* idea today to show human beings speaking to one another by rendering their actual words as a sound image near them (as opposed to depicting the characters silently in the act of uttering them and supplying the words as separate external dialogue or narrating them). Keep in mind, however, that until the early twentieth century, even until after the spread

Figure 2.15. *The Doings of Happy Hooligan*, May 6, 1900. (Image courtesy of San Francisco Academy of Comic Art Collection, Ohio State University, Billy Ireland Cartoon Library and Museum.)

of transdiegetic comics, there was no other medium that did this—likely the primary reason for comics' enormous success in the early twentieth century. The other immensely popular visual entertainment medium of the late nineteenth and early twentieth century besides graphic narrative, the cinema, had not yet come up with a viable way of featuring speech simultaneously with its human originators. It took until 1927's *The Jazz Singer* for sound to become a regular part of feature-length films (though there were earlier experiments), and even subtitles were not used until 1922's *Mireille*.[41] Before then, speech had to be represented with the help of *inter*titles, which functioned in a way similar to picture stories, with the dialogue text separated from the intradiegetic images (spatially in picture stories, temporally in film). As the history of transdiegetic sound in cartoons before 1900 demonstrates, to depict characters actually speaking to one another via sound images of their speech was an idea so radically different from previous visual storytelling that it was able to take shape only step by step—evolving incrementally from the voice-speaker disconnect caused by the phonograph—over years.

That learning to use sound images to depict entire conversations took so long shouldn't be all that surprising if one considers that capturing image and sound simultaneously had been impossible for all of human history preceding the invention of film and sound recording. It is difficult to imagine what life was like before recorded sound, but as an analogy, it may help to consider what it would be like if most of us suddenly witnessed technology that could re-create virtually any taste on our tongues seemingly out of nowhere, as often as desired, without any actual food or beverage present. Try to find a comic or cartoon that features transdiegetic devices that make visible different tastes. Perhaps someone somewhere has actually attempted this before, but it definitely has not caught on yet, because so far, there has been no pressing need to depict gustation in images. But if "taste-recording technology" were to suddenly become a major social and cultural phenomenon, comics artists would certainly begin to experiment with ways to represent the experience of taste on the page. At first such "taste images" would be limited to comics that joke specifically about the new technology, but eventually, one artist would discover that these newly created taste images could also be used to enrich virtually all graphic narrative. Since we would by then all be familiar with the experience of taste reproducible even absent its original physical source, taste images would almost certainly quickly become a standard element of cartoons and comics. If existing comics/manga historiography is any indication, future generations would then likely search for "taste images" in older, pregustatory comics, since they would be unable to understand how no one could have thought of including taste in comics before their own age—after all, they would think that since taste itself has existed throughout human history, the concept of representing it in comics must hence be timeless, natural, and *obvious*.

Assuming that the effects of climate collapse, an economic system based on perpetual exponential growth, and resurgent fascism don't disrupt human civilization first, we *could* conceivably see taste images in comics one day. After all, the history of contemporary comics is not just the history of the sound image but the history of a multitude of transdiegetic signs that developed over time (such as motion, sensation, and sound) and there is no reason this shouldn't one day include taste. The history of transdiegetic signs did not end with the sound image. It continued with the creation of other inventive ways of making visual that which escapes direct visual apperception—such as the act of having an idea (represented by a light bulb), greed (pupils replaced by dollar signs), or love (the stylized heart shape)—and still continues today, with Japanese artists having been some of the most prolific inventors of new transdiegetic signs.

The rudimentary form of this transdiegetic stage—as fully audiovisual, mimetic storytelling on the page—was completed by Rudolph Dirks and Fred Opper when they made the sound image a regular part of their works, however. Their combination of motion and sound made comics the first audiovisual narrative mass medium and enabled artists to tell complex stories mimetically, without the need for external narration to fill in for what earlier forms of graphic narrative had not yet been able to express visually through transdiegetic content. It is hardly a coincidence that we find both the *Katzenjammer Kids* and *Happy Hooligan* among the audiovisual comics that followed *Bringing Up Father* to Japan—both as signature features of Japanese publications.

To better understand the popularity of American audiovisual comics in Japan in the 1920s, imagine that as taste-recording technology in your country of residence is becoming widespread, and before domestic cartoonists have fully engaged with the new technology, artists in another country have already had the time to figure out how to incorporate the sense of taste into their own comics, so much so that when you read these foreign comics, it is as if you can taste the taste images in your head. While this analogy is obviously far from perfect (not least due to the fact that, for most humans, hearing is a more important sense than gustation) it may help grasp what it must have been like for a Japanese person in 1923 to read her first audiovisual comic. For it was the radical expansion of what could now be related mimetically in these new fully audiovisual, transdiegetic comics—from static images to motion, emotion, and (above all else) sound—that explains their popularity both at home and abroad. This radical difference compared to preaudiovisual storytelling such as *manga manbun* picture stories is why Jiggs and Maggie's arrival in Japan represented more than a graphic narrative that simply "happened to use speech balloons." In contrast to *Shō-chan no bōken* (The adventures of little Sho), whose balloons arguably can also be understood as sound images but which still depended on external narration, *Bringing Up Father* was an entirely new form of storytelling. Comics scholar Brian Walker explains the effect that this new form of storytelling, and the paradigm shift from narration to mimesis, must have had on readers: "When dialogue was placed within speech balloons in the drawings, the characters appeared to speak with greater immediacy than when text was placed below the illustrations. Balloons transformed two-dimensional performers into personalities with thoughts and emotions, who could *speak and move simultaneously like real people.*"[42]

The establishment of chronographic, "mechanically recorded" cartoons in Japan by Imaizumi Ippyō in 1891 had laid important groundwork for the introduction of fully audiovisual comics. In addition, due to Japan's hunger for everything Euro-American after the Meiji Restoration in 1868 and the keen interest in American cartooning shown by figures like Imaizumi and Kitazawa Rakuten, the representation of motion and pain via lines and stars, too, was experimented with in Japan before the advent of Jiggs and Maggie in 1923. Kitazawa's *Tokyo Puck*, for example, featured not only the *Mr. Jack* episode mentioned in chapter 1 (fig. 1.1) and cartoons from American satire magazines such as *Judge* but also Japanese-drawn cartoons and short narratives that occasionally made isolated use of the pain stars, motion lines, and/or sound images seen in foreign works. In 1915, *Tokyo Puck* even included a somewhat clumsy attempt at an audiovisual comic strip drawn by Kitazawa's disciple Shimokawa Hekoten titled *Imokawa Mukuzō*, whose Euro-American influence is readily apparent from its header, which imitates those of American comic strips and gives the strip's title in English, as "Mukuzo Imokawa." But the strip was short-lived, perhaps because Japan was still lagging behind the United States in terms of society's permeation by audiovisual technology and entertainment, and the general public hence was not yet sufficiently receptive to storytelling via "audiovisual stage" and transdiegetic content.

For it was precisely the earlier spread of visual and aural technology that both made possible new forms of purely mimetic storytelling (such as pantomime strips that no longer relied on a narrator) and enabled them to become so successful where these new forms of visual art matched the local zeitgeist. The kinetoscope, for example, which had been invented by Thomas Edison in 1891 and had enabled and inspired *The Journal Kinetoscope* (fig. 2.1), was not demonstrated in Japan until late 1896, only about a week before the *New York Journal* would already print the first episode of its kinetoscope-based cartoon.[43]

Approximately twenty years after the first fully audiovisual comics had appeared in the United States, however, the necessary conditions for the medium's success had materialized in Japan as well. The country's first dedicated phonograph dealership had opened in 1899, and between then and 1923, the spread of phonographs (and movie theaters) had turned Japan into a nation accustomed to and enamored of recorded sound (and motion).[44] Historian Andrew Gordon describes this rise of modern popular culture in Japan as part of a "political, social, and cultural flowering of the 1910s and 1920s," during which "Hollywood and Japanese movies began to draw huge audiences to hundreds of theaters nationwide" and "the record player and jazz music enjoyed huge popularity as well."[45] Umeda Haruo, author of a book on the phonograph's history in Japan, similarly refers to the Taishō period (1912–1926) as the local record industry's "first golden age" (*daiikki zenseijidai*).[46] Whereas in 1899 a phonograph had still been a precious luxury good unattainable by an ordinary Japanese person,[47] by the Taishō period, it had become significantly more affordable and within reach of many Japanese.[48] By 1923, mass culture based on sound reproduction and motion pictures thus had become a firm part of everyday life for many Japanese, at least in the major cities, creating a fecund environment for audiovisual comics, just as had been the case in the United States by the late 1890s. Because at the time of *Bringing Up Father*'s importation, there were yet few Japanese artists able and willing to deliver domestically produced audiovisual manga of the same quality—after all, American artists had had a head start of nearly a quarter century when it came to the new form—Jiggs and Maggie were only the beginning of the Japanese public's appetite for foreign audiovisual comics.

CHAPTER 3

WHEN KRAZY KAT SPOKE JAPANESE

JAPAN'S MASSIVE IMPORTATION OF FOREIGN AUDIOVISUAL COMICS

Since the idea of transdiegetic, audiovisual manga, of watching and hearing characters act and speak on the page, was so well-received by their audiences, Japanese publications printed dozens of additional foreign comic strips to attract readers after the *Asahi Graph*'s success with *Bringing Up Father*'s translation. It is uncertain whether Japanese artists would have adopted audiovisual comics as the dominant form of narrative manga before World War II without the ubiquity and popularity of these additional foreign comic strips. Though McManus's strip remained the most popular manga in 1920s Japan, many of these other comics were successful in their own right and helped popularize the audiovisual model. Jimmy Swinnerton's *Little Jimmy*, for example, the second American strip to be serialized in Japan, was published by the *Kokumin Shinbun* for over three years (April 1923 to June 1926), beginning a mere two weeks after the first issue of McManus's strip in the *Asahi Graph*. From our perspective today, a runtime of three years may not appear all that impressive; after all, some comic strips in the United States, like *Bringing Up Father* or the *Katzenjammer Kids*, lasted multiple decades. But according to data compiled by prewar-manga scholar Jo En on narrative manga in eight major Japanese newspapers, among works published in these eight publications continually and regularly during the 1920s, very few manga reached their three-year anniversary, and only a single domestically produced one did (Asō Yutaka's *Nonki na tōsan*, which was directly inspired by *Bringing Up Father* and became the first successful Japanese-drawn fully audiovisual comic strip).[1] Serialization extending beyond three years was hence extremely rare and must be taken as a sign of significant popularity.[2]

The fact that *Little Jimmy*'s Japanese translation was one of the longest-running manga of the 1920s and 1930s thus suggests that it was also one of the most successful works at the time and quite influential despite being omitted from virtually all histories of manga. One factor contributing to this lack of historical recognition may be the fact that the *Kokumin Shinbun* did not actually name the strip but rather created an individual title for each episode, such as "Jimī no obu'u" (Jimmy's bath) for the first episode, and a label as "American manga,"[3] though this eventually was changed to *Jimī manga* (fig. 3.1; Jimmy is the boy who appears in the final panel). Based on the "American manga" label's central positioning and large font size in early episodes, it appears that the *Kokumin Shinbun* considered the proclamation of *Little Jimmy* as American manga more important than even the title of the strip, which speaks to the significant popularity of the new form that *Bringing Up Father* had introduced to the Japanese readership. In other words, *Little Jimmy* was popular less because it was *Little Jimmy* specifically but because it was an "American" manga, and given the scarcity of culturally specific content—the first episode is about Jimmy bathing his dog instead of taking a bath himself as requested by his mother—"American manga" here can safely be read as signifying "audiovisual comic."

Out of the first wave of these American comics arriving in Japan, *Bringing Up Father* curiously was the only one to at least temporarily use Japanese reading directions. *Little Jimmy* employed the original American

Figure 3.1. *Little Jimmy, Kokumin Shinbun*, February 18, 1925. (Image courtesy of Yorutori Bunko.)

reading direction for panels, titles, and dialogue in translation from its first episode (and continued this practice until the last), when the *Asahi Graph* was still figuring out how to reconcile *Bringing Up Father*'s panel order with traditional Japanese ways of reading.[4] It is thus possible that the translators and editors of *Bringing Up Father* were inspired by *Little Jimmy*'s example when they began doing the same from May 16, 1923, onward and that *Little Jimmy* was instrumental in establishing this practice, which was observed by all other translations of American comic strips until the 1930s. Left-to-right has become the standard reading direction for horizontal Japanese today, but remember that in the early 1920s, it was extremely rare. The decision by editors to preserve the foreign reading direction in these first audiovisual comics proved quite consequential, as left-to-right horizontal reading became so associated with these comics that even many of the first domestically drawn audiovisual comic strips would use it—all of which may have been the result of the *Kokumin Shinbun*'s refraining from trying to adapt *Little Jimmy* to traditional ways of reading Japanese.

Little Jimmy's readership expanded dramatically when publishing house Kōdansha decided to feature the Sunday edition of Swinnerton's strip in its monthly flagship magazine *Kingu* (King)—Japan's most popular and eventually the first to achieve a circulation of over one million—beginning with its inaugural issue in January 1925 and continuing through March 1926. The translation's title alternated between various renderings of "Little Jimmy" into Japanese (such as *Rittoru Jimī* or *Jimī-san*) but sometimes featured the original English title as well. It was not marketed as specifically American but rather as generally "foreign"—*gaikoku manga*, in bold—and, unlike the daily version in the *Kokumin Shinbun*, was labeled an "exclusive." In another reflection of the prestige of these new foreign comic strips, and similarly to the *Kokumin Shinbun*'s translation, the label *gaikoku manga* was almost always written in a larger font than any other part of the header, including the strip's title.

An astonishing number of audiovisual comic strips imported from abroad were advertised in similar ways. The Tokyo edition of the business newspaper *Chūgai Shōgyō Shinpō* (precursor to today's *Nihon Keizai Shinbun*), for example, introduced Jimmy Murphy's comic strip about the eponymous married couple Toots and Casper (as *Tsūtsu to Kyasupā*) in its Sunday family supplement *Katei Nōto* (Family notebook) in July 1923 as an "American [*beikoku*] manga" and a "company exclusive." *Tsūtsu to Kyasupā* is also noteworthy as the first example of a complete full-page Sunday comic strip in Japan—the *Asahi Graph* first printed *Bringing Up Father*'s Sunday edition on November 14, 1923, several months later—showing the rapid speed with which different formats of American newspaper comics were imported in the wake of *Bringing Up Father*'s immediate success. Similarly to the other translations in print at the time, the *Chūgai Shōgyō Shinpō* kept *Toots and Casper*'s American panel order and reading direction, even in a brief added Japanese introduction to the strip—a highly unusual step at the time that suggests the appeal of audiovisual comics' different *look*, which was primarily due to the inclusion of sound and other transdiegetic content but appeared inseparable from looking "Western" and "modern" more generally. *Toots and Casper*'s replacement in the paper, A. C. Fera's *Just Boy* (also known as *Elmer*), translated as *Chame no Erumā-kun* (January to June 1924), too, continued the use of the "American manga" label, showing that the decision to emphasize this fact had by no means been arbitrary.

The women's monthly *Fujokai* picked up *Toots and Casper* after it was dropped by the *Chūgai Shōgyō Shinpō* and published it from February 1924 to January 1925, with four full pages per issue, making it the Japanese magazine with the most space devoted to audiovisual comics at the time (fig. 3.2 shows two pages from the September 1924 issue). Like the American comic strips published in translation by its competitors, *Fujokai* kept the American reading direction for text and panels in *Toots and Casper*, which posed a problem given that, like virtually all Japanese magazines and books at the time, *Fujokai* itself was read from right to left, requiring the reader to flip pages from left to right (the opposite of American publications). In addition to clearly numbering the panels, *Fujokai* also added a small note to the middle of each four-panel row in order to avoid confusion, informing the reader that the comic strip is to be read from the left page to the right (as in fig. 3.2). Though virtually all comic strip translations in Japanese publications at the time featured labels promoting their status as "exclusive" and "American," *Fujokai* went one step further by reminding readers on *each* of the two double-page spreads per issue that the comic strip before them was one or both of those things (depending on the issue).

A translation of Billy DeBeck's *Barney Google* (as *Gūtaro-kun to aiba*, literally "Gūtaro and His Beloved Horse") published in the *Chūgai Shōgyō Shinpō*'s Osaka edition (from December 1924 to October 1925) likewise featured a boxed header with the "company-exclusive American comic" designation. The translation's first issues mistakenly listed author Billy DeBeck as "Bīkū Debekku," likely due to a misunderstanding based on someone's unclear handwriting, as the katakana characters for the syllables *ku* and *ri*—the closest phonetic approximation to the sound *li*—can look similar when written quickly by hand (fig. 3.3).[5] This mishap indicates how eager newspaper editors were to find something to match Asahi's success with *Bringing Up Father*, even if they themselves were largely unfamiliar with American comic strips and their authors.

Figure 3.2. *Toots and Casper, Fujokai*, September 1924. (Image courtesy of Yorutori Bunko.)

Despite this obvious unfamiliarity on the part of at least some of them (or perhaps because of it), editors generally preferred publishing comics in translation that had already proven successful in their country of origin. The first wave of foreign transdiegetic comics thus also included such influential works as Cliff Sterrett's *Polly and Her Pals*, which first appeared daily in the *Tōkyō Nichi Nichi Shinbun* (July 1 to August 19, 1923). Despite its brief duration compared to other foreign strips, this iteration of *Polly and Her Pals* is one of four comic strip translations explicitly referenced in cartoonist Shishido Sakō's 1929 book *Amerika no yokoppara* (America's flank), demonstrating that it left an impression on one of the *mangaka* (manga artists) who would later embrace and help further popularize audiovisual comics in Japan.[6] Coincidentally, the same year that Shishido's book was published, *Polly and Her Pals* appeared once more, in English in the *Japan Times* (November 1929 to July 1930), succeeding Jefferson

Figure 3.3. *Barney Google, Chūgai Shōgyō Shinpō* (Osaka edition), December 6, 1924. (Image courtesy of Hara Akihiko, *Nihon Keizai Shinbun*.)

Machamer's *The Doings of Patty* (June to October 1929), another of the few comic strips then to feature a female protagonist.[7] Though *Polly and Her Pals*'s translation in the *Nichi Nichi Shinbun* was historic as the very first audiovisual manga to have a female protagonist—at least nominally, given that Polly did not herself figure prominently in the strip—editors may not have cared about its specific content: like the translation of *Little*

Jimmy, Polly and Her Pals appeared each time under a different title related
to the day's episode, without a title for the strip itself (Shishido, who knew
the original, refers to it as *Porī to otomodachi*—literally, "Polly and Her
Friends"), likewise implying that having *a* comic strip, at least to some
newspapers, was more important than having a specific character's strip.[8]

On October 2, 1924, Tokyo's *Chūgai Shōgyō Shinpō* introduced its third
American comic strip: Russ Westover's *Tillie the Toiler*, as *Oshare no Chirī*
(Fashionable Tillie), whose titular female character was, unlike Polly, also
its narrative protagonist and far more successful in Japan. In contrast to
Toots and Casper and *Just Boy*, *Tillie the Toiler* was published in the newspaper as a daily four-panel strip and significantly longer, for over two
years, until December 19, 1926. Like other translated comics, it kept the
American panel order and reading direction for the strip itself, with only
the title written in the traditional Japanese right to left. Although, unlike
Bringing Up Father's protagonists, Little Jimmy and Tillie did not star in
advertisements themselves, both characters' strips were popular enough
to warrant the creation of a dedicated ad space underneath them (see the
lower part of fig. 3.1, for example). The *Chūgai Shōgyō Shinpō* and *Kokumin Shinbun* were independent of each other, which means that the identical ad spaces likely were the idea of the advertising agency in charge of
them.[9] Clients for the ad spaces included major companies like Sapporo
Breweries (as in fig. 3.1) or cosmetics maker Shiseido, which frequently
advertised under both comic strips. Audiovisual comic strips targeted at
newspapers' educated adult readerships were hence expected not only to
draw in more readers but also to help sell products to those readers, as was
the case with Jiggs and Maggie's appearances in advertisements.

The same ad space as under *Little Jimmy* and *Tillie the Toiler* can also
be found underneath the *Chūō Shinbun*'s Japanese translation of *The
Newlyweds* (October 1925 to November 1926), a comic strip created by
George McManus but taken over by his brother Charles. It had originally
been brought to Japan by the *Tōkyō Asahi Shinbun* on January 1, 1924,
as *Kobonnō* (Child troubles), featuring the familiar "paper exclusive" and

"American manga" labels. For reasons not specified, *The Newlyweds* never appeared in the *Tōkyō Asahi Shinbun* again after the single January 1 issue, however. Instead, it joined *Bringing Up Father* in Asahi's weekly tabloid, the *Asahi Graph*, without explanation the following day. The page on which it was printed featured photos of George and Charles McManus as well as an introduction to *The Newlyweds* that emphasizes the strip's popularity in the Western world, claiming that it is read in various newspapers across the United States and by several million households every day—after all, if something was popular in the West, it was expected to appeal to the average educated Japanese person as well. The introduction to *The Newlyweds* also briefly summarizes the narrative's basic premise (a newlywed couple trying to figure out how to deal with their adorable infant Snookums) and suggests that readers partial to *Bringing Up Father* will likewise appreciate *The Newlyweds*.

Although it also disappeared from the *Asahi Graph* without warning on September 23, 1925, *The Newlyweds* reappeared as surprisingly a month later in the *Chūō Shinbun*, a newspaper not connected to the Asahi group, featuring the same ad space as *Little Jimmy* and *Tillie the Toiler*. The *Chūō Shinbun*'s translation of *The Newlyweds* stood out among all contemporaneous comic strip translations due to its exclusive use of the katakana syllabary and lack of more difficult kanji characters, which suggests that the newspaper was trying to make the strip accessible to children as well, though this is not reflected in the ads run underneath it.

Whereas *The Newlyweds* switched from the *Asahi Shinbun* to the *Asahi Graph* after a single episode, the reverse had happened two years earlier to Bud Fisher's *Mutt and Jeff*, which first appeared in Japan across the top of the *Graph*'s title page (fig. 3.4) on the fateful day of the Great Kantō Earthquake (September 1, 1923) that severely disrupted the *Asahi Graph*'s publication. The page featuring *Mutt and Jeff* included an introduction to Fisher and his work underneath the strip that extols Fisher as a world-famous American comics artist who ushered in "the new age of the daily comic strip."[10] In another instance of the familiar pattern of using a comic

Figure 3.4. *Mutt and Jeff* in the *Asahi Graph*, September 1, 1923.

strip's popularity in "the West" to advertise it to Japanese readers, it also
claims that among readers of foreign newspapers, there was none who had
not already heard of *Mutt and Jeff*, which was "even welcomed by daily
newspapers in Europe" and had been turned into motion pictures and
stage plays. The text also announces that Asahi had purchased the Japanese
rights to *Mutt and Jeff* and that the strip would from then on be featured
daily in the *Asahi Graph* alongside *Bringing Up Father*. Due to the Great
Kantō Earthquake occurring the same day, this prediction did not come
true, and when the *Asahi Graph* became a weekly publication and again
featured drawn humor on November 14, *Mutt and Jeff* were absent from it
and would never appear in it again.

   Instead, on November 11, the *Ōsaka Asahi Shinbun*'s evening edition dis-
played a front-page article with a drawing of Mutt and Jeff, announcing that
the two characters would be gracing its pages soon. The announcement
retained some elements of the previous, shorter *Asahi Graph* version, such
as extolling *Mutt and Jeff*'s worldwide fame. The announcement unsurprisingly references *Bringing Up Father* in the paper's Tokyo edition but also
unexpectedly mentions Harold Knerr's version of Dirks's *Katzenjammer
Kids*, which does not seem to have been translated by 1923 (though it would
be later).[11] McManus and Knerr are cited as examples of an elite group of

American comic strip artists to which Fisher belongs as well. A reference to Jimmy Swinnerton, whose *Little Jimmy* was appearing in the *Kokumin Shinbun*, would seem more natural than one to Knerr, but the Asahi newspaper probably wanted to avoid inadvertently advertising for its competitor.

Two days later, on November 13, another announcement featuring a drawing of Mutt and Jeff appeared on the front page of the *Ōsaka Asahi Shinbun*'s evening edition. This second announcement promised readers that *Mutt and Jeff* would "finally" appear regularly in the evening edition "starting tomorrow." In addition to depicting Mutt and Jeff, the announcement also contained a photograph of Bud Fisher. The relatively brief text emphasized again, like the previous announcement in the same newspaper and that in the *Asahi Graph*, that *Mutt and Jeff* was published in major European newspapers. That this claim is repeated in all three announcements hints at just how much cultural cachet the editors expected "popularity in the West" to carry for their audience. The announcement ends with a concise preview of the first translated episode, relaying that Mutt and Jeff will suffer at the hands of Mrs. Mutt and her rolling pin, "the primary weapon of the American woman."

Mrs. Mutt's rolling pin indeed featured in the first episode of *Mutt and Jeff* published in the *Ōsaka Asahi Shinbun* the following day (November 14, 1923) and illustrated the difficulties of intercultural translation in an audiovisual medium like transdiegetic comics. In the episode, Jeff visits Mutt at their favorite hangout, the Lion Club, and inquires whether Mutt's wife was furious when he returned home late last night. Mutt responds that although he went home around three in the morning, his wife didn't say anything. Jeff is surprised by this, but Mutt laconically adds that today he'll have to have two teeth pulled, causing Jeff to imagine Mutt's mouth being struck by a rolling pin hurled at him. The strip features two explanations by the translator or editor, one on the role of social clubs as "men's only safe zone in the country of Ladies First" (meaning the United States) and one on the use of the rolling pin as the primary weapon of the American housewife, wedged in between the panels. It was not the last time that *Mutt and Jeff*'s translation would require added explanations of culturally specific elements.

In fact, out of all translated comic strips in prewar Japan, *Mutt and Jeff* featured the most intercessions on the part of the translator/editor in the form of explanatory notes added to the strip to clarify American cultural, social, or political references for its readership. That the *Asahi Shinbun* continued publishing *Mutt and Jeff* despite the difficulty of its intercultural translation, instead of publishing a picture story drawn by Okamoto Ippei for example, can be understood as a testament to the raw appeal of audiovisual comics to their 1920s audience accustomed to film and sound recording and enamored of audiovisual mass entertainment, though said audience's curiosity about life in the United States may have played a role in this as well. During the translation's first three months alone, editorial intervention to understand the comic strip was necessary five more times: on November 17, 1923, for example, Mutt and Jeff begin a series of efforts to win the American Peace Award of $100,000 that had been inaugurated earlier that year by editor and Pulitzer Prize–winning author Edward William Bok.[12] The money was to be awarded to whomever was to come up with the best plan to further global peace, and according to the *Ōsaka Asahi Shinbun*'s lengthy explanatory note, the award had become popular material for American cartoonists. On November 25, during the same story line, a walnut is depicted in a thought balloon emanating from Mutt's head as he listens to Jeff's idea on how they will win the Peace Award. An editor's note explains that it is customary in America to refer to fools as "nuts" or "coconuts."

A different story line about a strength potion on January 10, 1924, refers to then-boxing World Heavyweight Champion Jack Dempsey, whom Mutt attempts to knock out after consuming the strength potion but who was not known well enough in Japan, thus requiring another explanatory note by the editor. Nine days later, on January 19, Mutt and Jeff appear to have hit rock bottom, as they are broke and unable to afford food or pay their rent. When Mutt bemoans the fact that they are going to perish without even a proper tombstone, Jeff suddenly pulls a bundle of dollar bills out of his sock and tells Mutt not to worry, because he will purchase proper graves for the two of them. The next panel shows Jeff on the floor sporting a black eye while Mutt walks away with the money, informing him that he has changed his mind about dying. A note helpfully educates readers on the American practice of hiding money in one's socks to protect it from theft.

A purely linguistic explanation concerning an untranslatable idiom, on the other hand, could be found on January 30, 1924: Jeff has decided to run for president of the United States and visits his friend Mutt to solicit his political advice. In the episode, Mutt draws a circle on the floor and counsels Jeff to toss his top hat in the center, so that he can properly announce to "have thrown his hat into the ring" (when Jeff follows the advice, Mutt jumps on his hat because they are now political enemies). Since the expression does not exist in Japanese, but the episode depicts it graphically and revolves around it, the need for an explanation to prevent confusion among the Japanese readership is obvious.

It is possible that *Mutt and Jeff*'s greater utilization of editorial notes compared to other strips like *Bringing Up Father* and *Little Jimmy* stemmed from an unwillingness to discard episodes that did not translate well, such as the "hat in the ring" one. Suzuki Bunshirō, after all, asserts that this is what he did to ensure the success of *Bringing Up Father*, which obviated a need for complicated editorial explanations. It is also possible that *Mutt and Jeff*'s prevalence of added explanations was necessitated by Bud Fisher's tendency to incorporate real-world news into his strip to a far greater extent than other cartoonists did—a tendency that dates back to the very origins of *Mutt and Jeff*, when the strip was called *A. Mutt* and its plot consisted of Mutt's betting on real horse races and his reactions to the actual results in future episodes. Despite the difficulty of its translation, *Mutt and Jeff* appeared in the *Ōsaka Asahi Shinbun* for almost two years, from November 1923 to July 1925, alternating for a while with *Bringing Up Father*.[13] From December 1925 to March 1928, *Mutt and Jeff* continued (with occasional absences) in the Asahi Kansai-area women's monthly *Zen-Kansai Fujin Rengōkai*, where it was introduced together with McManus's *Bringing Up Father* and—of course—again with a special note relating Fisher's fame overseas.

The initial sudden disappearance of *Mutt and Jeff* from the *Asahi Graph* in 1923 after just one episode and without explanation led to confusion on the part of at least one Tokyo reader, resulting in a fascinating, rare case of public correspondence between a reader and an editor regarding a comic strip translation. On December 11, 1923, the *Tōkyō Asahi Shinbun*, in the "Memo" column underneath *Shō-chan no bōken*, published a letter from a Tanaka Yoshio, who asks why *Mutt and Jeff* has appeared in the *Asahi Graph* only once and why the (Tokyo) *Asahi Shinbun* and *Graph* are not publishing it despite the hilarious nature of the September 1 episode. The editor responding informs Mr. Tanaka that *Mutt and Jeff* is already appearing in the evening edition of the Osaka version of the *Asahi Shinbun*. That a reader was demanding more *Mutt and Jeff* a whole two months after having seen only a single episode showcases the kind of impression these audio-visual comics left on 1920s Japanese readers and how different the comics must have appeared from the existing tradition of narrative manga (i.e., *manga manbun* picture stories) in order to stand out to this extent. Tanaka's bewilderment at the strip's disappearance is understandable, given that Tokyo Asahi readers had not been notified of the decision to publish *Mutt and Jeff* only in the Kansai area (the region around Osaka and Kyoto). The editor's response was not the end of this reader's confusion, however.

In a second letter published in the "Memo" column on February 15, 1924—another two months later—the same reader complains that he purchased a copy of the *Ōsaka Asahi Shinbun* five to six days earlier, but contrary to his expectation, *Mutt and Jeff* was not found in it (nor was any other manga).[14] The editor responds that although both Mutt and Jeff are alive and well in the paper, depending on the articles published in each issue, there are some days on which they won't appear. This statement is a rare surviving explanation of the occasional temporary absence of serial-ized graphic narratives from prewar publications. Unfortunately, it is too vague and brief—and in light of its purpose of reassuring an upset reader, potentially dishonest—to shed much light on the question of why news-papers and magazines would sometimes omit a continuing narrative from one of their issues. The inability to finish a translation in time, technical difficulties, or testing the readers' response to the absence, as claimed by Suzuki Bunshirō, appear more likely reasons.[15]

In addition to Mr. Tanaka's letter writing, *Mutt and Jeff*'s significant popularity in Japan is evident also from the fact that it is among the hand-ful of manga whose protagonists were featured in third-party advertise-ments at the time, as seen with *Bringing Up Father* in chapter 1. Although Mutt and Jeff did not appear in nearly as many ads as Jiggs and Maggie did, and although their ads appear to have been limited to the *Ōsaka Asahi Shinbun*, Fisher's strip is the only prewar manga to have inspired two sepa-rate newspaper pages consisting mostly of advertisements based on it (on June 17 and July 8, 1924).[16] The first of these pages featured twelve unique advertisements (fig. 3.5), all starring Mutt and Jeff, while the second dis-played twelve ads, with a majority (but not all) including Mutt and Jeff, surrounding a central panel with the two characters and the names of all the products advertised.[17]

The perhaps most fascinating aspect of the juxtaposed *Mutt and Jeff*–based advertisements is their great variance in drawing styles and degrees of resem-blance. Although all renderings can be clearly identified as Mutt and Jeff, some are much closer to Fisher's original characters than others, which suggests that multiple artists were involved in creating the ads and must have been familiar with the strip. Unfortunately, it is unlikely that we will ever know how these ads were commissioned, but Mutt and Jeff were obviously expected to be pop-ular enough to entice readers to purchase the products with which they were affiliated.

The Japanese public's enthusiastic reception of American audiovi-sual comics was not lost on Kitazawa Rakuten, Japan's most influential manga creator and editor during the preaudiovisual era (see prologue and chapter 1). Realizing that featuring audiovisual comics had proved a boon to several competing newspapers, on January 11, 1925, Rakuten began to

Figure 3.5. Advertisements featuring Mutt and Jeff in the *Ōsaka Asahi Shinbun*, June 17, 1924.

feature Fred Opper's *Happy Hooligan*—history's first comic strip to consistently use the fully audiovisual form—in his weekly *Jiji Manga* Sunday supplement to the *Jiji Shinpō* newspaper. *Happy Hooligan*'s translation consisted of twelve panels, occupying the bottom half of the page in its first issue, then filling the entire page (along with a topper panel or one of Opper's topper strips during some periods) beginning with the second and until the last issue on January 26, 1930, outdoing other newspapers in the sheer amount of page space devoted to transdiegetic comics (see fig. 3.6 for an example).[18] Its runtime of five years makes *Happy Hooligan* the second-longest-running Japanese-language manga of the 1920s, after *Bringing Up Father* and ahead of all domestically produced manga (including both picture stories and audiovisual comics).[19]

Similar to other comic strip translations, *Happy Hooligan*'s first episode was adorned by a brief introduction to the strip, which announced the strip's official contracting for the newspaper and that it would appear in

Figure 3.6. *Happy Hooligan*, *Jiji Shinpō*, July 12, 1925. (Image courtesy of Yorutori Bunko.)

every *Jiji Manga* issue from then on. Reminiscent of other introductions to translated comics, the introduction to *Happy Hooligan*, too, emphasized the strip's popularity overseas (calling Happy "the American manga world's most popular character"), again showing that popularity in the United States was expected to pique the average Japanese reader's interest, much as popularity in Europe was emphasized in the Asahi introductions to *Mutt and Jeff*.

Manga historian Takeuchi Osamu, in briefly discussing a few translated comic strips, refers to *Happy Hooligan* as the beginning of "serious" (*honkakuteki na*) translation of newspaper comics in Japan, though he does not elaborate on the reasons for this assessment and why previous translations do not qualify.[20] One reason may be the noticeably verbal nature of the strip's humor compared to others (once Opper had become more accustomed to the transdiegetic model, *Happy Hooligan* became far wordier than its first episodes had been). It is not uncommon for more than half of a 1920s *Happy Hooligan* panel to consist of text-filled speech balloons. Hand-lettering small-font text is easier to do in the Roman alphabet than in Japanese, due in large part to the presence of kanji consisting of many separate strokes. It hence must have been difficult to fit all the translated text into the existing speech balloons during the editing and copying process.

In fact, translating and copying a comic strip in the 1920s was a rather complicated endeavor, both linguistically and technologically. First, many comic strips were replete with slang and colloquialisms that made them harder to translate than other types of texts (several such expressions actually were coined in comic strips and some of those are still with us today, such as *milquetoast* or *heebie-jeebies*). Second, without digital editing and copying technology, translations had to be edited manually on paper and copied using a photomechanical process called photoengraving.

The complexity of the overall process becomes easily apparent when comparing translated comic strip episodes with their originals. For example, in the *Happy Hooligan* translation that appeared on July 12, 1925 (fig. 3.6), it appears that panels and speech balloons were enlarged to accommodate the greater need for writing space in the Japanese translation.[21] The translation differs from the source in other respects as well: the English title has been moved to the right to make room for the Japanese title and the phrase "Registered U.S. Patent Office" underneath the original title has been moved with it (but has been preserved rather than removed completely). Several details in the drawings that differ between original and translation are evidence of additional manual editing. In the original, a plate shown in panel 4 is partially cut off by the panel's left-hand border, whereas the translation displays it in its entirety. One character's nose in panel seven is noticeably more pointed in the translation, and his pants are black, whereas they are white in the original. The left-hand panel borders of panels 2 and 5 are furthermore connected (they cut across the gutter between them), which appears to have been a mistake on the part of the person copying or editing the panels (similar to a shading mistake in the first translated *Bringing Up Father* episode; see fig. 1.6). The panel boundaries have been changed in the translation; all panels have been elongated upwards in order to provide more room for speech balloons, which have also been redrawn, albeit in a style mimicking Opper's.

Despite these differences and unlike for example the 1908 translation of a *Mr. Jack* episode by Kitazawa Rakuten (see fig. 1.1), the panels do not seem to have been copied by hand in their entirety, given that the printed copyright information in panel 10 is preserved identically in the translation, which would be difficult to do by hand. The most likely explanation for the differences between original and translation is that panels were manually cut, then resized and rearranged onto a new sheet of paper, and that their borders were redrawn (which explains the panel border line accidentally crossing the gutter). The English title and copyright information were likely cut and pasted into their new location as well. Changes to the images themselves, such as different speech balloons, the Japanese text, and other graphical changes such as the altered nose must then have been accomplished with correction fluid and ink, while differences in shading likely happened during manual editing at the photoengraving stage.

The precise process by which translated cartoons and comic strips were copied by Japanese publications in the 1920s and 1930s is unclear,[22] but a March 1926 *Popular Mechanics* article, "How Cartoons Are Syndicated," describes how comic strips were printed in American newspapers at the time: finished proofs of comic strips first had to be photographed onto a metal plate and engraved (etched) into it, in order to then produce a paper-based negative of the engraving (called a matrix), into which molten type metal was poured to create a printing plate.[23] Based on the *Happy Hooligan* translation described above, it can be assumed that Japanese newspapers used a similar process.

Though the process is called photoengraving, it is actually an etching process, during which a metal plate, usually made of zinc or copper, is coated with a photosensitive liquid, which in the case of line art is illuminated through a negative of the original image to be reproduced.[24] The light shines through the transparent parts of the negative (which correspond to the black parts of the original art) and hardens the parts of the photosensitive liquid beneath these parts. The nonhardened areas of the photosensitive liquid are then removed, leaving only those parts of the metal plate coated that correspond to the black parts of the original copy. After an engraver/etcher manually edits the coating (by adding or removing coating, for example) to make sure it reproduces the original image as accurately as possible, the plate is then etched (submerged in or sprayed with acid) in multiple steps. During the etching process, the coated parts of the plate remain protected from the acid, while the noncoated parts (corresponding to the white areas in the copy) are eaten into by the acid, creating a relief printing surface that serves as the basis for the eventual printing plate.

When juxtaposed with the corresponding originals, a stretch of *Bringing Up Father* episodes from the *Tōkyō Asahi Shinbun* in November and December 1923 further supports the hypothesis that comic strip translations like these were first edited by hand and then reproduced for printing via photoengraving as described above. Compare, for example, the original and translated episode of *Bringing Up Father* shown as figures 3.7 and 3.8, where details in the former have been copied too precisely in the latter to have been traced by hand, which implies a photomechanical process. Replacing the English with Japanese text and enlarging some speech balloons, however, is unlikely to have been done directly on the metal plate and was almost certainly done on paper beforehand, using correction fluid and ink. This process explains how panel numbers were added and the copyright information and handwritten date removed. Other differences between the original and the translation likely occurred during the engraving/etching process: namely, the lack of shading on Jiggs's chair and one character's legs in the first panel, the added shading on the door frame in panel 2 (though not the part of the door frame at the very bottom) and on Jiggs's car's fenders in panel 3, and the lack of shading on the judge's desk in the last panel in the translation. For copying line (i.e., black-and-white) art, a bichromatic solution was used for photographing the image onto the metal plate, meaning that the liquid either hardened or not depending on the amount of light reaching it. The gray and crosshatched areas in the original hence may not have been dark enough to make the corresponding areas on the photo negative sufficiently transparent to allow the liquid behind them to harden. In other words, all gray and crosshatched areas would have ended up white in the translation without intervention by the engraver, who for gray areas most likely used staging ink (coating fluid that would harden and protect the metal from the acid) to create many small dots (stippling) on the metal plate. After etching, these dots would remain raised and hence end up printing black dots on the white paper, giving the illusion of gray. For crosshatching, the engraver probably simply drew lines onto the metal plate with the same type of ink.

Considering that nearly identical crosshatching was used for Jiggs's vest in the original and translation, the engraver must have referred to the paper

Figure 3.7. *Bringing Up Father*, November 1, 1923.

copy when editing the metal plate, and the differences in shading between
original and translation can be explained either by sloppy work or by the
engraver substituting his own judgment for accuracy (or a mixture of both,
given the inconsistent shading on the door frame). There is also a small
chance that the image the engraver had to work with was smudged in a way
that made it difficult to guess which parts were supposed to be gray and
which white. After all, remember *Asahi Graph* vice editor in chief Hata Sankichi's claim that Nakazato Tomijirō, the translator for *Bringing Up Father*,
"sometimes corrected his words more than ten times."[25] Assuming heavy

Figure 3.8. *Bringing Up Father*, December 7, 1923, translation of the November 1, 1923, original. (Image courtesy of Yorutori Bunko.)

editing directly on the comic strip image later used for photoengraving, the finished translation may have ended up smudged to such a degree that it prevented the engraver from assigning the correct shading to some areas.

Today, when anyone with access to an image scanner (or even just a smartphone camera) and a basic image-editing application is theoretically able to produce a "scanlation" of comics written in a different language, it is easy to forget not only what a labor- and cost-intensive process the printing of *untranslated* newspaper comics used to be but also how much more difficult it was to publish *translated* comics nearly every day. That Japanese newspapers decided to feature so many translated comics despite these immense difficulties suggests that editors expected a commensurate benefit that justified these costs, which in turn implies that readers showed profuse interest in those translated audiovisual comics.

After transdiegetic comic strips became more common in the 1920s and as Japanese artists started to supply domestically produced transdiegetic manga, the 1930s saw a shift away from importing a broad spectrum of audiovisual comics and toward a greater focus on individual popular characters, in particular Mickey Mouse, Betty Boop, Popeye, and Felix the Cat. Many newspapers gave up on translated material to the benefit of original Japanese strips, though there was an increase in translated comic strips in magazines. One reason for the shift toward a limited number of specific characters was their popularization through American animated films, which were extraordinarily well-received in Japan in the early 1930s, as evidenced by numerous advertisements featuring the characters or announcing so-called manga festivals (*manga-sai*)—screenings of Disney and/or Fleischer animated films, as the word *anime* had not been created yet and so such films were instead referred to as *manga eiga*, or "manga movies."

Happy Hooligan was not among these new "anime" stars, and thus the *Jiji Shinpō* on January 26, 1930, featured a separate panel superimposed on parts of the final four *Happy Hooligan* panels announcing that beginning the following week, Felix the Cat would become Happy's substitute. It was extremely rare for a strip's end to be announced to its readership, instead of the more usual sudden and unexplained disappearance, and the reason in this case was likely that Felix was expected to be even more popular than Happy. The Felix announcement also displayed the familiar *honsha tokuyaku* (company exclusive) and *beikoku manga* (American manga) labels, which the actual strip would sport as well beginning with its first issue the following week on February 2, 1930, showing that American comics had not yet relinquished their significant popularity. Though the Felix announcement was written in the traditional top-to-bottom, right-to-left direction, the actual strip continued the established use of the "modern," American left-to-right, top-to-bottom writing style.

Together with *Felix the Cat* (fig. 3.9 shows a rare silent episode) the *Jiji Shinpō* also began publishing the comic strip *Laura*, which, like *Felix the Cat*, was produced by the Pat Sullivan Studio. (Though the comics were actually created and drawn by Otto Messmer, studio boss Pat Sullivan took credit for his employee's work, so the published strips ended up bearing Sullivan's signature instead.) *Laura*, a strip about a talking parrot (as we saw in chapter 2, an unthinkable concept before the invention of the phonograph, absent a supernatural element), was published on a separate page from Felix under the name *Oshaberi Porī* (Chatty Polly). Both appeared on Sundays, *Laura* until February 28 (with an additional appearance on June 19) and *Felix* until July 3, 1932. *Felix the Cat* then continued as a daily four-panel strip until December 31, 1932.

Felix the Cat was one of the most significant American strips to be translated into Japanese because it was the first work of graphic narrative appearing in Japan regularly (as opposed to the single *Mr. Jack* issue published in *Tokyo Puck*, for example) that featured an anthropomorphic animal as its protagonist. Other manga had featured talking animals before, such as the squirrel in *Shō-chan no bōken*, but these characters had always physiologically remained wholly animal, despite their ability to communicate with humans (Laura the parrot, too, could talk but was not anthropomorphic). Felix had actually appeared in Japan as early as 1929, when translated *Felix the Cat* comic strips were published in the magazine *Hachisuzume* in May and June.[26] After the end of his strip's run in the *Jiji Shinpō*, Felix also later reappeared in April 1934 as part of the *Shinseinen* translations, which we will get to in a bit.

Other anthropomorphic animal protagonists were brought to Japan from abroad by none other than *manga manbun* picture-story writer Okamoto Ippei, who edited the twenty-third volume of the *Shōgakusei zenshū* (Elementary school student complete works) book series, titled *Jidō manga-shū* (Children's manga collection), which featured a mixture of Japanese and foreign material and was published in August 1927. In the editor's introduction, Okamoto writes that children need manga just as they need their *oyatsu* (a midafternoon snack) and that being able to enjoy

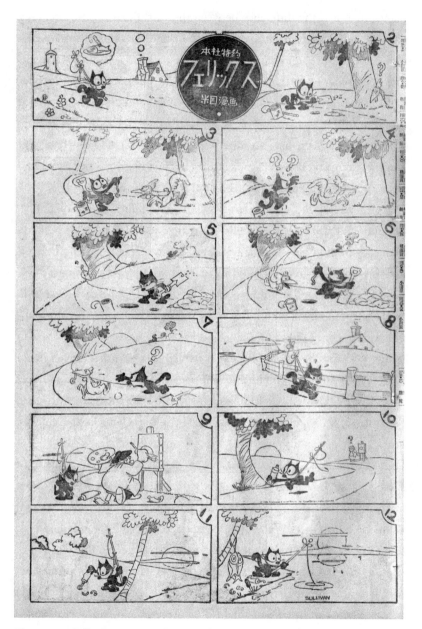

Figure 3.9. *Felix the Cat, Jiji Shinpō*, February 2, 1930. (Image courtesy of Yorutori Bunko.)

manga or not is the difference between the world's rising and declining
nations, showing that a perceived need to defend the value of comics, cartoons, and picture stories existed before our own time. Okamoto remarks
that due to his own unfamiliarity with foreign children's manga, he solicited the help of *Shō-chan no bōken* writer Oda Nobutsune, a supposed
expert in this area.[27]

One of the foreign manga featured with which Oda should have been very
familiar was Austin Bowen Payne's *Pip, Squeak and Wilfred*, which, according
to Suzuki Bunshirō, had generated the idea for Oda's *Shō-chan no bōken*.[28]
The protagonists Pip, Squeak, and Wilfred are an anthropomorphic dog,
penguin, and rabbit. Two more British manga included in the "Children's
Manga Collection" also have animal protagonists. The first is an unidenti-
fied three-panel strip about a pig and a snake finding a way to use a single
pair of roller skates for both of them. The second is an issue of George E.
Studdy's comic strip about a dog called *Bonzo*, which later was also published in the comics and cartoon magazine *Manga Man* from August 1929 to
March 1930 and the *Kokumin Shinbun* (which had published *Little Jimmy*)
from July to August 1933. The *Jidō manga-shū* of course included multiple
American audiovisual comic strips as well: Gene Byrnes's *Reg'lar Fellers*,
Fontaine Fox's *Toonerville Folks*, and Milt Gross's *Nize Baby*, each occupying
four to six pages. It also featured Oscar Jacobsson's *Adamson* (also known
in the United States as *Silent Sam*), which would become one of the most
successful prewar narrative manga (fig. 3.10). The strip was originally from
Sweden but labeled here as German, ironic given that the volume's actual
German contribution, Wilhelm Busch's picture story *Plisch und Plum*, was,
despite Okamoto's affection for Busch's oeuvre, proclaimed Russian.

Adamson had first been published in Japanese a few months prior, from
March to June 1927 in *Kingu*, the popular monthly magazine that before had
contained the Sunday edition of *Little Jimmy*. *Kingu*, too, had labeled *Adamson* German, which suggests that the strip first became known in Japan via
a German publication. On the other hand, when *Adamson* appeared in the
Asahi Graph from September 5, 1928, to October 16, 1940, the translation

Figure 3.10. *Adamson, Jidō manga-shū*, 1927.

featured (at least in some cases) copyright information listing a post office box
in Copenhagen, Denmark. The *Asahi Graph* published *Adamson* in parallel
with *Bringing Up Father*, adding the subtitle *Oyaji ichidaiki* (Chronicles of
a middle-aged man), perhaps so that it might benefit from the popularity
of McManus's strip appearing under the Japanese title *Oyaji kyōiku*. Despite
its long run in the *Asahi Graph*, making it the second-longest-running prewar graphic narrative (including both foreign and Japanese-drawn manga)
in Japanese history after *Bringing Up Father*—even outlasting McManus's
strip, which ended on June 31, 1940—Suzuki Bunshirō does not mention
it in his writings on manga. It therefore remains unclear how and via what
country the *Asahi Graph* or any of the other Japanese publications that
printed it acquired *Adamson*.

   Adamson is often considered a "silent" strip due to its general lack of
transdiegetic sound. Because it nevertheless did not require narrative text
to explain what happens in its panels (usually a misadventure of some sorts

by the unfortunate titular character), it was likely sufficiently "modern" to be embraced by Japanese readers as a "filmic" strip in the vein of *The Journal Kinetoscope* despite its aural scarcity. (Episodes did feature sound when the joke required it; see Adamson playing the violin in fig. 3.10.) On the other hand, *Adamson*'s relative silence may explain why it never reached the same popularity as *Bringing Up Father*, as evidenced by the absence of references to it in popular culture apart from Adamson's appearance in one advertisement for Misono Oshiroi face powder alongside *Bringing Up Father*'s Jiggs and Maekawa Senpan's character Kuma-san (from the eponymous strip *Awatemono no Kuma-san*). *Adamson*'s lack of text and culturally specific references—recall the need for explanatory notes in the translation of *Mutt and Jeff*—nevertheless rendered it particularly easy to translate compared to all the wordy audiovisual comic strips, which explains why *Adamson* could be found in at least six different Japanese publications during the 1920s and 1930s.[29]

In contrast to newspapers and magazines, books featuring foreign comics were rare, but in 1929 another *Shōgakusei zenshū* volume consisting of manga, called *Manga e-monogatari* (Manga picture stories), featured Charles McManus's *Newlyweds* and Rudolph Dirks's *The Katzenjammer Kids* (see chapter 2). The importation of the *Katzenjammer Kids*, along with that of *Happy Hooligan* by the *Jiji Shinpō*, ensured that both of the two original fully audiovisual/transdiegetic comic strips were now a part of manga history themselves and no longer only through the intermediary of *Bringing Up Father* and other audiovisual comics derived from Dirks's and Opper's work. The same year that the *Manga e-monogatari* volume introduced Rudolph Dirks's Katzenjammer Kids to Japan, Harold Knerr's version of the "Katzies" (which William Randolph Hearst had commissioned after Dirks left to draw his strip under the names *Hans and Fritz* and later *The Captain and the Kids* for Joseph Pulitzer) also appeared in Japanese translation.

The magazine that published it, though short-lived, would play an important role in the development of Japanese manga. Started by a group of manga enthusiasts in August 1929 to bring (even more) American comics to Japan and showcase work by Japanese *mangaka* that could rival these American comics, *Gekkan Manga Man* (Monthly manga man) was published by the publisher Tōkyō Manga Shinbunsha (Tokyo Manga Newspaper Company), which the group had established for this purpose. The two driving individuals behind it were Kubo Akira, a former journalist with the magazine *Bungei Shunshū* and *Manga Man*'s listed publisher,[30] and Matsui Komazō, who wrote the first issue's editorial statement. In the editorial statement, Matsui proclaims himself an enthusiastic consumer of domestic and foreign manga for many years and a fan in particular of the *American Weekly*, the Sunday supplement to the *San Francisco Examiner*, of which Matsui had collected issues going back almost thirty years. Knerr's *Katzenjammer Kids* was taken from these issues and published in *Manga Man* as *Ohitoyoshi no senchō-san to kodomo-tachi*, "The Soft-Hearted Captain and the Children"—possibly based on *The Captain and the Kids*, the eventual title Rudolph Dirks gave his creation after the rights to the original one had been accorded in court to his erstwhile employer Hearst.[31]

Matsui also references the two most successful American comic strips in Japan—*Bringing Up Father* in the *Asahi Graph* and *Happy Hooligan* in the *Jiji Shinpō*—writing that both were part of the *American Weekly* as well. The shorter-lived strips in the *American Weekly* would run for more than ten years, the longer ones for over thirty, Matsui writes, admiringly citing this as evidence of American readers' patience and authors' creativity, an understandable assessment given the generally short lives of manga in Japan at the time, with the vast majority appearing for no more than a few months at most. Matsui had been hoping that one day, a similar manga newspaper would emerge in Japan but was disappointed. As a result, he decided to create *Manga Man*, hoping to contribute to Japan's comics culture. As announced in advertisements in Tokyo newspapers in early May (1929, presumably), *Manga Man* had first been planned as a weekly publication.[32] A different ad in July promised over ten pages of foreign manga (likely counting both comic strips and cartoons), testifying to the continuing appeal of (mostly) American audiovisual comics.

Inspired by American comics like those found in the *American Weekly*, *Manga Man* was an attempt to popularize the visual splendor of color comics in Japan.[33] Correspondingly, *Manga Man* (at first, at least) appeared in double *shirokuban* format (approximately 38 × 26 cm), featuring over a dozen pages printed entirely in color. *Manga Man*'s visual content (as opposed to its articles and stories) consisted of a combination of foreign "nonsense" cartoons (as opposed to political cartoons or those depicting scenes from everyday life) and audiovisual comic strips, both translated ones and works by Japanese artists in the same style. The magazine's most iconic feature was Harold Knerr's aforementioned *The Katzenjammer Kids* (fig. 3.11), which ran on a color-printed, full double-page spread during *Manga Man*'s color period from August 1929 to January 1930 and remained a feature in black and white until May 1930. *Manga Man* also featured other foreign audiovisual strips[34] and cartoons, as well as domestic comic strips by authors that included Asō Yutaka and Shishido Sakō.

Although *Manga Man* was read by turning pages from left to right just like other Japanese magazines, it preserved the original reading direction for all translated comics and even used this direction for nearly all strips by Japanese authors. Almost all comic strips in *Manga Man*, both translations and original, also used a three-by-two equiform panel arrangement, with a topper strip or cartoon above. This uniform page design, in conjunction with similarities in coloring among different translations and an absence of original dates, signatures, or copyright information, implies that the foreign strips were traced and edited in their entirety by hand, instead of being edited with correction fluid on a copy of the original as appears to have been the case for virtually all translations appearing in newspapers (see the examples of *Happy Hooligan* and *Bringing Up Father* discussed above). This hypothesis is buttressed by Minejima Masayuki's biography of Japanese cartoonist Kondō Hidezō, which is based on autobiographical writings by Kondō. According to Minejima, publisher Kubo Akira relied on Japanese artists to trace and edit the foreign material he wanted to include in *Manga Man*, sometimes even creating color versions of previously black-and-white works. Minejima also

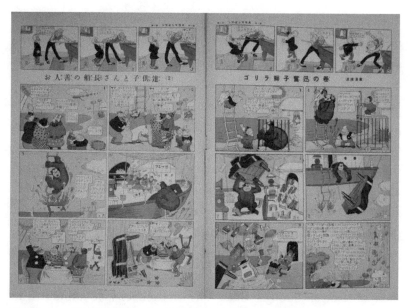

Figure 3.11. *The Katzenjammer Kids, Manga Man*, September 1929. (Image courtesy of Noda Kensuke.)

writes that Kondō and others working for Kubo had to change the original reading direction of panels, which sounds odd given that *Manga Man* did not invert foreign strips to fit the Japanese right-to-left reading order, but perhaps the statement is referring to the altered order of panels required to accommodate the magazine's preferred three-by-two grid.

Manga Man's aspirations as a large-format color magazine were frustrated by financial concerns within months after its establishment. Although its second issue in September 1929 optimistically proclaimed that the first one had sold out and that a circulation of ten thousand to fifteen thousand issues should be achievable in the future, the magazine's fourth issue in November 1929 featured an apology for a 20 percent price increase from twenty-five to thirty sen, justifying it as the only option to keep the magazine afloat due to the high cost of color printing.[35] In February 1930, the magazine changed strategy and lowered its price to twenty sen while shrinking its format and abandoning color printing.

This decision may have been made in order to better compete with other manga magazines, intense competition by which appears to have been a significant reason for *Manga Man*'s short life span.[36] The *Shuppan nen-kan* publication directory for the year 1930, for example, lists all of *Manga Man*'s competitors at a unit price of twenty sen in February 1930.[37] It is possible that readers were not able or willing to pay 50 percent more than the price of a smaller black-and-white competitor for *Manga Man*'s large color comics. Although *Manga Man*'s adoption of the new business model appears, based on circulation numbers printed in the back of the magazine, to have led to significant sustained growth in circulation for a while, the magazine's size was reduced further in December 1930, and *Manga Man* disappeared from newsstands five to six months later.[38]

With the demise of *Manga Man* another monthly magazine became the central organ through which American comics were introduced to Japan throughout the 1930s: *Shinseinen*, a literary magazine founded in January 1920 by publisher Hakubunkan that focused primarily on translations of foreign detective stories. We know more about comics publication in *Shinseinen* than in any other contemporaneous publication thanks to Inui Shin'ichirō, whose *"Shinseinen" no koro* (Then at *Shinseinen*), a book about his time at the magazine, is by far the most extensive of the few surviving original sources on the prewar translation of foreign comics. Inui had been hired by *Shinseinen* editor Mizutani Jun about a year before *Manga Man*'s end, and one of his main responsibilities in the new job was the copying and translation of foreign manga.[39] The reason for *Shinseinen*'s embrace of predominantly American comics and cartoons, according to Mizutani, was that they were an easy way of giving the magazine the "modern" appearance it was striving for.[40] "Old-school" Japanese cartoonists in the mold of Kitazawa and Okamoto were seen as too old-fashioned and behind the times to be appropriate for *Shinseinen*.[41] Mizutani considered American comics and cartoons more advanced than others primarily because they had sought to "drive out" explanatory text as much as possible and instead relied mostly on visual means of conveying information.[42]

As seen from early pantomime strips (e.g., *The Journal Kinetoscope*) that pioneered the telling of stories through the "mechanical recording of human action" without the need for a narrator, such foreign manga were indeed inherently modern in that their emergence was closely connected to modern technologies that had made possible such "mechanical record-ing," which Mizutani seems to have understood at least intuitively.

It would have been difficult to find someone more qualified for the task of selecting American comics for publication in *Shinseinen* than Inui Shin'ichirō. Inui had been born near Seattle, Washington, in 1906 and lived in the United States until, at seven years of age, he was sent to attend school in Japan against his will. Due to his foreign upbringing, he was treated as an outsider there and missed the land of his birth, eagerly consuming American books and magazines sent by his mother.[43] Although Inui wanted desperately to return to his native Seattle, this was made impossible by the anti-Japanese Immigration Act of 1924. Forced to stay in Japan, he hoped to study English literature at Aoyama Gakuin University but because of his caretaker uncle's fierce opposition had to enroll in the university's economics department instead. As a college student, Inui discovered and became a fervent reader of *Shinseinen*, which was publishing translations of foreign detective and humoristic novels. Inui enjoyed the translations so much that he decided to try his hand at literary translation himself. Despite not expecting his work to be received particularly well, he submitted it to *Shinseinen*, which pub-lished his translations of P. G. Wodehouse's short story *The Romance of a Bulb-Squeezer* and of a story by Ellis Parker Butler in May of 1928.[44]

Two years later, Inui had become a regular employee at *Shinseinen* and its manga editor. As a student, Inui had wondered why the "new-style manga" that he had grown up with in the United States were not appear-ing in Japan, and he had searched bookstores for copies of English and American magazines "to quench my thirst for manga."[45] Inui's duties as manga editor consisted largely of cutting comic strips and cartoons out of a pile of foreign magazines at *Shinseinen* and editing them for reproduc-tion. Although unlike other publications at the time, the magazine did not publish any translated comics in narrative continuity over successive issues, it provided by far the greatest overall diversity in foreign manga material found in prewar Japan. *Shinseinen* had begun to feature foreign cartoons already prior to Inui's tenure at the magazine, but it started featuring transdiegetic comic strips only after his arrival.

The first foreign example of graphic narrative or humor in *Shinseinen* appeared in August 1925: a three-panel cartoon about a man evading a lion, which in turn is devoured by a crocodile. The cartoon was labeled *beikoku manga* (American manga) and used external narration to comment on the action depicted in the images, though it also employed some transdiegetic content in the form of motion lines. Considering that at this point in time, translations of *Bringing Up Father*, *Little Jimmy*, *Polly and Her Pals*, *Mutt and Jeff*, *The Newlyweds*, *Toots and Casper*, *Tillie the Toiler*, *Just Boy*, and *Happy Hooligan* (in addition to *The Gumps*, untranslated, in the *Japan Times*) had already appeared (and with most of them still in print), *Shinseinen* was significantly behind the vanguard of Japan's comics culture at the time.

After occasional foreign cartoons during the mid-1920s, *Shinseinen* began including a regular feature called *manga no pēji* (manga pages) in August 1928. The feature usually consisted of eight pages of mostly single-panel cartoons. In 1930, *Shinseinen* started to also publish American comic strips, which coincides with Inui's arrival at the magazine. It is likely that Inui became involved starting with the January 1930 issue, since it featured *Shinseinen*'s first audiovisual comic strip. This strip, by Rube Goldberg, shows Saint Peter and Archangel Gabriel despairing up in the clouds over an earthly lack of response to Gabriel's trumpet. In the end, the two solve their quandary by playing jazz, which suddenly compels humans to seek entrance into heaven. Compared to previous cartoons printed in *Shinseinen*, which had been single-panel scenes or multipanel comical vignettes featuring archetypical characters in humorous situations, Goldberg's cartoon exhibits a new level of narrative complexity. The following month's issue continued the trend toward greater complexity in content (compared to single-panel cartoons focusing on immediately obvious visual gags) by

featuring some of Dr. Seuss's "Life's Little Educational Charts," which had
originally appeared in *Life*.

Should Inui not have been responsible for picking the above cartoons by
Goldberg and Dr. Seuss, he must have been in charge of manga selection
by June 1930 at the latest, when *Shinseinen* featured George Herriman's *Krazy
Kat* for the first time. In the United States, *Krazy Kat* eventually became the
first comic strip to garner academic recognition as art, and rumor has it that
it only survived for as long as it did because of William Randolph Hearst's
personal patronage. Its language use is so nonstandard that it is improbable
that anyone at *Shinseinen* besides Inui, who had been born and raised in the
United States, would have been able to appreciate it in the original. *Krazy Kat*
appeared in three additional *Shinseinen* issues: in April and May 1931, as well
as in December 1934. The June 1930 issue featured a single eight-panel *Krazy
Kat* strip underneath the table of contents in which Ignatz Mouse's eager
consumption of *Shinseinen* leads other characters to demand the magazine
as well (liberties seem to have been taken with the translation here). The April
1931 issue included six four-panel strips over four full pages in red, white, and
blue (fig. 3.12 shows the first two pages), while the May 1931 and December
1934 issues featured single four- and three-panel strips, respectively.

The April 1931 issue also boasted a full four pages of Floyd Gottfredson's
Mickey Mouse comic strip. During the 1930s, Mickey Mouse became hugely
popular in Japan, largely due to the importation of Disney animation.
Mickey Mouse strips were also featured in *Shinseinen* in May and September 1932, all preceding Mickey's appearance in advertisements in newspapers, which begin in early 1933. Given that the earliest mention of Mickey
Mouse in the *Asahi Shinbun* happened on April 22, 1931, when a column
reported that censors in Denmark had prohibited screenings of Mickey
Mouse films, the April 1931 issue of *Shinseinen* may well be the first-ever
nationwide appearance of Mickey Mouse's image in Japan. Though many
publications later printed plagiarized images of Mickey Mouse and some
featured comic strips reverse engineered from animated Disney films,
Shinseinen appears to have been the only publication in prewar Japan to

Figure 3.12. *Krazy Kat, Shinseinen*, April 1931 (two of four pages).

have printed the actual Mickey Mouse comic strip drawn for Disney by Floyd Gottfredson.

Shinseinen under Inui Shin'ichirō's tenure as manga editor featured an enormous variety of foreign audiovisual comics, including among others Clarence D. Russell's *Pete the Tramp* (February 1931 and April 1936), Otto Soglow's *The Little King* (April 1931, November 1933, December 1934, June 1937, July 1939, and likely others), *Felix the Cat* and *Laura* (both known from the *Jiji Shinpō*), and E. C. Segar's *Thimble Theatre* (fig. 3.13), better known under the name of its eventual main character, Popeye (all three: April 1934), as well as Bud Counihan's *Betty Boop* (December 1934). Like Mickey Mouse, Popeye and Betty Boop were familiar characters in 1930s Japan, known mostly from animated films and broadly plagiarized. While other publications printed comic strips starring the three that were adapted from animated shorts, *Shinseinen* again was the only Japanese publication to print their original comic strips.[46]

Figure 3.13. *Thimble Theatre, Shinseinen*, April 1934 (two of four pages).

One *Shinseinen* translation of particular note is Alex Raymond's *Secret Agent X-9*, which appeared in July 1937 (fig. 3.14). In the late 1920s, the first adventure strips had appeared in the United States as a new genre that gained in popularity throughout the 1930s and laid the groundwork for noncomical comics. These adventure strips featured more realistically drawn characters and privileged mystery, action, and adventure over humor. Popular examples include Phil Knowlan and Dick Calkins's *Buck Rogers*, Milton Caniff's *Terry and the Pirates*, as well as Raymond's *Flash Gordon*. Somewhat strangely, *Secret Agent X-9* is the only one of these new strips that made it to Japan. An important factor likely was that its first scripts were written by Dashiell Hammett, which must have increased the strip's appeal for *Shinseinen*, given the large number of detective stories it published in translation. In fact, though Raymond's name only survived in his signatures featured at the end of each original strip, Hammett's name is featured in bold underneath the title (which is not the title of the strip but rather of the story line featured: "Kaimadan," meaning "Group of sea devils"). This new adventure strip genre appeared so different to the editorial staff at *Shinseinen* (even Inui, who had grown up with American comics, had left the United States more than a decade before the appearance of adventure comics) that instead of labeling it a comic (manga), they decided to call it a "detective novel / illustrated talkie" (*tantei shōsetsu / sashie tōkī*). *Secret Agent X-9* was prominently featured on page 1 of the issue in which it appeared and consisted of a full forty-eight pages but did not lead to further adventure comics published in 1930s Japan.

Though the lack of additional adventure comics following *Secret Agent X-9* is emblematic of a larger decline in the number of American comic strips in Japan during the 1930s, *Shinseinen* was not the only publication still occasionally introducing new foreign comic strips. The *Kokumin Shinbun*, for example, ran Grace Dayton's *Dolly Dimples and Bobby Bounce* from December 1929 to November 1930, whereas the *Nichi Nichi Shinbun* featured Walter Berndt's *Smitty* from November 1931 to January 1932. After *Dolly Dimples and Bobby Bounce*, the *Kokumin Shinbun* also briefly published Chic Young's *Blondie* (February to June 1933) and George E. Studdy's *Bonzo* (known from *Manga Man* and the *Jidō manga-shū*, July to August 1933). The *Tōkyō Nichi Nichi Shinbun* published Carl Anderson's *Henry* from December 1936 to August 1937, and a version of *Mickey Mouse* from December 1936 to January 1937 (plus a *Donald Duck* strip on December 20, 1936). The *Mickey Mouse* published in the *Tōkyō Nichi Nichi Shinbun* does not appear to be the comic strip drawn by Floyd Gottfredson and is either a plagiarized Japanese strip (plenty of plagiarized Mickey Mouses, Betty Boops, and Popeyes can be found in Japanese publications of the 1930s) or a comic strip adaptation of Mickey Mouse (and in one instance Donald Duck) animated films.

Such conversion of animated films into comic strips definitely happened in at least two publications. The monthly general-audience magazine *Hi no De* from December 1932 to February 1938 featured comic strips that were adapted from Fleischer Studios animated short films, starring Bimbo, Betty Boop, and Popeye, as well as one such Mickey Mouse adaptation in July

Figure 3.14. *Secret Agent X-9*, *Shinseinen*, July 1937 (first page). (Image courtesy of Yorutori Bunko.)

1933. The first of these comic strips (featuring mostly Betty Boop) usually were given Japanese titles derived from those of their animated originals; the later ones (starring mostly Popeye) featured the English titles of the originals. All the Fleischer-based strips profess to be *Hi no De* exclusives, implying that they were licensed in some way. The plots of these animated-film adaptations sometimes diverged significantly from their originals, as is the case with the very first Fleischer Studios strip to appear in *Hi no De*: *Betei-hakase to Haido* (Dr. Betty and [Mr.] Hyde), based on the animated short *Betty M.D.* The animated film (which is in the public domain and can be found online) is approximately seven minutes long and was condensed into twenty-two panels spread over four pages. Because much of the story is told through song and dance in the original, liberties have been taken with the adaptation. Much of the original plot is relayed via newly created dialogue and scenes have been arranged in a different chronological order. The panels must have been copied by hand from still images from the film, since backgrounds were sometimes omitted and details redrawn. Some of the later adapted strips feature an increased amount of transdiegetic content like sound effects (first in English, later exclusively in Japanese), free-floating question or exclamation marks, vision lines, and motion lines.

Similarly to *Hi no De*, the women's magazine *Shufu no Tomo* from May to October 1934 printed *Mickey Mouse* comic strips adapted from animated films like *Playful Pluto* (fig. 3.15), *Mickey Shanghaied*, and *Giantland*, later followed by strips adapted from Dick Huemer's *Scrappy* animated shorts, published under the title *Sukurappī bebī* from November 1934 to between December 1934 and February 1935.[47] The Fleischer, Disney, and *Scrappy* strips in *Hi no De*, *Shufu no Tomo*, and (likely) the *Tōkyō Nichi Nichi Shinbun* might be considered examples of transcreation rather than translation. While most of the visual content in the comic strips was retained from the original, much of the text was newly created rather than a translation of existing dialogue (just compare fig. 3.15 to the actual *Playful Pluto* animated short). These adaptations may also be the first film-to-comic adaptations and as such hold an important place in the history of

Figure 3.15. *Mickey Mouse* animated-film-turned-comic-strip, *Shufu no Tomo*, August 1934 (first page).

cross-media adaptations. More importantly, they are an apt illustration of the audiovisual nature of transdiegetic comics, since the adaptations described here are literal sound films that have been converted to the page.

A significant number of prewar comic strip translations in Japanese publications remain undiscovered. After all, an article published in the magazine *Manga no Kuni* in July 1937 claims that after the *Asahi Graph* began publishing *Bringing Up Father*, daily newspapers competed to publish foreign comics.[48] The same article also asserts that old copies of foreign comics magazines and Sunday supplements were available in used bookstores in Japanese cities. Considering the frequency of piracy in comics translation at the time (see, for example, the many plagiarized Mickey Mouse, Popeye, and Betty Boop cartoons in Japanese publications then), this means that it was easy for publishers not constrained by copyright concerns to incorporate foreign material. In his October 19, 1938, article in the *Asahi Graph*, Suzuki Bunshirō furthermore mentions that in addition to Tokyo and Osaka newspapers, regional papers also began publishing foreign comic strips due to the popularity of Jiggs and Maggie. Given that almost all the newspapers currently known to have featured foreign comics were based in Tokyo or Osaka, this means that even more translated transdiegetic comic strips are waiting to be rediscovered.

The immense number of Japanese translations of foreign audiovisual comics unearthed during the research for this book nonetheless conclusively establishes that foreign audiovisual comics were a major form of entertainment in 1920s and 1930s Japan. Given their popularity, it is obvious why Japanese-drawn manga changed to look like these "foreign manga": Since importing and translating foreign works was both difficult and expensive, Japanese publications had ample incentive to encourage the domestic production of comparable audiovisual comics. Simultaneously, the widespread availability of a diverse range of foreign comic strips supplied Japanese artists with a broad spectrum of examples of the audiovisual form to study and imitate, making it little surprising that manga, concurrently with the success of Japanese translations of foreign audiovisual comics over the course of the 1920s and 1930s, came to closely resemble these comics.

CHAPTER 4

FROM ASŌ YUTAKA TO
TEZUKA OSAMU

HOW MANGA MADE IN JAPAN ADOPTED THE FORM OF
AUDIOVISUAL COMICS

The immense popularity of imported audiovisual comics among the Japanese population after the introduction of *Bringing Up Father* quickly induced editors to urge local artists to adopt the form and produce similar material. Because of this, over the course of the 1920s and 1930s, following the success of *Bringing Up Father* and other audiovisual comics imported from abroad, more and more narrative manga drawn by Japanese artists began to use the audiovisual form to tell stories mimetically rather than via illustrated text. Due to the increasing prevalence of this new form between 1923 and 1940, the word *manga* came to refer primarily to audiovisual comics rather than picture stories and single-panel cartoons. Japanese artists' embrace of the audiovisual form turned "audiovisual comics" into the most common meaning of *manga*, demonstrating that contemporary Japanese manga share a common ancestry with early American audiovisual comics more so than with older Japanese art.

A central factor in the development and rapid spread of the audiovisual form in the United States at the turn of the century between the 1890s and 1910s had been intense competition between different print media outlets (most notably the newspaper war between Hearst and Pulitzer),[1] amid which newspapers strove to distinguish themselves from rival publications by providing their readers with more popular comic strips. Unsurprisingly, audiovisual comics spread in similar fashion in Japan, starting with one newspaper editor's urging a Japanese artist to create the first domestically drawn fully audiovisual comic strip and take on Japan's (foreign-drawn) most popular manga at the time. According to *Asahi Graph* editor Suzuki Bunshirō, Takada Tomoichirō, editor in chief of the newspaper *Hōchi Shinbun*, reacted to the success of the *Asahi Graph*'s translation of *Bringing Up Father* within weeks of its first issue by requesting that cartoonist Asō Yutaka come up with something in the same vein that would be able to compete with McManus's strip.[2] The result was the first successful Japanese-drawn audiovisual comic strip, *Nonki na tōsan*, which would become one of the most popular manga of the 1920s in its own right. It would also be the first and perhaps most important step in the shift of *domestically produced* narrative manga from picture stories to audiovisual comics, helping ensure that the word *manga* would still primarily refer to audiovisual comics even after the disappearance of foreign comics from Japan by 1940.

At the time of *Bringing Up Father*'s first appearance in Japanese on April 1, 1923, Asō Yutaka was writing a series of multi-image stories featuring a little girl called Dadako for the *Hōchi Shinbun*. These stories generally followed the picture-story model of intradiegetic images next to extradiegetic narrative text.[3] In response to his editor's request, however, Asō abandoned the Dadako stories and created the completely new, audiovisual comic strip *Nonki na tōsan*. Asō's strip, often colloquially shortened to *Nontō* and rendered in English most commonly as "Easygoing Daddy" or "Carefree Dad," began serialization in the *Hōchi Shinbun* on April 29, 1923. It was the first major strip by a Japanese author to fully embrace the American format (fig. 4.1), only four weeks after the appearance of *Bringing Up Father*. Unlike *Shō-chan no bōken*, *Nontō* did not feature extradiegetic narration and instead made extensive use of transdiegetic content beyond speech balloons, such as sight and motion lines, music notes, pain

Figure 4.1. Asō Yutaka, first *Nonki na tōsan*, *Hōchi Shinbun*, April 29, 1923.

stars, and "briffits" (a term created by cartoonist Mort Walker to describe dust clouds indicating movement).

Many of the first Japanese-made audiovisual comics copied translations of American comic strips so closely that they even adopted their foreign reading direction (left to right), providing concrete evidence of the cause-and-effect relationship between the appearance of American audiovisual comics in Japan and the ensuing paradigm shift to the audiovisual form in narrative manga.[4] That Asō was closely following *Bringing Up Father* is obvious from his quick adoption of its changing reading order, for example. The *Asahi Graph*'s translation of *Bringing Up Father* (*Oyaji kyōiku*) had originally preserved the American reading order only for panels and speech balloons (left to right, top to bottom) while using the traditional Japanese order for dialogue (top to bottom, right to left), but since conflicting reading directions (such as reading speech balloons from the left to the right, but the text within them right to left) are obviously confusing to the reader, *Oyaji kyōiku* switched to rendering Japanese dialogue in the original English reading direction on May 16, 1923.[5] Beginning with

June 3, *Nonki na tōsan* likewise suddenly featured dialogue written from left to right. Since left-to-right Japanese writing was extremely uncommon in the early 1920s, the only plausible explanation for why Asō would adopt this foreign reading order for Japanese text is that he was imitating *Bringing Up Father*.

Unsurprisingly, two weeks later, on June 17, Asō also changed the order of panels to match that of McManus's strip, and in the following issue of the "Easygoing Daddy" (June 24) even changed the reading direction of the title to match the American reading direction of the rest of the strip. In addition, Asō added his signature in the Latin alphabet, given name first—"YUTAKA ASO"—the same way American comic strip artists signed their works (fig. 4.2, last panel). The signature did not become a permanent feature, but *Nonki na tōsan* kept the American reading order for title, panels, and balloon text until the very end of its run in the *Hōchi Shinbun*. On October 28, Asō lowered the number of panels from eight to six and started a daily four-panel version on November 26, 1923, which made it look even more like its American equivalent. The six-panel Sunday version ended on December 2, 1923, while the daily strip continued for three more years, until December 11, 1926.

Asō Yutaka himself later spoke freely about the inspiration he had derived from *Bringing Up Father*, though the histories of manga that acknowledge the connection between it and *Nonki na tōsan* tend to downplay this influence by claiming that it was only *after* Asō had already created *Nonki na tōsan* that editor Takada requested a new kind of manga and Asō began imitating *Bringing Up Father*. Manga historian Shimizu Isao, for example, quotes Asō as saying,

During the time that the first newspaper comic strip [*shinbun rensai manga*, "newspaper serial manga"] in Japan, "Jiggs and Maggie (*Bringing Up Father*)" was published in the *Asahi Graph*, I had just started working as a new *mangaka* at the *Hōchi Shinbun*. After the Great Kantō Earthquake on September 1, 1923, the editor at the time, Takada Tomoichirō, told me to write a comic strip [*rensai manga*] to comfort the earthquake's victims.

Figure 4.2. Ninth *Nonki na tōsan*, *Hōchi Shinbun*, June 24, 1923.

I had been looking at Asahi's *Bringing Up Father* and tried to avoid the
request because I wouldn't be able to compete with it, but I was ordered to
write and picked up the pen, the result being *Nonki na tōsan*. Fortunately,
it was popular as the first comic strip drawn by a Japanese author, but the
Hōchi made me take this plunge [*bōken saseta*] in response to the popularity of Asahi's *Bringing Up Father*.[6]

The quotation reportedly is from an interview with Asō in the third issue
of 1957 of the newsletter *Asahi Kyūyū Kaihō*, of which no copy exists in the
public record, making it impossible to verify, but since it has been used
as a basis for denying the obvious link between *Bringing Up Father* and
"Easygoing Daddy," let us examine it. Shimizu's claim that Asō began imitating *Bringing Up Father* only after the September earthquake begs the
question of what would have been left for Asō to imitate by then, when he
had already adopted the strip's audiovisual form from the first issue and,
by June, even its American reading and panel order.

   In the above-cited quotation, Asō mentions that he was following *Bringing Up Father* even before he was instructed to copy it. Understood literally, this would mean that despite already being familiar with *Bringing Up
Father*, it was sheer coincidence that Asō both created Japan's first successful audiovisual comic strip four weeks after its appearance *and* changed
his own strip's panel order and text direction to that of McManus's. This

is rather implausible. For one, it is difficult to imagine any other reason than *Bringing Up Father*'s success for why Asō would take the extremely unusual step of imitating its foreign reading direction. Furthermore, by September 1, there was little of significance left for Asō to copy. Shimizu Isao attempts to resolve the chronological conundrum posed by his Asō quotation by claiming that the two elements copied from *Bringing Up Father* were the number of panels (four) and the frequency of appearance (daily). However, after the earthquake, *Nontō* reemerged on October 28 (with an episode about the quake) as a weekly strip with six panels and did not become a daily four-panel strip until November 26, which means that the earthquake was not the immediate reason for this change.[7]

The more plausible explanation for the chronological conundrum is that what Asō meant in the interview—assuming the quotation is accurate—is that he was already imitating *Bringing Up Father* from the beginning, but that his editor asked him to make his strip daily rather than weekly in order to make it compete with *Bringing Up Father* more directly, and that this was why Asō was hesitant to comply—that is, that he felt either that he would not be able to draw a daily strip or that his daily strip would not match the quality of McManus's. Suyama Keiichi's *Nihon manga 100nen* contains a related quotation by Asō (with no source provided): "When I went to the newspaper offices again after a long absence, Mr. Takada, the salt-and-pepper-haired editor, asked me if we couldn't serialize a manga to cheer up the Great Kantō Earthquake survivors, so I decided to start serializing *Nonki na tōsan*, which I had been drawing as a Sunday manga, daily."[8] Considering Suzuki Bunshirō's account that Asō told him that *Nonki na tōsan*'s creation had been the result of Takada's asking him to create something akin to *Bringing Up Father*, it appears that Shimizu's quotation from the *Asahi Kyūyū Kaihō* newsletter conflates two separate events: first, in April, Takada asked Asō to create an audiovisual comic strip modeled after *Bringing Up Father*, and second, in September Takada asked Asō to change the frequency of this strip from weekly to daily and use it to provide comfort to earthquake survivors.

Asō Yutaka's adoption of *Bringing Up Father*'s audiovisual form turned *Nonki na tōsan* into an immediate and lasting success, so popular that even after the "Easygoing Daddy" disappeared from the *Hōchi Shinbun* in December 1926, the comic strip resurfaced one and a half years later in the May 1928 issue of the magazine *Kingu* (which had previously printed *Little Jimmy*). Panels and dialogue were now in Japanese reading direction, but Asō kept the audiovisual form—separating a nonessential element copied from American audiovisual comics from the essential ones. After in turn disappearing from *Kingu* following the December 1928 issue, *Nontō* once more reappeared in the *Yomiuri Shinbun* in June 1930, following a brief attempt by Asō at a more matriarchal manga in the comic strip *Kaachan* (Mommy) from June 2 to 21. *Kaachan* was executed only half-heartedly—even lacking backgrounds—and perhaps Asō deliberately sabotaged it in order to get a chance to finish the saga of his "Easygoing Daddy" by giving *Nontō* a proper send-off instead: in its last installment on October 15, 1930, seven and a half years after its inception, *Nonki na tōsan*'s protagonists break the fourth wall, say goodbye to their readers, and walk off into the distance. Such a conclusion to a serialized comic strip was a rarity, since strips would usually disappear without warning. Despite this conclusion, however, *Nontō* would return one more time, in the monthly *Fujin Kurabu* (Ladies' club) from January to December 1939, supporting the Japanese war effort. The strip was so popular that it even spawned what is perhaps manga's first spin-off: a comic strip called *Jinsei benkyō* (The study of life) featuring Nonto's son, published in the *Tōkyō Asahi Shinbun* from May 1933 to July 1934.

Given *Nonki na tōsan*'s status in Japanese graphic narrative history as the first significant attempt at a domestically produced audiovisual comic strip, it is perhaps unsurprising that in secondary literature Asō's name is rarely mentioned in other contexts, but his impact on the development of Japanese comics did not end with this strip. An extensive list of audiovisual comic strips drawn by Asō Yutaka demonstrates that he was far from a "one-hit wonder" limited to *Nonki na tōsan*, instead remaining a popular artist well into the 1930s, more than a decade after creating "Easygoing Daddy," and that he must be credited not only with drawing the first regular and successful domestically produced Japanese audiovisual comic strip but also with playing a significant role in establishing the form over the course of more than a decade.[9] While still writing *Nontō* for the *Hōchi Shinbun*, for example, Asō began another comic strip called *Mamaa to teishu* (Mom and husband) in *Kingu* in January 1925, using a Japanese reading order but still relying on transdiegetic content instead of extradiegetic narration. Similarly, *Nontō*'s final episode in the *Yomiuri Shinbun* was followed eleven days later (October 26, 1930) with another comic strip by Asō called *Akachan kakka* (His majesty the baby). Asō stuck closely to the depiction of married and family life that he had taken over from McManus as the central premise of many of his later comic strips as well, such as for example in *Nonki na gofūfu* (Easygoing husband and wife; from January 1932) in the women's magazine *Fujokai, Hogaraka okusan* (Cheerful wife; July to December 1934) in the women's magazine *Fujin Kurabu*, and *Oyaji no seikatsu* (Father's life; September 1932 to August 1933) in the general-audience magazine *Hi no De*.[10]

As mentioned earlier, the most obvious evidence of the direct impact of the translations of *Bringing Up Father* and other foreign audiovisual comics on Japanese graphic narrative is *Nonki na tōsan*'s adoption of the American reading order, but Asō's manga was far from an isolated case in this regard. An astonishing number of other early Japanese comic strips also copied American audiovisual comics down to their reading order: Kitazawa Rakuten's disciple Nagasaki Batten, for example, began writing one of the first Japanese-drawn audiovisual comic strips, called *Pī-bō monogatari* (Pi's story; fig. 4.3), on January 27, 1924, in the *Jiji Shinpō*. On February 24 and March 2, this strip employed the Western reading direction and afterward alternated between American and Japanese orders depending on whether an issue appeared in four or six panels, respectively. *Pī-bō monogatari* was also one of the first strips to use an American-style header (i.e., separated from the strip's panels, stating title and author, and featuring some kind of decoration).

Figure 4.3. Nagasaki Batten, *Pī-bō monogatari, Jiji Shinpō*, March 2, 1924.
(Image courtesy of Yorutori Bunko.)

In some cases, the connection between American comics and the introduction of transdiegetic devices to Japanese manga reveals itself only upon
closer examination. One short-lived audiovisual comic strip drawn by
Hosokibara Seiki for the Tokyo *Chūgai Shōgyō Shinpō* (January 1–9, 1924),
for example, used the two traditional Japanese reading orders for speech
balloons and panels but also featured at least one left-to-right sound-
image balloon and another one filled with a horizontal row of exclamation points. In other 1920s manga, the association of the American reading
direction with transdiegetic sound is readily apparent at first glance, such
as in a January 1, 1925, manga in the *Chūgai Shōgyō Shinpō*, which combined external narrative text with speech balloons in a manner similar to
Shō-chan no bōken. Tellingly, this manga used the American reading direction for transdiegetic speech but a traditional horizontal Japanese reading
order (right to left) for the extradiegetic narration, showing how closely
the "audio" component in comics was associated with its foreign origins.
This manga was not the only one to insist on the use of the American
reading order for sound images even when this conflicted with the reading
order used for other elements and made following the story more difficult.
The fully audiovisual manga *Shinsetai* (New household; from May 1924)
by Kitazawa Rakuten's student Shimokawa Hekoten, for example, featured
panels arranged in the traditional Japanese order but nonetheless used
left-to-right writing for its transdiegetic dialogue.

In most audiovisual manga that employed left-to-right writing, the connection between this foreign writing direction and the audiovisual form is completely obvious. The comic strip *Soppa no ojisan* (Uncle Soppa; by Yuize Hidehiko), serialized in the *Otaru Shinbun* from March to April 1925, exclusively used left-to-right, top-to-bottom reading for the entire duration of its run. Between June 24 and August 14, 1924, the *Yomiuri Shinbun* published the comic strip *Jogakkōde no Fumi-chan* (Fumi-chan, girls' school graduate; fig. 4.4), one of the first Japanese-drawn comic strips featuring a female protagonist (and explicitly published as a women's manga), which did the same.[11] From its first episode, *Fumi-chan*'s panels and text were drawn and written in the American reading direction. The strip also underscores the point that transdiegetic dialogue need not use balloons, as its dialogue sound images were at first not encapsulated in speech balloons but underlined with a single line and connected to the corresponding speaker by a hook off said line.

Some audiovisual manga borrowed even more from translations of American comics than form or writing direction: the *Hōchi Shinbun* for example printed a comic strip called *Osora to Butaroku* by Ōta Masamitsu from November 1924 to February 1925, and the husband, Butaroku, appears to be based on Andy Gump (who was appearing in the *Japan Times*) and/ or Mutt's partner Jeff (from the *Ōsaka Asahi Shinbun*). Figure 4.5 shows the January 9, 1925, episode, in which Butaroku is ecstatic because he has grown back a single hair. Ōta's strip was running concurrently with Asō's *Nonki na tōsan* and used a similar graphic style for its speech balloon outlines, demonstrating influence by Asō as well. Interestingly, *Osora to Butaroku* also featured transdiegetic "heart" shapes on November 27 and December 30, 1924. The shapes appear to symbolize a racing heartbeat in the first example and joy in the second, rather than the now-conventional meaning of romantic love, but they are likely the first such shapes used in Japanese comics, predating the earliest use in a translated American strip and showing how quickly some artists moved from imitation to innovation.[12] *Osora to Butaroku* also featured several additional uses of transdiegetic content likely gleaned from American comics, such as "plewds"

Figure 4.4. Tanabe/Tabe Masaru/Shō (reading unclear), *Jogakkōde no Fumi-chan*, *Yomiuri Shinbun*, August 1, 1924. (Image courtesy of Yorutori Bunko.)

(sweat beads indicating distress) and font modulation to express volume or emphasis. The correlation between diversity of transdiegetic content and stylistic proximity to American comics (e.g., the similarity of Buta-roku to Andy Gump and Jeff) is unlikely to have been coincidental.

A further example of an early Japanese-drawn audiovisual comic that copied even the American reading order is *Gōketsu Yū-bō* (Yu the hero; by Mitsui Shūji, published from October 1925 to July 1926 in the newspaper *Yorozu Chōhō*), which used the left-to-right order for dialogue and occasionally even its title. *Gōketsu Yū-bō* also used a substantial amount of transdiegetic content beyond speech balloons, such as pain stars, question

Figure 4.5. Ōta Masamitsu, *Osora to Butaroku*, *Hōchi Shinbun*, January 9, 1925.

and exclamation mark emanata (transdiegetic devices showing emotion), motion lines, and hats flying off characters' heads to indicate excitement or surprise (see fig. 4.6, panel 4), like *Osora to Butaroku*. The strip illustrates how the impact of American comics on manga was not limited to sound images but included a broad range of transdiegetic content to tell stories as mimetically as possible. Incidentally, the *Gōketsu Yū-bō* episode in figure 4.6 was published on November 8, 1925, the year in which radio broadcasts started in Japan, and shows that the "voice-speaker disconnect," the "eeriness

Figure 4.6. Mitsui Shūji, *Gōketsu Yū-bō*, *Yorozu Chōhō*, November 8, 1925.

of hearing voices that can't be traced back to bodies" that had occasioned the introduction of sound to comics around 1899, was still very real for people in Japan at the time of the episode's publication. Commenting on the radio to which the characters are listening, the second man from the right in panel 2 remarks, "Soon, there'll be people jumping out of this horn."

The connection between the audiovisual form, audiovisual technology, and American influence is similarly encapsulated by a comic strip by Fujii Ichirō called *Roido no bōken* (Lloyd's adventures; between October 1925 and November 1927, *Shōnen Kurabu*), which starred Hollywood actor Harold Lloyd and occasionally colleagues of his, such as Charlie Chaplin. Though all issues of "Lloyd's Adventures" used the Japanese reading direction for the order of panels, some nevertheless rendered the transdiegetic dialogue text within the panels left to right.[13]

Even *Shō-chan no bōken*, though remaining primarily a picture story, became a part of the trend to adopt the reading direction of American comic strips on January 3, 1925, when its dialogue was switched to left-to-right in the *Ōsaka Asahi Shinbun*. One week later, on January 10, even the title and extradiegetic narration followed suit. This state of affairs continued for three months, until April 1, when the narration reverted to its former Japanese reading direction, but the dialogue continued in the American order for an additional three weeks, until April 24, and the title and subtitle even beyond that. The adoption of the American reading order even by picture stories like *Shō-chan no bōken* hints at the degree to which their creators saw the new foreign-born audiovisual comics as a threat to the popularity of such older forms of graphic narrative. Of course, the different reading direction was the least significant feature introduced by the American comic strip translations, since it is largely irrelevant to the content or function of a text whether it is written left to right or right to left (of course few languages even offer this option as Japanese does). This means that the new audiovisual form and its "modern," "Western" look were popular to such an overwhelming extent that *mangaka* became so eager to emulate this "modern" look that they assimilated the reading order associated with it as a by-product. The unconventional new reading direction must have been confusing for at least some readers, though, which is likely why artists eventually dropped it (see for example Asō's continuations of *Nonki na tōsan* in *Kingu*, the *Yomiuri Shinbun*, and *Fujin Kurabu*) and it did not become standard practice for manga in the end.[14] On the other hand, the sudden presence of left-to-right reading in popular comics, both foreign and domestic, likely contributed to the normalization of the left-to-right reading direction for horizontal writing in Japanese that began to emerge during the 1920s and 1930s, particularly in advertisements.

We have already seen how the adoption of the Western reading direction by many of the first Japanese-drawn audiovisual manga throughout the 1920s and early 1930s greatly facilitates tracing the link between translated American comics and *mangaka*'s embrace of their form. In the short-lived magazine *Manga Man* discussed in chapter 3, it even illustrates how an entire group of such *mangaka* was trained in the new form. *Manga Man*, notable especially for its Japanese translation of Harold Knerr's version of *The Katzenjammer Kids* and its full-page four-color comics, during its color period also featured a variety of comic strips by established and upcoming Japanese artists, almost all written left to right. These artists included Nagasaki Batten, Shishido Sakō and Miyao Shigeo, some of the biggest names in narrative manga at the time. Even Okamoto Ippei contributed a five-panel manga for the cover of *Manga Man*'s first issue—the only one in it that uses the picture-story model.

In 1929, the picture story was already in decline. Comic strips had eclipsed picture stories in popularity to such an extent that even someone like Miyao Shigeo, one of the artists featured in *Manga Man* and perhaps the picture story's most ardent adherent, was compelled to try out the new form. As Okamoto's most successful pupil, Miyao had inherited the *manga manbun* picture-story style from him and used it to great success before Japanese audiences' and authors' embrace of audiovisual comics.[15] Miyao's *Manga Tarō* and *Dangokushisuke*—both first published in the *Tōkyō Maiyū Shinbun* in 1922 and 1923, respectively—represented the height of the picture story's popularity in Japan. Like his teacher, Miyao strongly preferred picture stories over audiovisual comics, and the first installment of Miyao's comic strip *Hanashita Nobio-kun no ichinichi* (A day in the life of Nobio Hanashita) in *Manga Man* in August 1929 may represent his first-ever use of a speech balloon and the transdiegetic-stage form. Like most of the other American and Japanese comic strips in the same *Manga Man* issue, *Hanashita Nobio-kun no ichinichi* is written left to right, top to bottom, implying that Miyao used this form and format because *Manga Man*'s editors had requested it.[16] In contrast to the other comic strips in the magazine, Miyao's speech balloons are drawn noticeably awkwardly and (apart from a single exception) are superimposed on the background as a mere balloon outline with lettering, without the solid white filling of all other balloons in *Manga Man* (and comics in general), perhaps due to his lack of familiarity with the audiovisual form.[17] Miyao's apparent discomfort with the audiovisual form further suggests that he wrote his submission as a comic strip primarily because he was asked to do so by the magazine in order to adhere to the same look established by the American comic translations it was publishing, such as *The Katzenjammer Kids*, which, as the only strip to be afforded a full two pages, set the standard for what *Manga Man* expected a "modern" manga to look like.

The editorial staff knew that left-to-right reading might be problematic for some readers. An editorial statement in the back of the second issue solicited readers to write to the magazine to share their opinions regarding its content, mentioning specifically that the staff had decided to make all horizontal writing for color comics "European-script style" (i.e., left to right),[18] but that they would like to know if they should instead make it right to left or vertical, Japanese style (i.e., top to bottom, right to left). This statement evinces the state of flux into which the shape and form of narrative manga had been thrust during the mid-to-late 1920s by the popularity of American comic strips and the resulting shift from picture story to audiovisual comics.

After his work for *Manga Man*, Miyao Shigeo published a second comic strip called *Otomo no Micchan* in *Fujokai* in April 1931. The balloons look almost identical to those from the second issue of *Hanashita Nobio-kun*, though the reading direction conflict was resolved by ordering the panels to match the writing (top to bottom, right to left). According to Takeuchi Osamu, Miyao's popularity had begun to wane with the beginning of the Shōwa period (1926), so his experimentation with the comic strip, which was rapidly replacing the picture story as the dominant form of graphic narrative, was perhaps an effort to remain relevant as a *mangaka*.[19]

Other artists emerged from *Manga Man*'s brief existence more successfully than Miyao. In particular, the magazine brought about the creation of the New Manga Group (*Shin-manga-ha shūdan*) of artists, many of whom later prospered individually due to their embrace of the new American-style single-panel cartoons and audiovisual comics. These *mangaka*'s adoption of such cartoons and comics was greatly facilitated by *Manga Man*, including in the case of the New Manga Group's most famous member, Yokoyama Ryūichi. Early in his career, Yokoyama purchased one of the first *Manga Man* issues from a newsstand in Katase, outside of Tokyo.[20] Yokoyama had become a "manga fan" after he saw "foreign manga" (i.e., cartoons and/or comic strips) in magazines and liked their easy-to-understand humor and careful line work.[21] Intrigued by such models, Yokoyama began to submit his own "Western" work to *Manga Man* and soon became a regularly featured contributor.[22] Through the magazine, he met and befriended other artists working for it, most notably Kondō Hidezō, Yazaki Shigeshi, Yoshida Kanzaburō, and Sugiura Yukio. All of these would later become members of the New Manga Group and, like Yokoyama, were influenced by foreign comics. Sugiura, for example, explicitly writes in his autobiography, "I was inspired to become a *mangaka* by the American manga *Bringing Up Father* and such."[23]

Regarding the prewar translation of foreign comics and cartoons by Japanese publications, Yokoyama recalls that "Japanese magazines at the time weren't aware that foreign manga were copyrighted and reprinted them freely. This meant that we were able to see a lot of great foreign manga, but eventually, syndicates complained, and [magazines] started paying for translation rights from then on. Because of this, we weren't able to enjoy good manga in magazines anymore. So depending on your perspective, it seems like you could say that we were able to learn a lot thanks to the editors who prepared pirated copies."[24] When Yokoyama speaks of learning from foreign manga, he is talking about more than just reading them. One of the tasks given to the permanent *Manga Man* artists was to trace, copy, and edit the foreign cartoons and strips for publication in translation. This was true for Kondō Hidezō and Yazaki Shigeshi, for example.[25] It is hence likely that some of the foreign manga—not only cartoons but also *The Katzenjammer Kids* or *Adamson*—in *Manga Man* were traced and edited by Yokoyama and that through this process he acquired hands-on experience drawing in this new format. *Manga Man*'s comics were not the only ones to which Yokoyama had a direct connection: around the year 1933, he even lettered Nakazato Tomijirō's translations of *Bringing Up Father* for the *Asahi Graph*, work that Yokoyama writes paid better than drawing original material for most magazines.[26]

Manga Man had been important for the emerging artists who would later form the New Manga Group not only because it acquainted them with foreign comics and cartoons but also because it was one of the few magazines that would print work by authors who were yet unknown to the public.[27] With *Manga Man*'s disappearance from circulation in 1931, these artists' most important venue of publication vanished. Forced to find ways of marketing their work to publications reluctant to feature less established artists, in response, Yokoyama and the *mangaka* he had befriended at *Manga Man* founded the New Manga Group the following year, electing Yokoyama as their leader. Although the New Manga Group turned out a success, Yokoyama had already become a rising star on his own. In January 1931 Inui Shin'ichirō, editor for the monthly magazine *Shinseinen* (see chapter 3), saw the current *Manga Man* issue at a newsstand at Ōtsuka station, much like Yokoyama had over a year earlier in Katase.[28] Inui purchased a copy of the magazine and liked Yokoyama's contribution so much that he decided to pay the *Manga Man* offices a visit to ask for the artist's address.

As luck would have it, the *Manga Man* address was within walking distance from the station and, unbeknownst to Inui, was actually Yokoyama's
personal address, which, in January 1931, *Manga Man* had begun to use as
its business address.[29] Yokoyama's work was then featured in the February
issue of *Shinseinen* and he as well as other members of the New Manga
Group became frequent contributors. The New Manga Group was now
replacing the older *mangaka* establishment dominated by Kitazawa and
Okamoto, substituting American-inspired cartoons and comics for the
caricatures and picture stories represented by Kitazawa (pre-1924), Okamoto, and Miyao Shigeo.[30] In addition to single-panel cartoons, Yokoyama
also wrote audiovisual comic strips for *Shinseinen*, such as *An-kō* (fig. 4.7)
between August 1933 and June 1934, which hints at his training via American comics and *Manga Man* through left-to-right speech balloon text
(despite a traditional Japanese panel order and a right-to-left title) and
one signature in the Latin alphabet. Though his early work has largely
been forgotten, Yokoyama in 1936 also created the popular character Fuku-
chan, whose comic strip turned out a long-running success both before
and after the war, eventually even surpassing *Bringing Up Father*'s longev-
ity in Japan and becoming a new template for Japanese newspaper comic
strips.[31] It is not altogether surprising that one character in *Fuku-chan*
bears a curious resemblance to the Captain from the *Katzenjammer Kids*
episodes published in *Manga Man*.

Similarly unsurprising should be that the rise of the New Manga Group
was enabled by the same publications (primarily *Manga Man*, the *Asahi
Graph*, and *Shinseinen*) that played significant roles in the translation of
the American comics and cartoons that had inspired the group's members.
This connection is exemplified by a "New Year's meet of the world's popu-
lar manga characters" collaborative two-page spread created by the New
Manga Group for the *Asahi Graph*'s New Year's issue in 1937, which includes
many characters originally from overseas: Mickey and Minnie Mouse, Pluto,
Donald Duck, Felix the Cat, Bonzo, the Captain and the Katzenjammer
Kids, Oswald the Rabbit, Popeye, the Toonerville Skipper, Betty Boop, the

Figure 4.7. Yokoyama Ryūichi, *An-kō*, *Shinseinen*, November 1933 (first of several pages).

Little King, Dinglehoofer, Adamson, Jiggs and Maggie, Smitty, Andy Gump, and Skippy (and, for some reason, Benito Mussolini, who may have been included because of his appearances in political cartoons at the time). The majority of these characters had appeared in translated comic strips by 1937, though Oswald was likely known exclusively through animated films. The sheer abundance of foreign comics characters in this cartoon showcases the New Manga Group members' extensive familiarity with these characters and their comic strips. The New Year's cartoon hence constitutes further evidence that the primary source of inspiration for this new generation of manga artists was not traditional Japanese art, the picture stories of Okamoto Ippei, or cartoons in the older *Ponchi-e* tradition introduced by Wirgman's *Japan Punch*, but contemporaneous foreign comics and cartoons as well as Japanese-drawn manga influenced by these.

The New Manga Group is not the only case of a collaboration between *mangaka* that helped spread audiovisual comics in Japan. Between July and November 1930, none other than Asō Yutaka, creator of the "Easygoing Daddy," the first successful Japanese-drawn audiovisual comic strip, worked with fellow manga artists Tsutsumi Kanzō, Shishido Sakō, and Yanase Masamu to create a weekly full-page comic called *Shijūsō* (Quartet; presumably named so because of its four protagonists, who are based on the four authors; fig. 4.8). Besides Yanase, all these artists had written comic strips for *Manga Man*, which may be how the idea for *Shijūsō* arose. Like their comic strips in that publication, "Quartet" employed the American reading order for panels and transdiegetic text, visually emphasizing the lineage derived from *Bringing Up Father*, *Little Jimmy*, and so on and the break that such comic strips represented with pre-1923 narrative manga. Fittingly, "Quartet" was published in the *Asahi Graph*, which had jump-started the shift to audiovisual comics in Japan, and appeared in it concurrently with audiovisual manga's most influential ancestor, *Bringing Up Father*.

Publication of "Quartet" was likely arranged by Asō Yutaka, whose work had previously been featured in the *Asahi Graph*. That he took on a leading role in the creation of the four-author strip is evident from its use

Figure 4.8. Asō Yutaka, Tsutsumi Kanzō, Shishido Sakō, and Yanase Masamu, *Shijūsō*, *Asahi Graph*, August 20, 1930.

of Asō's trademark horizontally elongated speech balloons. Considering that at that point in time, Asō was also the most successful out of the four *mangaka*, it is easy to imagine that the other three would have been willing to defer to his judgment and learn from him. Like Asō's earlier audiovisual manga, "Quartet" abounds with a variety of transdiegetic content, such as motion lines, speech balloons changing shape to indicate different tones or attitudes, different font sizes to emulate volume, squiggly lines emanating from a character's head to show annoyance, and music notes to visualize the sound of music. In terms of drawing style, too, *Shijūsō* differs distinctly from the pre-1923 manga lineage of Okamoto Ippei and Kitazawa Rakuten in that it uses clear pen-drawn lines, shading, changes of perspective, and detailed backgrounds (which Okamoto, in his 1933 *Manga kōza*, proclaimed typical for American comics but unnecessary in Japanese ones).[32] By the end of their collaboration, all four of the "Quartet" authors were thoroughly experienced in using transdiegetic content to create audiovisual comics. According to *Asahi Graph* vice chief editor Hata Sankichi in the October 17, 1932, *Japan Times*, Asō and Tsutsumi later also influenced the work of other Japanese cartoonists through direct tutelage: "Now about twenty young catoonists [*sic*] including women, are studying zealously under the instruction of Messrs. Asou and Tsutsumi under the patronage of the Asahi." Within less than a decade, Asō Yutaka had gone from being the only Japanese *mangaka* drawing audiovisual comics (in April 1923) to teaching a new generation of aspiring *mangaka* the use of this medium (by 1932).

While working on "Quartet" with the other three, Asō also drew his continuation of "Easygoing Daddy" for the *Yomiuri Shinbun* until October 15, 1930. On October 26, the *Yomiuri Shinbun* then debuted a new Sunday comics supplement, which featured audiovisual comic strips by both Asō and Yanase Masamu. Yanase's contribution showed that Asō Yutaka was not the only member of the Quartet who took direct inspiration from Jiggs and Maggie: the strip he drew for the *Yomiuri Shinbun* was called *Kanemochi kyōiku* (Bringing up a rich man), an obvious reference to *Oyaji kyōiku*, the Japanese title of McManus's strip in the *Asahi Graph*. Shishido Sakō joined his Quartet coauthors in the *Yomiuri*'s manga supplement a week later on November 2 with an audiovisual strip of his own and, on December 7, added a second such comic strip called *Supīdo Tarō* (Speed Taro), which would become one of the most popular manga of the 1930s and make Shishido Sakō one of the most influential prewar *mangaka*.

"Speed Taro" is often credited with having introduced "movie-like effects" to Japanese comics.[33] As Ōtsuka Eiji has pointed out, what most manga scholars mean by "filmic effects" boils down to depth of field and elements of montage (such as close-ups and changes in perspective, presumably).[34] Though "Speed Taro" was not the first Japanese-language comic strip to use either—the *Kokumin Shinbun*'s translation of *Little Jimmy* had already made extensive use of both in some episodes, as had "Quartet" and even Shishido's earlier strip for the *Yomiuri*—it employed such means more regularly than other manga at the time, demonstrating audiovisual comics' versatility and further popularizing the medium. With "Speed Taro," Shishido Sakō helped lay the groundwork for the great variety of visual effects seen in manga today.

Though Shishido Sakō is one of the few early Japanese creators of audiovisual comics whom manga historians generally recognize as having been influenced by American comics, it is usually suggested that this happened during Shishido's stay in the United States. But while Shishido was certainly influenced by comics he saw during his travels in the 1920s, he was also following translated audiovisual strips appearing in Japanese publications at the time. In *Amerika no yokoppara*, the 1929 book he wrote about his time in the United States, he specifically mentions the Japanese translations of *Bringing Up Father*, *Mutt and Jeff*, *Happy Hooligan*, and *Polly and Her Pals* and their places of publication (see chapter 3).[35] Shishido even describes other comic strips, including the *Katzenjammer Kids*, and writes that many of them were sold in Japan by syndicates like King Feature Service, which means that it is possible that Shishido was aware of further comic strip translations that have yet to be rediscovered.

As cartoonist Adam Buttrick has pointed out to me, the Speed Taro character also resembles Little Jimmy closely enough to suggest some degree of direct influence. Despite his early familiarity with American comic strips, however, Shishido completely embraced audiovisual comics only after his work for *Manga Man* and as part of the Quartet, having occasionally used the picture-story format as late as February 1930 (in *Kingu*), long after audiovisual comics had already begun to dominate the world of narrative manga. Perhaps he never would have created "Speed Taro" had it not been for his collaboration with Asō, Tsutsumi, and Yanase.

Due to the success of earlier audiovisual comics like "Speed Taro," especially *Bringing Up Father* and "Easygoing Daddy," by 1930, transdiegetic/audiovisual comics were already outnumbering picture stories in Japan,[36] a remarkable development given that the first regularly published audiovisual comic strips had appeared only seven years earlier. This change was not lost on Kitazawa Rakuten and Okamoto Ippei, formerly Japan's foremost *mangaka*, who both began to draw audiovisual comic strips after the immense success of *Bringing Up Father* and other such works in Japan. The earliest such comic strip in which Kitazawa was involved, apart from his early unsustained experiments with the form, was *Hitorimusume no Hineko-san* (Hineko the only daughter) in the *Jiji Shinpō* in 1924, though Kitazawa is credited only as having assisted his student Nagasaki Batten on it. The first known audiovisual comic strip Kitazawa drew by himself was *Tonda Haneko*, between 1928 and 1931, likewise in the *Jiji Shinpō*. During this time, the newspaper, with Kitazawa as its manga editor, was also publishing Fred Opper's *Happy Hooligan* and *Mr. Dough and Mr. Dubb*, as well as the accompanying topper strips *And Her Name Was Maud* and *Our Antediluvian Ancestors* (1925 to 1930), and Otto Messmer's *Felix the Cat* and *Laura* (1930 to 1932). While Kitazawa's work as artist and editor did not evince particular affinity for the audiovisual comic strip form prior to 1923, after the success of *Bringing Up Father*, he helped accelerate the triumph of the new form not only by publishing two of the most influential Japanese translations of American comics (*Happy Hooligan* and *Felix the Cat*) but also by eventually adopting the transdiegetic form himself in *Tonda Haneko* and other audiovisual manga. That Kitazawa had been familiar with audiovisual comics at the latest by 1907, but had resisted using the form until after the massive importation of American comics in translation, suggests that he did not embrace audiovisual comics due to personal preference but in order to stay relevant as a *mangaka* (as we also saw happen with Miyao Shigeo and his work for *Manga Man*).

Okamoto Ippei's stance vis-à-vis the newly dominant audiovisual comic strip appears to have been ambivalent. Even after 1923, Okamoto continued drawing political cartoons for the *Tōkyō Asahi Shinbun* and picture stories for various other publications, without adopting the new transdiegetic form. Nevertheless he also wrote a contribution titled "*Katei manga kōza*—the Home A.B.C of Cariature [*sic*]" for the April 6, 1927, *Asahi Graph* in which he discusses favorably the new genre of *renzoku* (continuing/serial) *manga*. In the piece, Okamoto describes *renzoku manga* as refraining from *setsumeibun* (external narration), instead using speech balloons for dialogue, stars to indicate when someone is struck, music notes for sound, and question marks for confusion—in short, replacing extradiegetic narration with transdiegetic devices. The two four-panel strips drawn by Okamoto to illustrate his essay use the left-to-right order for their panels, showing that he was not immune to the influence of American comics. Okamoto does not mention any Japanese audiovisual comics but asserts in the introduction that the *renzoku manga* style is used by most American comics, citing the *Asahi Graph*'s own *Bringing Up Father* translation as an example and discussing the character of Jiggs in particular. The positive tone of the essay suggests that Okamoto eventually relented in his initial opposition to American audiovisual comics, and in February 1930, he surprisingly even published an audiovisual comic strip called *Katei no yōkō* (A family's visit to the West) in *Fujokai*, which had previously published some of his picture stories. *Katei no yōkō* was limited to a single issue, but from July to September, a strip called *Jochū-san no yōkō* (A maid's visit to the West) followed. Although *Jochū-san no yōkō* ran for only three months, it consisted of a total of fourteen full pages.[37] Its backgrounds were fairly detailed, which is surprising considering that Okamoto would later describe detailed backgrounds as an American idiosyncrasy and unnecessary for Japanese comics. The discovery of *Katei no yōkō* and *Jochū-san no yōkō* certainly refutes the prevailing assumption that Okamoto rejected audiovisual comics until the end.[38] That all three of Japan's formerly decidedly nonaudiovisual *mangaka*—Miyao, Kitazawa, and Okamoto—had given up their opposition to audiovisual comics signaled that the new medium's victory over the picture story was complete. The picture story never completely disappeared, of course, and many hybrid works using elements of both continued to be published throughout the 1930s and beyond, but the *standard* form, the paradigm, of narrative manga by this point had shifted to audiovisual comics.

The most significant change in narrative manga brought about by the translation of American comics was this shift from picture story to audiovisual comic strip, but the foreign comics published by Japanese newspapers and magazines also exerted influence on style and content. Such influence hints at the extent of the impact of 1920s and 1930s translations of these comics on the historical development of narrative manga. Some manga almost directly copied characters and linework from translated American comics, as was for example the case with a cartoon in the *Miyako Shinbun* from September 17, 1925, whose characters all bear a striking resemblance to Jiggs; a strip in *Yōnen Kurabu* in April 1936 by Nagasaki Batten that appears inspired by Grace Dayton's *Dimples*; or a strip called *Genki no Genchan* in May 1939 in the same publication that borrows from *Skippy* and/or *Reg'lar Fellers*. The strips drawn by Ichikawa Toshi for *Fujokai* from 1932 to 1939 likewise all exhibit linework and content reminiscent of *Bringing Up Father* (even featuring an almost exact copy of a black cat from McManus's strip in April 1935), while the strip *Bonzō to Suiko-san* in the *Tōkyō Asahi Shinbun* on June 6, 1932, copied George E. Studdy's *Bonzo* down to its actual title, and *Shōnen Shōjo Manga Kurabu* in August 1933 featured an imitation of the *Katzenjammer Kids*. Throughout the 1930s, many Japanese strips even starred plagiarized versions of Mickey Mouse, Popeye, and Betty Boop (who during that decade replaced Jiggs and Maggie as the most popular foreign characters).[39]

American comics also introduced racist caricatures of Black people to manga, as seen in translated issues of *Bringing Up Father*,[40] *Mutt and Jeff*,[41] *Little Jimmy*,[42] *Barney Google* (fig. 3.3), and several of the *Katzenjammer Kids* episodes published in *Manga Man* (see fig. 3.13). These caricatures were usually bald (if male), their mouths a large white oval with a line or circle in the middle—that is, a set of large, tube-like white lips—in stark contrast to their pitch-black skin (apart from large white eyes). This racial carica-ture is almost exactly that later found in several Japanese manga, most nota-bly Shimada Keizō's (in)famous picture story *Bōken Dankichi* (Adventure Dankichi), in which a plucky Japanese boy educates primitive island natives. American comics in 1920s and 1930s Japan hence not only introduced a new medium but also influenced its content.

The most lasting stylistic influence was the "cutification" of Japanese com-ics. As Jo En points out, the "cute" (*kawaii*) drawing style in Japanese comics developed during the 1920s and 1930s. Jo uses Kitazawa Rakuten's 1902 Dekobō (a character similar to Chame) as an example of a pre-cute character and Yokoyama Ryūichi's 1936 Fuku-chan as a cute one, relying on a partial defini-tion of "cute" by Thierry Groensteen ("drawing the head disproportionally large").[43] What happened between these two ways of drawing child charac-ters in manga was the introduction of American comic strips (and animated films), which strongly influenced, if not caused, the initial development of the *kawaii* aesthetic in manga. After all, the proportions of Yokoyama's Fuku-chan and contemporary *kawaii* characters like Doraemon resemble those of Little Jimmy (see Jimmy and his animal companion in panel 4 of fig. 3.1) and Felix the Cat (see fig. 3.9) much more closely than those of Dekobō and Chame. Even the large eyes of Japanese comics characters today, seen as representative of a particularly Japanese drawing style, were introduced with American char-acters like Mickey Mouse (see fig. 3.15) and Felix the Cat (see fig. 3.9). It's not that the eyes of Japanese manga characters became significantly larger after the war, but that American characters' eyes became smaller: today's Mickey Mouse, for example, has much smaller eyes than his prewar version.

As briefly discussed in chapter 3, American comics via characters like Mickey Mouse and Felix the Cat also introduced anthropomorphic animal protagonists to Japanese manga. Though such anthropomorphic cartoon animals were essentially unheard of in Japan before Felix's appearance in *Hachisuzume* in 1929 and the *Jiji Shinpō* in 1930, from 1930 on, they proliferated due to the influence of *Felix the Cat* and other foreign comics.[44] Shimada Keizō's comic strip *Nekoshichi-sensei* (Cat seven sensei) between 1939 and 1940 in the *Tōkyō Nichi Nichi Shinbun*, for example, was more or less a direct copy of Felix the Cat.[45] The biggest difference is that Shimada's cat wears shorts, gloves, and shoes, which may reflect the influence of Disney's Mickey. The historically most significant of the new breed of Japanese anthropomorphic animal protagonists imitative of Mickey and Felix was a stray dog, however.

This stray dog by the name of Norakuro (fig. 4.9; often translated as "Stray Black") would surpass Asō's Easygoing Daddy as Japan's most popular native-born character and his comic strip's success turned its creator, Takamizawa Nakatarō—today better known under his eventual pen name Tagawa Suihō—into the most popular Japanese *mangaka* of the 1930s.[46] Though not the sole reason for its popularity, *Norakuro*'s audiovisual nature certainly contributed to its immense success, which in turn further cemented audiovisual comics as the standard form for narrative manga.[47] Coming up with *Norakuro*'s successful formula took time, however. In contrast to many of the New Manga Group artists, Tagawa became a *mangaka* only in his late twenties and not out of a long-standing interest in cartoons, picture stories, or comics. Having begun his artistic career as a member of the radical art group MAVO (alongside Yanase Masamu), he next turned to writing *rakugo* (traditional humoristic storytelling) stories until an editor suggested that given his training in painting and talent for crafting funny stories, he might be good at creating comics as well.[48]

Unlike Asō Yutaka when he was urged to imitate *Bringing Up Father* or the *Manga Man* artists who had been told to copy the American comic strips

Figure 4.9. Tagawa Suihō, *Norakuro*, *Shōnen Kurabu*, June 1931 (last page). (Image courtesy of Yorutori Bunko.)

published by the magazine, Tagawa did not have a clear template for creating graphic narratives when he started his career as a *mangaka*. His first published narrative manga in 1928 and 1929 experimented with various combinations of picture story and audiovisual comics but rarely distinguished visually between dialogue and narration, used little transdiegetic content, and did not synchronize dialogue to the action depicted, making them look outdated for their time. Since Tagawa enjoyed neither the tutelage of a more experienced *mangaka* well versed in the new popular medium of audiovisual comics like Asō nor an opportunity to collaborate with such a person, he instead had to study foreign and Japanese-drawn manga that made use of this freshly dominant form. Tagawa's studies of audiovisual manga resulted in a steadily growing vocabulary of transdiegetic devices, which he gradually enlarged from pain stars and motion lines to emanata (such as question marks to show confusion or surprise), dust clouds to show movement (what Mort Walker called "briffits" and Tagawa termed *keridashi*), and sound-image speech balloons. When Tagawa abandoned extradiegetic narrative in favor of transdiegetic content and synchronous sound and action and added Japan's first homegrown anthropomorphic animal protagonist, he had created his first and biggest hit.

Norakuro thus was the product of imported audiovisual comics in more than one way, given that Tagawa's audiovisual manga about the clumsy dog rising through the ranks of the canine military despite many comical mishaps, which began appearing in *Shōnen Kurabu* in January 1931, was precipitated by the popularity of *Felix the Cat*[49] but also the result of Tagawa's study of the form of such comics. Though he unfortunately wrote very little about his own work and influences,[50] shortly before his death in 1989, Tagawa reportedly confirmed during a radio interview that he got the idea for Norakuro from Felix the Cat.[51] His familiarity with American comics is also suggested by his occasionally signing comic strips in the Latin alphabet (similar to how Asō Yutaka had once signed *Nonki na tōsan* "YUTAKA ASO"), using his legal name "Takamizawa" or "Mizawa" (e.g., in the last panel of fig. 4.9),[52] and by his publication of a comic strip named

Oyaji kyōiku (in the magazine *Kaitaku*, April 1940), the exact Japanese title of *Bringing Up Father*. Tagawa furthermore submitted some of his *rakugo* stories to *Kingu*, which between 1925 and 1926 had featured a translation of *Little Jimmy*. That Tagawa would emulate foreign comics is unsurprising when one considers a 1979 interview in which he claimed to have had a cultural inferiority complex toward European and American culture earlier in his life—another instance of the by-now-familiar Japanese prewar conflation of "Western" and "advanced."[53]

Tagawa eventually turned the originally rather innocuous *Norakuro* into a glorification of military conquest as Japan escalated its Fifteen Years War against China (in particularly with the beginning of the Second Sino-Japanese War in 1937). In 1941, he was nevertheless prohibited from continuing it, purportedly in order to reduce the number of *Shōnen Kurabu* copies sold and thus save paper, which was becoming scarce. The influence Tagawa exerted on manga between 1931 and then was immense.[54] While drawing *Norakuro*, he also produced a large number of other audiovisual comics, such as the popular *Tako no Yacchan* (Eightie the octopus) about an octopus trying to live as a human, or *Gasorin Oyoshi* (Gasoline Oyoshi) about a woman who loves cars and planes. Quickly refining his artistic and narrative skills, Tagawa developed a unique visual style marked in particular by the use of rectangular (as opposed to pointed) appendices for speech balloons and briffits/*keridashi*, which was in turn copied by numerous other *mangaka* hoping to emulate Tagawa's success. He also tutored Hasegawa Machiko, who in 1946 would create the best-selling comic strip *Sazae-san*, and helped her publish her first manga in 1935.[55] Despite his comparatively late entry into the world of manga, Tagawa's preeminent status and influence as a creator of popular manga in the 1930s was rivaled only by *Fuku-chan* creator Yokoyama Ryūichi (of *Manga Man* and *Shinseinen* fame), having surpassed George McManus, Asō Yutaka, and other previously dominant artists. His legacy was continued after the war not only by Hasegawa Machiko but by many other aspiring young *mangaka*, including one who would come to be referred to as "the god of manga."

This god of manga, whose human name was Tezuka Osamu, after the end of World War II created such best sellers as *New Treasure Island*, *Lost World*, *Astro Boy*, *Black Jack*, and *Buddha*, through which he ensured that *manga* would be essentially synonymous with audiovisual comics in the mind of the general public until the present day. Although Tezuka today is often portrayed as the originator of contemporary Japanese comics, it is more accurate to say that he further popularized a medium that he inherited both from Japanese *mangaka* like Yokoyama Ryūichi and Tagawa Suihō, as well as via translations of *Bringing Up Father* and other American comics. By the time Tezuka began publishing manga in 1946, audiovisual comics had already become the norm for narrative manga and Tezuka's first published work, *Maa-chan no nikkichō* (Maa-chan's diary)—serialized in the Osaka edition of the *Mainichi Shōkokumin Shinbun* beginning January 4, 1946—was a typical four-panel strip in the vein of *Bringing Up Father* and *Nonki na tōsan*.[56] Tezuka was born in 1928, five years after the influx of translated American comics into Japan had begun, but his father kept a well-stocked comics library in his study, where Osamu would discover and read collected issues of publications like *Shinseinen*, the *Asahi Graph*, and the *Asahi Shinbun*, which thoroughly acquainted him with foreign audiovisual comics.[57] Tezuka has talked specifically about reading *Bringing Up Father* in the *Asahi Shinbun* and being influenced by George McManus.[58]

His intimate familiarity with Jiggs and Maggie at a young age is documented in one of Tezuka's earliest (at the time unpublished) longer stories. The 1945 *Shōri no hi made* (Till the day of victory) features Jiggs and Maggie falling victim to a Japanese airstrike (fig. 4.10; the speech balloons' angular appendices used here by Tezuka are those pioneered and popularized by Tagawa Suihō). In addition to Jiggs and Maggie, *Shōri no hi made* also includes other Japanese and American characters.

A crowd scene from Tezuka's 1948 comic *Lost World* similarly underscores Tezuka's familiarity with both domestically created characters and ones from foreign comic strips that had appeared in Japanese translation (fig. 4.11).[59] It includes Jiggs and Maggie, Blondie and Dagwood, Mickey Mouse and Donald

Figure 4.10. Jiggs and Maggie in Tezuka Osamu's *Shōri no hi made* (reprint).

Duck, Popeye and Betty Boop, the Little King, Henry, and Adamson—all of whom had starred in translated comic strips during Tezuka's childhood—along with Japanese characters like Nonto (the Easygoing Daddy), Fuku-chan, and Norakuro. *Lost World* also features Tezuka characters that are obvious copies of Mickey Mouse and Popeye, whereas the recurring Tezuka character Ham Egg is based on the villain from Milt Gross's *He Done Her Wrong*, which Tezuka had seen in *Shinseinen*.[60] During his childhood, Tezuka must have been fond of Adamson in particular, given that in 1944, he hand-wrote a twenty-page booklet about the character, titled *Adamson—Manga dokushū shidō* (Adamson—Guide to the self-study of manga).[61]

Besides copying characters from foreign comics, Tezuka has also recalled drawing skyscrapers based on those in *Bringing Up Father*.[62] Even the

Figure 4.11. Crowd scene from Tezuka Osamu's *Lost World*.

opening scene of Tezuka's *New Treasure Island*, famously cited by *Doraemon* creator duo Fujiko F. Fujio as their inspiration for becoming comics artists,[63] shows the influence of American comic strips, as the protagonist's car appears to be based on similar drawings of cars in motion found in the December 7, 1923 (fig. 3.8), and January 2, 1924, episodes of *Bringing Up Father* in the *Tōkyō Asahi Shinbun* and the *Asahi Graph*, respectively, or the *Mickey Mouse* strip featured in the April 1931 issue of *Shinseinen*.[64] Noguchi Fumio has documented—well-supported with visual evidence—even more ways in which *He Done Her Wrong* and *Bringing Up Father* influenced Tezuka's work, such as by providing him with a template for crowd scenes.[65]

One reason Tezuka is sometimes treated as the point of origin for contemporary narrative manga may be that his active period coincided with the postwar divergence of Japanese comics from American ones during a period of little exchange between the two that lasted until the late 1980s.[66] However, rather than create or reinvent contemporary manga,

Tezuka Osamu continued a form of graphic narrative that had been introduced from abroad in 1923 and domesticated over the years by the likes
of Asō Yutaka, Yokoyama Ryūichi, and Tagawa Suihō. Given the lack of a
connection between Tezuka's oeuvre (i.e., transdiegetic, audiovisual comics) and the pre-1923 narrative works of Kitazawa Rakuten or Okamoto
Ippei (i.e., illustrated stories) other than the umbrella term *manga*, the
two can hardly be claimed to represent an uninterrupted, coherent lineage,
as posited by proponents of manga as a continuous Japanese art form. In
terms of their structural (and many stylistic) conventions, Tezuka's manga
and virtually all narrative manga that have followed them have their origins not in Okamoto's *manga manbun*, but in the *gaikoku*, *beikoku*, and
amerika manga that brought the form created by Dirks and Opper, that
of the audiovisual stage, to the Land of the Rising Sun and popularized it
there.

The trend audiovisual narrative manga are thus neither a premodern nor a
post–World War II phenomenon. They instead were introduced in 1923
(when *Bringing Up Father* started the large-scale importation of audiovisual comics from abroad) and steadily gained ground against picture
stories throughout the 1920s, turning picture-story manga into an endan-
gered species by the late 1930s.[67] This rise of audiovisual comics and
decline of the picture story has been documented statistically by Jo En
in her research on the graphic narratives published in eight Tokyo newspapers between 1902 and 1942.[68] Jo's data do not classify manga as picture
stories or audiovisual comics but do specify whether a manga featured
speech balloons, narrative text, or both, and beginning in 1923, the number of graphic narratives featuring speech balloons steadily rose, while the
frequency of external narration decreased. By 1937, only a single graphic
narrative still employed extradiegetic narrative text, and in the following
years, all narrative manga used speech balloons exclusively (in the eight
newspapers examined; there were exceptions elsewhere).

The trend captured in these statistical data thus mirrors manga's shift
from picture story to transdiegetic, audiovisual comic strip, as initiated

by translations of American comics and unfolding over the 1920s and 1930s (described in detail in the preceding chapters). The diminishing share of picture stories among narrative manga is likewise reflected in the representative 1935–1936 eight-book series *Gendai renzoku manga zenshū* (Modern serial comics anthology), each book of which featured work by a different pair of well-known *mangaka*, including Asō, Shishido, Tagawa, and Yokoyama. Out of the sixteen manga in the series, only three did not use the transdiegetic-stage form.[69] Tellingly, the three most popular *mangaka* of the 1930s (Shishido, Tagawa, and Yokoyama) all were among the thirteen authors who wrote their contributions as audiovisual comics.

It is possible and even likely that, as audiovisual technologies became more widespread forms of entertainment in the early twentieth century, narrative manga would have gradually turned audiovisual even without the influence of foreign comics and that the introduction of American comic strips merely hastened this transition. As discussed in chapter 2, audiovisual comics developed in response to new conceptions and technologies of vision and hearing, much like the cinema did, with the invention and spread of the phonograph being particularly essential to the creation of audiovisual comics. Audiovisual comics can even be seen as the successful attempt by cartoonists to beat cinema to the punch when it came to the inclusion of sound, given that the first major American talkie appeared only in 1927 and the first Japanese one in 1931, long after audiovisual comics had already become mainstays of entertainment in each country. By abandoning narration and instead showing (rather than telling) as much as possible through visual, transdiegetic means, audiovisual comics represented a more immediate form of narrative than picture stories and arguably even silent films. In Japan's increasingly audiovisual culture of the early twentieth century, Japanese *mangaka* eventually would likely have begun experimenting with sound images on their own. As popular entertainment shifted from reading to watching and from listening to storytellers to listening to records, such mimetic, audiovisual manga would have constituted a more attractive form of entertainment to the general public than the picture story even without their additional appeal of being "Western" and "modern" at a time when Japanese middle-class consumers craved both.

As it happened, however, it was the introduction of audiovisual comics from abroad that caused manga's paradigm shift from picture story to audiovisual comics, and the perception of foreign comics as a superior form of storytelling by virtue of being "Western" and "modern" certainly helped their success. As touched upon in the introduction, in the late nineteenth and early twentieth century, Japan was eagerly importing both technology and culture from the United States and the European powers. Motion pictures arrived in Japan as "cutting-edge" Western technology and, like the modern novel, were seen as a symbol of the West's advanced culture,[70] an attitude reflected in Tagawa's cultural inferiority complex. It is understandable that audiovisual comics, as a similar "modern" medium, were perceived in a similar fashion. The reason for *Shinseinen*'s embrace of predominantly American comics and cartoons according to editor Mizutani Jun, for example, was that such comics and cartoons were an easy way to give the magazine the "modern" appearance to which it aspired.[71] Japanese cartoonists adhering to the established tradition of caricatures and picture stories in the vein of Kitazawa Rakuten and Okamoto Ippei were seen as old-fashioned and rooted in a past that the new generation was eager to move beyond.[72] This view is also evident from comments in the October 17, 1932, *Japan Times* by *Asahi Graph* vice chief editor "and well-known patron of Japanese cartoonists" Hata Sankichi, who acknowledges Okamoto Ippei and Kitazawa Rakuten as erstwhile pioneers who "brought up many disciples to succeed them" but bemoans that eventually "the topics they dealt with, however, were too much out of date—that is, they could not get out of the bounds of the puns and jokes of the man in the street. Besides, their followers too did their best to imitate their master's [sic] and, as a necessary result, they lacked originality." Though Hata's comments focus primarily on content, those by *Shinseinen*'s Mizutani make evident that form was similarly important. According to Mizutani,

American comics and cartoons were seen as more advanced than others not primarily because of their superior humor but because they had
sought to "drive out" explanatory text as much as possible and rely instead
mostly on purely visual means of conveying information. The change
described by Mizutani is of course precisely the difference between a narrated picture story and a mimetic audiovisual comic.

The belief that the United States in particular was the most advanced
comics culture and that Japan had to catch up to it was surprisingly common among those responsible for producing and publishing manga at the
time.[73] To some, the state of manga represented a political issue of historical
import. In the introduction to the 1927 *Jidō manga-shū* (see chapter 3), even
Okamoto Ippei, accused of being behind the times by Hata and Mizutani,
connects the status of a nation's manga (i.e., cartoons and comics) to its prosperity and historical trajectory. Okamoto writes that the prospering peoples
of the world are enjoying comics (manga) but that the ones in decline have
no such leeway.[74] As historian Harry Harootunian summarizes the state of
the country coming out of World War I, "Japan was transformed into an
industrial power equal to most European nations like France, England, and
even Germany, according to leading indices of development, ahead of soci-
eties like Italy and the Soviet Union but trailing the United States."[75] It makes
sense then that the United States, both more prosperous than Japan and
home to the world's dominant comics culture, was the obvious model to
emulate for a new wave of manga editors and artists.[76] Even if an editor
or artist had not been primarily interested in the medium of transdiegetic,
audiovisual comics itself, an eagerness to emulate and copy material from
the United States, where it had already become universal, meant that its
adoption in Japan was only a matter of time.

In his comments in the *Japan Times*, Hata Sankichi recounts how "after
the Great Earthquake of 1923, there was a sudden demand for cartoons
on the part of the Japanese public to satisfy their sense of humour. Japanese
papers desired to meet this demand, but they couldn't find a cartoonist
skillful enough to give readers satisfaction. So it became essential to train

young cartoonists to meet this need." This imbalance between supply and demand explains the immense volume of foreign comic strips imported during that time period until more Japanese *mangaka* like Asō Yutaka had become proficient in the new form. In fact, there was such a dearth of *mangaka* able to satisfy demand that many newspapers and magazines in the 1920s and 1930s solicited submissions from readers, and crowned winners. *Manga Man*, whose founder Kubo Akira according to *Manga Man* contributor and New Manga Group member Kondō Hidezō was trying to help raise a new generation of Japanese comics artists with his magazine, explicitly instructed its readers that potential submissions should be guided by the comics the magazine was publishing: American comic strips and imitations of them. The struggle to catch up to the United States as a comics culture thus became—without explicit instruction or coordination from political forces—part of Japan's larger national project of "modernization."

In retrospect, this project was successful both economically and in terms of the global influence exerted today by Japanese comics. In the postwar era, the United States' comics industry was crippled by the aggressive anticomics movement of the 1950s, while Japanese comics were able to develop more or less unhampered, allowing Japan's comics industry to eventually outgrow its American competition. When Japanese comics were first translated into English on a commercial scale in the 1980s, the direction of influence was suddenly inverted. Not only did Japan become the world's biggest exporter of comics, but foreign comics, including many created in the United States, began to imitate the look of Japanese ones. The shared roots of American and Japanese comics in prewar comic strips had largely been forgotten at that point.

The reason the rediscovery of these shared roots is so significant is that it demonstrates that contemporary manga and other audiovisual comics are in fact one and the same medium and did not emerge from mutually alien traditions, as far too many histories of comics and manga would have one believe. Several decades of relative isolation from each other have of course led to the development of some characteristics unique to one or the other:

Someone only familiar with American comics will for example be bewildered by some manga scenes that feature nosebleeds, not knowing that a nosebleed in the Japanese comics tradition can serve as a visual shorthand for sexual arousal (perhaps because depicting a nosebleed is substantially more acceptable to most mass-market publishers than drawing an erection).[77] Similarly, cloud-like bubbly balloons signify thought in American comics, but whispering in Japanese ones. And most noticeably, after World War II, mainstream drawing styles diverged significantly between the two. But such differences are largely superficial and do not detract from the underlying shared form. Few of us would use peculiarities of style or content in Japanese literature not generally found in American literature as grounds for referring to Japanese literature exclusively as *bungaku*, and it is time to acknowledge that today's narrative manga are in fact comics whose origins can be traced back to the same first audiovisual comic strips drawn by Rudolph Dirks and Fred Opper at the close of the nineteenth century, just like other audiovisual comics around the world today.

That the medium first appeared in the United States does not make audiovisual comics/manga a specifically American medium. Nor does it mean that American cartoonists were somehow smarter or more inventive than cartoonists elsewhere. Audiovisual comics are a universal but specifically modern medium, and their initial creation in the United States was nothing more or less than the logical consequence of a confluence of certain material conditions (a developed and competitive newspaper industry, the popularity of cartooning and graphic narrative, widespread experience with motion pictures and sound recording) that occurred earlier there than elsewhere. As long as one takes a materialist view of history (as opposed to an idealist one, in which history is driven by "greatness" rather than material circumstances), the history outlined in this book neither diminishes nor enhances the quality of individual works, whether American or Japanese.[78] All it does is enable us to better understand their shared origins in a specific time in history.

EPILOGUE

THE MYTH OF MANGA AS A
"TRADITIONAL MODE OF EXPRESSION"

Given not only the overwhelming evidence that contemporary audiovisual manga derive from the translations of foreign audiovisual comics so common in Japan after 1923 but also pre-1923 manga's close connections to foreign cartooning and illustrated stories, it may at first be astonishing how prevalent and accepted claims that tie contemporary manga to Hokusai's sketches or medieval picture scrolls remain. But there are multiple reasons for the success of such ahistorical historiographies. For one, many manga historians—both foreign and Japanese—have a vested interest in portraying manga as something both older and more specifically Japanese than it really is. If contemporary audiovisual manga are the descendants of medieval picture scrolls, they are not only inherently more culturally valuable to study, but they can—and must—be studied in a uniquely Japanese context, which saves both the study of manga from being infringed upon by non-Japanologists, and manga historians from having to study the history of caricature, cartooning, and comics outside of Japan. The global popularity of contemporary manga and the resulting attempts to harness said popularity for the projection of Japanese soft power also make it tempting for Japanese organizations (including the government) to emphasize contemporary manga as quintessentially Japanese rather than as simply another local variant of a universal medium.

The theory that manga goes back hundreds of years persists in part also because of a long pedigree. Though *Jiji Shinpō* manga editor Imaizumi

Ippyō's claim that various works throughout Japanese art history could be retroactively classified as "manga" simply based on elements of humor or caricature was quickly forgotten, others were not. The first published book-length attempt at a history of "manga," Hosokibara Seiki's 1924 *Nihon mangashi* (Japanese manga history), which similarly uses the word to describe older works, has had a powerful impact lasting nearly a century (and counting). Cataloging a broad variety of traditional domestic art as "manga," Hosokibara's book established the familiar claim of a centuries-old history of manga. This legacy is somewhat ironic given that in the preface, Hosokibara himself cautions that he hesitated to call his study a "history of manga" (*mangashi*) due to the fact that "no independent art called 'manga' has existed in Japan since ancient times." Hosokibara admits that even after Katsushika Hokusai's sketches popularized the word *manga*, it was not used by itself to describe an art form or genre and that "Hokusai's manga generally were not what we call 'manga' today" (Hosokibara here, in 1924, is describing the difference between Hokusai's use of the word *manga* as "sketches" and Imaizumi's use as "caricature").[1]

Hosokibara nonetheless decided in favor of compiling a "history of manga" due to his belief that other, older pictorial forms like *Toba-e*, *giga*, or *kyōga*, "contain much of the meaning of what is called 'manga' today."[2] Predictably, grouping together diverse artworks without a common lineage proved difficult: "When asked what the thing we call 'manga' today [i.e., in 1924] is, I have to pause for a bit. This is because there is no general definition for manga."[3] As a solution, Hosokibara borrowed a metaphysical definition from Okamoto Ippei: "*Manga* refers to pictures that express the beauty resulting from dissecting the present state of all things in the universe and their true relations to each other."[4] Hosokibara interprets Okamoto's abstruse and vague description to mean that the defining characteristic of manga is a search for truth, distinguishing it from what Hosokibara calls "genuine art" (*junsei bijutsu*), which is "fixated on [material] beauty."[5]

Defining manga in opposition to such "kaleidophilic" art then makes its historiography a matter of listing disparate graphic works interpreted as "dissecting truth" rather than tracing the history of a particular pictorial (and/or narrative) form with a coherent lineage. Hosokibara is well aware of this, explaining that manga are a product of their respective periods and not based on a continuing lineage like a particular school of art would be.[6] He posits that manga began with the twelfth-century "Scrolls of Frolicking Animals" (the *chōjūgiga*), but "flourished and withered, appearing intermittently like beats of a drum" in between the twelfth century and 1924. The *chōjūgiga* (more precisely, its first scroll, which is what most manga historians are referring to when they discuss the *chōjūgiga*) is a single continuous image showing different animals engaged in a variety of human activities. It looks neither like a narrative manga in the 1891–1923 sense of the word nor like a post-1923 audiovisual one. For one, it does not have identifiable protagonists or a discernible narrative shown via multiple images. Unlike contemporary audiovisual comics, it is also entirely silent and features no dialogue.[7]

Hosokibara's intent hence was less to trace historical influences than to anchor the various works published under the label of "manga" in his time (such as caricatures, cartoons, picture stories, and recently introduced audiovisual comics) within a long, primarily domestic tradition—the same endeavor that still dominates most histories of manga today. He likely picked the *chōjūgiga* as his first listed work because it was at the time the oldest widely known Japanese work of art that contained elements of cartooning (the older temple graffiti in Nara had not yet been discovered in 1924), though he claims that he was actually hesitant to call the *chōjūgiga* "manga" to begin with, due to the "quests for truth and for beauty being roughly evenly represented in it" (see the definition Hosokibara borrowed from Okamoto). The decision to nevertheless begin his chronology with the *chōjūgiga* left a lasting impact on the field of manga historiography, creating what Ōtsuka Eiji has called the "*chōjūgiga* origin theory [*kigensetsu*]"—that is, the perception of the *chōjūgiga* as Japan's first or oldest manga.[8] Still today, nearly a century later, it is difficult to find a history of Japanese comics that does not point to the *chōjūgiga*. Try an internet search for "history of manga" or "oldest manga" and the *chōjūgiga* will invariably pop up. Even the consulate-general of Japan in New York proclaims on its website,

> Japan is at the epicenter of today's worldwide *manga* (comics) craze. But you may be surprised to learn just how far back in history the genre spans. Osamu Tezuka (1928—1989), creator of *Astro Boy*, is often called "the father of manga" for his innovative techniques and influence in the field. Going further into the past, there are even *manga* drawn by Hokusai Katsushika, the celebrated Edo-era *ukiyoe* artist (1760—1849). But the roots of *manga* can actually be traced back centuries.
>
> It is generally acknowledged that Japan's first *manga* was the Choju Giga ("The Scroll of Frolicking Animals").[9]

This continuing impact of Hosokibara's history is unsurprising given that it was the starting point of manga historiography and its foundational text, and is still referenced by historians today.[10] Although Hosokibara himself rejected the idea of a coherent lineage connecting the *chōjūgiga* and modern manga, virtually all later iterations of the *chōjūgiga* origin theory do make an implicit or explicit assumption of such a lineage, which is a central reason the perception of contemporary manga as something rooted in centuries of Japanese visual culture persists today.

Given the lack of concrete historical evidence for any meaningful connection between the *chōjūgiga* and post-1891 manga, the attempts to connect the two rely on tenuous claims, such as that the *chōjūgiga* "can be considered the originator of contemporary manga and anime [...] *as the source of manga and anime in the sense that it anthropomorphizes animals and develops a narrative.*"[11] Of course, considering that the *chōjūgiga* consists of collected scenes of animals engaging in various activities and does not actually develop a narrative beyond individual scenes, it is difficult to see the picture scroll as a narrative in the same way as either a *manga manbun* picture story or a contemporary audiovisual comic. The absence of anthropomorphic animal protagonists from manga until Japanese translations of *Felix the Cat*, *Mickey Mouse*, and *Krazy Kat* in the 1920s and 1930s likewise undermines the hypothesis that the *chōjūgiga*'s anthropomorphic animals exerted any influence on the history of manga.[12]

Another connection posited between the *chōjūgiga* and contemporary manga is the claim that the former features speech balloons (*fukidashi* in Japanese). For example, Brigitte Koyama-Richard, author of the tellingly titled *One Thousand Years of Manga*, asserts that "an initial avatar of the word balloon is already clearly identifiable in the twelfth-century Frolicking Animals and People."[13] Both Koyama-Richard and Japanese manga historian Shimizu Isao point to the image of a monkey reading a sutra toward the end of the first scroll as a supposed example of an early speech balloon. In said image, a set of undulating lines has been drawn in a manner that makes them appear as if coming out of the monkey's mouth, without forming a balloon-like shape or containing any script. One could, like Shimizu, call it a *fukidashi* if one interprets the word strictly literally—as something to the extent of "breathing out"—but it cannot be said to function in the same manner as a contemporary speech balloon, because it does not render sound through writing. One cannot rule out entirely that the author of the *chōjūgiga* meant the lines to represent some kind of sound, but this would have been highly unusual in his time. It is far more likely that the lines represent the air exhaled by the monkey during its recitation. In a similar, earlier instance in the *chōjūgiga*, during the famous sumo scene in which a frog has successfully wrestled a hare to the ground, lines similar to those in the sutra recitation scene are seen emerging from the frog's mouth. Koyama-Richard interprets these as "steam (representing the animal's exertions) hiss[ing] out of the winner's mouth." To the immediate left of the defeated hare, three frogs are seen in poses described by Koyama-Richard as "great laughter." Though the three frogs' mouths are open, no lines similar to the winning frog's can be seen emerging from them.

If the *chōjūgiga* author had intended the "*fukidashi*" lines to represent sound, it is strange that the image of the laughing frogs contains no such lines. Their absence implies that in the case of the winning frog and the chanting monkey, the lines in question are meant to indicate something other than sound. Matsushima Masato, Tokyo National Museum Curator of Japanese Painting, explains these lines as manifestations of a concept from Japanese antiquity by the name of *kotodama* (soul of language), the belief that words contain spiritual power and gain material substance when uttered.[14] According to Matsushima, the lines exiting the monkey's mouth are meant to represent such a manifestation of the recited sutra's words themselves (rather than their sound). As for the victorious frog, Matsushima speculates that instead of a yell the lines may actually represent a kind of spell enunciated by the frog to topple its opponent. This interpretation would explain the absence of lines connected to the laughing frogs, given that the laughter is mere sound and would hence not have been considered in possession of *kotodama*. Of course, even if one were to agree with Shimizu and Koyama-Richard and see the aforementioned lines in the *chōjūgiga* as an actual type of speech balloon, this would still require an explanation of why speech balloons remained otherwise absent from manga for approximately *eight centuries*.

I am not the first to point out the silliness of tying the *chōjūgiga* to contemporary manga.[15] Art historians not invested in manga as their primary field of research have been particularly explicit in rejecting the idea of a continuous manga lineage that connects post-1891 manga to older forms of Japanese art. Adam L. Kern, for example, with regards to modern manga and *kibyōshi* (late eighteenth-century picture booklets) categorically denies "any direct causal or historical link between the two forms or between their corresponding visual cultures."[16] Curator Matsushima Masato even devoted an article to the question "Did the *Chōjūgiga* Give Birth to Manga?" ("Chōjūgiga ga manga wo unda no ka?") in the 2015 *Masterpieces of Kosan-ji Temple: The Complete Scrolls of Choju Giga, Frolicking Animals* exhibition catalog, answering no, in stark contrast to some of the posters advertising the exhibition, which featured the phrase "Japan's oldest manga." Matsushima, too, traces the *chōjūgiga* origin theory back to Hosokibara and rejects any connection to present-day manga: "To put it plainly, the *chōjūgiga*, drawn in the Kamakura period, and manga, brought in from the West, are obviously not chronologically connected in any immediate sense."[17]

The lack of evidence for the proposed link between the *chōjūgiga* and modern manga begs the question of why the *chōjūgiga* origin theory has been—and continues to be—so successful. Manga critic Kure Tomofusa suspects that continuing support for it (and for the similar claim that modern manga originated with Hokusai) stems from a desire both to "enlighten" those readers and artists who are used only to low-brow contemporary works and to fight back against anticomics movements.[18] The appeal of connecting medieval picture scrolls to modern narrative manga is obvious: as Adam L. Kern writes in "Manga versus *Kibyōshi*," about attempts to connect older works like *kibyōshi* to modern manga, it is "understandably tempting for those with a vested interest in overcoming the conservative cultural criticism of the latter to argue for an historical continuity with the former."[19] Such a link transfers some of the cultural cachet of traditional high-culture artifacts to a medium that has been considered of little cultural or educational value—and even viewed as potentially harmful to its consumers and the national body at large as early as 1938, when the Ministry of the Interior published its General Directives Concerning the Improvement of Juvenile Reading Materials (*Jidō yomimono kaizen ni kansuru shijiyōkō*).[20]

The posited connection between contemporary manga and older artworks is also sometimes used in reverse, to arouse interest in traditional art by drawing on the popularity of Japanese comics: the 2015 *chōjūgiga* exhibition by the Tokyo National Museum, which advertised the picture scroll at its center as Japan's oldest manga, is one example of this strategy. Similarly, a 2019 exhibition on "manga" by the British Museum and Citigroup[21] that featured both audiovisual comics and traditional art would likely have drawn fewer visitors had its title and main theme been "Emakimono" (picture scrolls) instead of "Manga." Likewise, the Sumida Hokusai Museum from November 25, 2020, to January 24, 2021, held a special exhibition, curated by none other than Shimizu Isao and called "GIGA

MANGA: From Edo Giga to Modern Manga," which professes that "giga, a form of caricature from the Edo Period (1603–1868), provided the starting point for what is now known as manga."[22] Since there is no direct connection between Edo-period *giga* and "what is now known as manga," the exhibition is forced to rely on the common sleight of hand of pointing at superficial similarities to assert a common lineage (akin to the "speech balloons" in the *chōjūgiga*). A collage of four different images by Hokusai, for example, is presented as the "source" (*genryū*) of modern four-panel cartoons, despite the nonnarrative nature of said collage and the absence of any gradual development that could be traced from it to the first modern four-panel manga such as figures P.1 and P.2, which Imaizumi Ippyō imported from abroad.[23]

Ōtsuka Eiji has claimed that the focus on manga as either postmodern or having its roots in premodern art is popular in Japan primarily because it avoids discussion of the country's fascist past (i.e., the 1930s and 1940s).[24] While this precise claim is difficult to corroborate, there certainly exists a correlation between an embrace of the *chōjūgiga* origin theory and a kind of "manga nationalism"—a desire to see manga as emblematic of the comparative value of Japanese culture or even its superiority. Among authors writing on manga history, those fully embracing the theory are also most likely to emphasize the quality or status of Japanese works, particularly vis-à-vis the rest of the world. Such claims include that manga, "at the same time as representing a uniquely Japanese culture, have become a global lingua franca,"[25] that "since Toba Sōjō Kakuyū drew the *chōjūgiga* scroll in ancient times, masterpieces and great works have appeared one after the other, and beginning with the introduction of *ukiyo-e* [Edo-period woodblock prints and paintings] abroad, Japanese manga have garnered the world's attention," and that "Japanese manga have a long history, and the world has finally begun to realize that they are rich in creativity even compared to various foreign countries."[26] The catalog for the 1996 Kawasaki City Museum exhibition *Nihon no manga 300nen* (300 years of Japanese manga), which also traces manga back to the *chōjūgiga* (and also the Hōryūji temple graffiti, because why not?), even purports that "the history of manga as reproducible art extending over three hundred years is long even from a global perspective, so much so that a *Toba-e* book published at the beginning of the eighteenth century is considered the world's oldest manga book. Manga culture thus started blossoming in a Far East island nation ahead of the world."[27] Other proponents of the *chōjūgiga* origin theory boast that "there is no other country with as rich a variety [of manga] as ours, and Japan can thus truly be called the manga kingdom."[28]

The *chōjūgiga* origin theory is essential to this pride in manga. In the words of Shimizu Isao, the *chōjūgiga*'s "outstanding descriptive power, as the starting point of manga and as the beginning of *story manga* [contemporary Japanese comics], demonstrates that Japanese people have had outstanding taste and the ability to create manga since a thousand years ago."[29] Traditional Japanese art thus serves as proof of manga's greatness and of Japanese creativity. As Shimizu recounts elsewhere, "I have often been told that Japanese people's sense of humor is lacking or that they are not creative, but when you get to really know the world of Edo-period manga [1603–1868], such prejudices are eradicated. Even just by looking at *yōkai-e*, *Toba-e*, Hokusai's *manga*, the late Edo period *awate-e*, and others, one understands well just how rich the Japanese were in creativity and how excellent their sense of humor was."[30]

The legitimacy of the *chōjūgiga* origin theory has been buttressed by its adoption by the Japanese government. As Paul Gravett writes in *Manga: Sixty Years of Japanese Comics,*

> To what extent are modern manga continuous with Japan's long tradition of narrative art? The Japanese government seems to think entirely so. Since April 2000, the new national art curriculum for junior high schools has insisted that manga be brought into the classroom. In its accompanying explanatory textbook, the Ministry of Culture and Education affirmed that "manga can be called one of Japan's traditional modes of expression." Art teachers are supplied with a three-page illustrated

history to help them convey the uninterrupted continuity between historic picture scrolls and prints and manga. Alas, in this visual material,
the portrayal of contemporary manga was limited to one wordless sequence by Tezuka and a pin-up of Dragon Ball, with not a speech balloon or sound effect in sight.[31]

The relative absence of contemporary material in the teaching materials
evinces the continuing low social status of contemporary narrative manga,
and the Ministry of Culture and Education appears to be trying to harness its popularity to arouse students' interest in more "respectable" art
while remaining suspicious of manga's educational value. This continued
denigration of contemporary manga explains why authors like Shimizu
are eager to discover speech balloons or multipanel narratives in more
"legitimate" works like the *chōjūgiga* or Hokusai's sketches. The embrace
of manga as not simply contemporary comics, but as something *tradi-
tionally* Japanese by a conservative government is similarly unsurprising:
the passage from the Ministry of Culture and Education's Explication of
Middle School Instruction Guidelines cited by Gravett reads in its entirety,
"Manga are pictures expressing figures through simplification, symbolism, exaggeration, and so on. In Japan, the *chōjūjinbutsugiga* scrolls, the
shigisan engi picture scroll, the Hokusai manga, which depict the life of
Edo-period people in a manga style, and others have survived until today
and can be called *one of Japan's traditional modes of expression*."[32]

Note the Instruction Guidelines' exceedingly vague definition of manga,
without which the argument that manga represents "one of Japan's traditional modes of expression" would be impossible. It is difficult to think of
drawings that do *not* express figures through any "simplification, symbolism or exaggeration," but given that the *chōjūgiga*, Hokusai's sketches, and
Dragon Ball share few characteristics of form and function, grouping all
three together and proclaiming them part of a single "mode of expression" *requires* a definition this broad and vague.[33] Instead of representing
the sober conclusion of a thorough review of the history of visual and

narrative art in Japan, the assessment of manga as "one of Japan's traditional modes of expression" more likely preexisted a search for evidence that could be made to support it.

This tendency to lump together disparate visual and narrative forms as "manga" obscures more than it elucidates. Even among artwork called "manga" at the time of its creation—to say nothing of works that have been labeled as such only retroactively, such as the *chōjūgiga*—a landscape sketch, a caricature of a politician, a wordless gag cartoon, a written story illustrated with a few drawings, and an audiovisual comic strip work very differently from one another. The impulse to bolster the prestige of these oft-diminished forms of expression by tying them to universally respected "real art" is understandable but counterproductive to evidence-based historiography, since such genealogical claims feed into the myth that manga is metaphysical and ahistorical on the one hand and uniquely and essentially Japanese on the other. As we saw at the beginning of this book, the word *manga* in the contemporary sense of caricature, cartooning, and/or stories at least partially told through pictures does not date back further than 1891. The *Ponchi-e* tradition of caricature in Japan seems to have had little influence on Kitazawa Rakuten and Okamoto Ippei and the development of narrative manga like Okamoto's *manga manbun*, but even if one were to include this tradition under the broader umbrella of manga as caricature, cartooning, and sequential art, this would lead us back at most to 1862 and certainly not to older, domestic works like the *chōjūgiga*.

None of this is to say that Japanese-made manga—whether preaudiovisual or post-1923, audiovisual manga—aren't "really" Japanese but that neither the medium of preaudiovisual picture stories nor that of audiovisual comics developed out of a centuries-old domestic tradition. This does not make any manga "less Japanese." Few would claim that the tea ceremony is "less Japanese" because its origins can be traced to China.[34] Or to use a comparison with another narrative medium, a Japanese-made motion picture may be "thoroughly Japanese" and appreciated as a specifically Japanese cultural product (if one so desires) without seeking the origins of *eiga* (film) in Noh theater.

Though the history presented in this book will be met with resistance by those who prefer to romanticize manga as a uniquely Japanese tradition reaching back to feudal times, *Bringing Up Father* and "Easygoing Daddy" undeniably have far more in common with each other than either does with the picture stories of Wilhelm Busch and Okamoto Ippei, let alone the Bayeux Tapestry or *chōjūgiga*. Notwithstanding the pervasive view of graphic narrative as a "lesser" form of both artistic expression and storytelling (just compare the number of universities with programs in literary and film studies to that of those with comics studies departments), contemporary Japanese comics are just as much a "legitimate," "respectable" medium capable of producing both "trash" and "high art" as any other, without having to be related to medieval picture scrolls.[35] If anything, it is both fascinating and impressive how quickly Japanese and other people around the world assimilated "foreign" forms of visual art and storytelling and used them to tell jokes and stories of their own. That narrative and humoristic manga were part of a global culture of visual art and unconstrained by national borders from their very beginnings should not lessen our enjoyment of them but increase it.

As George McManus would say, *Banzai.*

APPENDIX

LIST OF FOREIGN COMICS IN JAPAN, 1908–1945

Original title	Author	Place of publication	From/in	Until
Adamson / Silent Sam (Sweden)	Oscar Jacobsson	Asahi Graph	September 5, 1928	October 16, 1940
Adamson / Silent Sam (Sweden)	Oscar Jacobsson	Kingu	March 1927	June 1927
Adamson / Silent Sam (Sweden)	Oscar Jacobsson	Shōgakusei zenshū, Jidō manga-shū	1927	
Adamson / Silent Sam (Sweden)	Oscar Jacobsson	Yōnen Kurabu	June 1936, November 1936	
Adamson / Silent Sam (Sweden)	Oscar Jacobsson	Manga Man	August 1929	January 1931
Adamson / Silent Sam (Sweden)	Oscar Jacobsson	Gendai manga taikan, Tōzai manga-shū	1928	
And Her Name Was Maud	Fred Opper	Jiji Shinpō	June 6, 1926	January 26, 1930
Barney Google	Billy DeBeck	Ōsaka Chūgai Shōgyō Shinpō	December 5 (possibly 1), 1924	October 19, 1925

Original title	Author	Place of publication	From/in	Until
Betty Boop	Bud Counihan	Shinseinen	December 1934	
Blondie	Chic Young	Kokumin Shinbun	February 11, 1933	June 30, 1933
Bonzo (U.K.)	George E. Studdy	Shōgakusei zenshū, Jidō manga-shū	1927	
Bonzo (U.K.)	George E. Studdy	Manga Man	August 1929	March 1930
Bonzo (U.K.)	George E. Studdy	Kokumin Shinbun	July 9, 1933	August 6, 1933
Bringing Up Father	George McManus	Asahi Graph	April 1, 1923	July 31, 1940
Bringing Up Father	George McManus	Tōkyō Asahi Shinbun	October 25, 1923	November 21, 1925
Bringing Up Father	George McManus	Ōsaka Asahi Shinbun	February 15, 1924	April 22, 1925
Bringing Up Father	George McManus	stand-alone anthology, vol. 1	1924	
Bringing Up Father	George McManus	stand-alone anthology, vol. 2	1925	
Bringing Up Father	George McManus	Zen-Kansai Fujin Rengōkai	December 1925	March 1928
Clarence	Crawford Young	Gendai manga taikan, Tōzai manga-shū	1928	
Dinglehoofer und His Dog	Harold Knerr	Manga Man	August 1929	January 1930
Doings of Patty, The	Jefferson Machamer	Japan Times	June 19, 1929	October 1, 1929
Dolly Dimples	Grace Dayton	Kokumin Shinbun	December 24, 1929	November 6, 1930

Original title	Author	Place of publication	From/in	Until
Donald Duck (animated film adaptation)	unknown	Tōkyō Nichi Nichi Shinbun	December 20, 1936	
Felix the Cat	Otto Messmer	Jiji Shinpō	February 2, 1930	December 31, 1932
Felix the Cat	Otto Messmer	Shinseinen	April 1934	
Felix the Cat	Otto Messmer	Hachisuzume	May 1929	June 1929
Fleischer cartoon comics: Betty Boop, Bimbo, Popeye (animated film adaptations)		Hi no De	December 1932	February 1938
Gumps, The	Sidney Smith	Japan Times	December 27, 1923	July 3, 1928
Happy Hooligan	Fred Opper	Jiji Shinpō	January 11, 1925	January 26, 1930
He Done Her Wrong	Milt Gross	Shinseinen	July 1937	
Henry	Carl Anderson	Tōkyō Nichi Nichi Shinbun	December 6, 1936	August 29, 1937
It's Papa Who Pays!	Jimmy Murphy	Manga Man	December 1929	
Just Boy / Elmer	A. C. Fera	Chūgai Shōgyō Shinpō	January 20, 1924	June 8, 1924
Katzenjammer Kids, The	Rudolph Dirks	Shōgakusei zenshū, Manga e-monogatari	1929	
Katzenjammer Kids, The	Harold Knerr	Manga Man	August 1929	May 1930

Original title	Author	Place of publication	From/in	Until
Krazy Kat	George Herriman	*Shinseinen*	June 1930, April 1931, May 1931, December 1934	
Laura	Otto Messmer	*Yōnen Kurabu*	June 1936	
Laura	Otto Messmer	*Jiji Shinpō*	February 2, 1930	February 28, 1932
Laura	Otto Messmer	*Shinseinen*	April 1934	
Little Jimmy	Jimmy Swinnerton	*Kokumin Shinbun*	April 16, 1923	June 8, 1926
Little Jimmy	Jimmy Swinnerton	*Kingu*	January 1925	March 1926
Little King, The	Otto Soglow	*Yōnen Kurabu*	June 1936	
Little King, The	Otto Soglow	*Shinseinen*	April 1931, November 1933, December 1934, June 1937, July 1939	
Little Lulu	Marge	*Shinseinen*	November 1938	
Mickey Mouse	Floyd Gottfredson	*Shinseinen*	April 1931, May 1932, September 1932	
Mickey Mouse (animated film adaptation)	unknown	*Tōkyō Nichi Nichi Shinbun*	December 6, 1936	January 17, 1937
Mickey Mouse (animated film adaptation)	unknown	*Shufu no Tomo*	May 1934	October 1934

Original title	Author	Place of publication	From/in	Until
Mr. Dough and Mr. Dubb	Fred Opper	Jiji Shinpō	August 30, 1925	January 30, 1927
Mr. Jack	Jimmy Swinnerton	Tokyo Puck	November 10, 1908	
Mutt and Jeff	Bud Fisher	Ōsaka Asahi Shinbun	November 14, 1923	July 17, 1925
Mutt and Jeff	Bud Fisher	Asahi Graph	September 1, 1923	
Mutt and Jeff	Bud Fisher	Zen-Kansai Fujin Rengōkai	December 1925	March 1928
Mutt and Jeff	Bud Fisher	Shinseinen	July 1939	
Newlyweds, The	Charles McManus	Shōgakusei zenshū, Manga e-monogatari	1929	
Newlyweds, The	Charles McManus	Asahi Graph	January 2, 1924	September 23, 1925
Newlyweds, The	Charles McManus	Tōkyō Asahi Shinbun	January 1, 1924	
Newlyweds, The	Charles McManus	Chūō Shinbun	October 22, 1925	November 18, 1926
Nize Baby	Milt Gross	Shōgakusei zenshū, Jidō manga-shū	1927	
Our Antediluvian Ancestors	Fred Opper	Jiji Shinpō	February 7, 1926	May 23, 1926
Pete the Tramp	Clarence D. Russell	Shinseinen	February 1931, April 1936	
Pip, Squeak and Wilfred (U.K.)	Austin Bowen Payne	Shōgakusei zenshū, Jidō manga-shū	1927	
Polly and Her Pals	Cliff Sterrett	Tōkyō Nichi Nichi Shinbun	July 1, 1923	August 19, 1923

Original title	Author	Place of publication	From/in	Until
Polly and Her Pals	Cliff Sterrett	Japan Times	November 1, 1929	July 31, 1930
Reg'lar Fellers	Gene Byrnes	Shōgakusei zenshū, Jidō manga-shū	1927	
Reg'lar Fellers	Gene Byrnes	Gendai manga taikan, Tōzai manga-shū	1928	
Scrappy (animated film adaptation)	Dick Heumor [Huemer]	Shufu no Tomo	November 1934	between December 1934 and February 1935
Secret Agent X-9	Raymond Williams	Shinseinen	June 1937	
Skippy	Percy Crosby	Yōnen Kurabu	June 1936	
Smitty	Walter Berndt	Tōkyō Nichi Nichi Shinbun	November 11, 1931	January 28, 1932
Smitty	Walter Berndt	Ōsaka Mainichi Shinbun	November 12, 1931	January 30, 1932
Thimble Theatre (starring Popeye)	E. C. Segar	Shinseinen	April 1934	
Tillie the Toiler	Russ Westover	Chūgai Shōgyō Shinpō	October 2, 1924	December 19, 1926
Tillie the Toiler	Russ Westover	Manga Man	December 1929	January 1930
Toonerville Folks	Fontaine Fox	Shōgakusei zenshū, Jidō manga-shū	1927	

Original title	Author	Place of publication	From/in	Until
Toots and Casper	Jimmy Murphy	*Tōkyō Chūgai Shōgyō Shinpō*	July 15, 1923	August 26, 1923
Toots and Casper	Jimmy Murphy	*Fujokai*	February 1924	January 1925
unidentified British strip	unknown	*Shōgakusei zenshū, Jidō manga-shū*	1927	
unidentified	unknown	*Manga Man*	August 1929	
unidentified	unknown	*Manga Man*	November 1929	
untitled	Rube Goldberg	*Shinseinen*	August 1927, January 1930	
Van Swaggers, The	Russ Westover	*Manga Man*	January 1930	

BRIEF CHRONOLOGY

1798   Santō Kyōden's picture book *Shiji no yukikai* uses the word *manga* as a verb meaning "to draw/sketch."

1862   The first issue of Charles Wirgman's satire magazine *Japan Punch* is published. The caricatures and cartoons featured in it come to be known as *Ponchi-e*, "Punch pictures."

1887   Parts of Wilhelm Busch's *Max und Moritz* are published in Japanese translation, providing a template for picture stories.

1891   *Manga* is first used to describe a (foreign) multipanel cartoon, by Imaizumi Ippyō in the newspaper *Jiji Shinpō*.

1896   In the *New York Journal*, R. F. Outcault initiates a trend of using sound images to ridicule the experience of hearing voices disconnected from human speakers for the first time in history. Other cartoonists follow suit.

1899   Rudolph Dirks's experimentation with sound images to joke about the "voice-speaker disconnect" in his *Katzenjammer Kids* cartoons culminates in the first conversation between intradiegetic characters. Frederick Burr Opper adopts this audiovisual storytelling form for his comic strip *Happy Hooligan* and audiovisual comics begin to proliferate in the United States.

1902   Kitazawa Rakuten becomes the *Jiji Shinpō*'s manga editor and starts a regular cartoon and graphic narrative section called *Jiji Manga*. *Manga* begins to replace *Ponchi-e* as the most common word for contemporaneous humorous drawings and starts to also describe picture stories.

1912   Okamoto Ippei begins writing picture stories, which he calls *manga manbun*.

1923   The tabloid *Asahi Graph* begins publishing *Shō-chan no bōken* (The adventures of little Sho), which becomes the first Japanese picture story to regularly feature word balloons. Shortly thereafter, the *Asahi Graph* also starts publishing George McManus's audiovisual comic strip *Bringing Up Father* in Japanese translation, which becomes the most successful narrative manga in Japanese history prior to World War II and brings about a paradigm shift in narrative manga, from picture stories to audiovisual comics, when Asō Yutaka and other Japanese cartoonists adopt its form for their own creations, such as Asō's *Nonki na tōsan* (Easygoing daddy). The translations of *Bringing Up Father* and other American audiovisual comics are frequently labeled "American manga."

1925   Kitazawa Rakuten begins publishing Opper's *Happy Hooligan* as part of *Jiji Manga*, eventually followed by Otto Messmer's *Felix the Cat*.

1929   The magazine *Manga Man* is founded. It stars the *Katzenjammer Kids* and solicits audiovisual comic strips from Japanese authors, several of whom found the New Manga Group, including Yokoyama Ryūichi. After working for *Manga Man*, Yokoyama later creates the popular audiovisual comic strip *Fuku-chan*.

1931   *Shōnen Kurabu* begins featuring Tagawa Suihō's *Norakuro*, inspired by *Felix the Cat*. *Norakuro* becomes the most successful Japanese-drawn manga since Asō's "Easygoing Daddy" and cements audiovisual comics as the standard form of narrative manga. By the end of the 1930s, picture stories have been largely replaced by audiovisual comics.

1946   Tezuka Osamu, influenced by prewar translations of foreign comics like *Bringing Up Father* as well as domestic audiovisual manga like *Fuku-chan* and *Norakuro*, starts publishing audiovisual manga. Tezuka ensures the success of audiovisual narrative manga in postwar Japan, even becoming known as "the god of manga."

ACKNOWLEDGMENTS

This book wouldn't exist without Akira Lippit, who helped me find a faculty position in Japan that allowed me to do the majority of the research upon which the book is based, and who has always been a comforting presence and outstanding mentor. While I was in Japan, Sasaki Minoru introduced me to people and resources, and I am immensely grateful for his generosity and the manifold ways in which he has contributed to this text. Niimi Nue and Noda Kensuke helped me with their excellent knowledge of prewar materials. Everyone at Josai International University who enabled me to reconcile my research with my teaching and other university duties there is also greatly appreciated, and I thank my colleagues and students for many enjoyable moments. I am furthermore greatly indebted to Tu Nguyen, Erik Henry, Ryan Pham, Ryan Khamkongsay, and Lei Iseya for their enormous help when I was moving back and forth between Los Angeles and Tokyo, as well as for their emotional support. The wonderful people at the Tokyo University gymnastics club and Mats Gymnastics in Los Angeles helped keep me sane as well.

My research could not have happened if it weren't for the diligent work of many different librarians, curators, and other staff at the National Diet Library, the Kyoto International Manga Museum (especially Watanabe Asako), the Kawasaki City Museum (especially Yoshimura Rei), the University of Southern California libraries (especially Danica Schroeder), and other institutions, and I thank every single one of them.

In addition to everyone already named (and in no particular order), Panivong Norindr, Vanessa Schwartz, Bertha Delgado Arce, Ryan Holmberg, Gennifer Weisenfeld, Adam Kern, Frederik Schodt, Craig Fischer, Ono Kōsei, Jo En, Hara Akihiko, Cameron Penwell, Adam Buttrick, Amanda Kennell, Shawma Chun, Lyr Colin, Endō Tōru, Kai Wataru, Christian Hansen-Hagge, Nikolas Scheuer, and several anonymous readers all provided valuable feedback and/or help with resources. Niimi Nue and Nikolas Scheuer kindly furnished many of the images you will find in this book, while Kevin Jiang deserves special credit and my eternal gratitude for his numerous careful rereads and extensive comments that helped make this text substantially more cohesive and easier to follow. Nicole Solano was an excellent editor and I thank her for believing in this book, as well as everyone else who helped put it in print.

The research upon which *Comics and the Origins of Manga* is based was partially supported by an Alpha Association of Phi Beta Kappa Alumni in Southern California International Scholarship, for which I will always be grateful. An early version of chapter 2 was published by the journal *ImageTexT*.

Finally, I thank my grandparents, Alfons and Hildegard Exner and Wilhelm and Lydia Großkurth, for making it possible for my parents to attend university, and my parents, Peter Exner and Ute Großkurth-Exner, for repeatedly looking up and scanning stuff for me in books I had left at their home—and for all their love and support throughout my life.

NOTES

PREFACE

1. Kerim Yasar, *Electrified Voices*, 3.

INTRODUCTION

1. Oyola, "International Comic Arts Forum 2016."

2. McCloud, *Understanding Comics*, 81.

3. I suspect it is in part due to the industrialized manner in which mainstream manga are produced today: mass-market manga are partially drawn by uncredited "assistants," and such a system works much better if every artist is trained in the same style.

4. Memmi, *Colonizer and the Colonized*, 152.

5. Weisenfeld, "Publicity and Propaganda," 13–14.

6. Some sources claim the first date of publication to have been December 8, Meiji 3 (1870 CE), but this was before Japan's switch to the Gregorian calendar in 1873 and so corresponds to January 28, 1871.

7. Estimated by Uchikawa in "Shinbun dokusha no hensen," 19.

8. Assuming that households generally did not purchase multiple newspapers. Statistical data from Statistics Bureau of Japan, "Population by Age."

9. Uchikawa, "Shinbun dokusha no hensen," 23–24.

10. Uchikawa, 25.

11. Weisenfeld, *Mavo*, 3.

12. Satō, *Nihon eigashi 1, 1896–1940*, 6–7.

13. Yomota, *Nihon eiga 110nen*, 44–49.

14. Yomota, 34.

15. For example, to describe artifacts as old as Trajan's Column, under Scott McCloud's famous definition of comics as "juxtaposed pictorial and other images

in deliberate sequence, intended to convey information and/or to produce an aesthetic response in the viewer." McCloud, *Understanding Comics*, 9. David Kunzle, author of a groundbreaking—and still the most extensive—historical study of European narrative prints, defines a comic strip as a sequence of separate images with a preponderance of image over text in a printed mass medium. Kunzle, *Early Comic Strip*, 2. Kunzle adds that the story told must be both "moral" and "topical," but these restrictions are negligible here. Kunzle's definition excludes Trajan's column but still permits the inclusion of works produced as early as the fifteenth century. Another common approach is to define comics based on the shared features between Rodolphe Töpffer's picture stories and what we think of as comics today, as done, for example, in Patricia Mainardi's *Another World*, which defines comic strips as one or more pages "each containing multiple frames of images narrating an original story" (131).

The above definitions are problematic for historical analysis given that all of them include works that look and function differently from today's prevalent model of comics. In Töpffer's stories, for example, it is not technically true that the *images* narrate a story. The primary narrative burden is borne by captions neatly separated from the images. In today's comics, however, the images truly do narrate a story by themselves—or perhaps more accurately, they *show* the story, with little need for a narrator.

16. Smolderen, "Of Labels, Loops, and Bubbles," 90–99.

PROLOGUE

1. All quotations taken from Japanese texts are my own translations.

2. The conflation of contemporary narrative manga with medieval picture scrolls was still common in 2019, as evidenced by the British Museum's heavily publicized exhibition *Manga* (May 23 through August 26, 2019).

3. See Kern, *Manga from the Floating World*, 12; on Kyōden, see Shimizu, *Manga no rekishi*, 17–19. The primary reason the claim that Hokusai coined the term persists (outside of Japan, at least) is likely that it is printed in Frederik Schodt's *Manga! Manga!*, which for a long time has been the primary (often the only) source for non-Japanese writings on manga.

The actual page from *Shiji no yukikai* can be found in the National Diet Library's digital collection (viewable at http://dl.ndl.go.jp/info:ndljp/pid/2534277, frame 5 out of 40, lower right). Shimizu Isao has found two earlier uses of *manga*: in Suzuki Kankei's 1771 *Mankaku zuihitsu* (viewable at https://kotenseki.nijl.ac.jp/biblio/100164421/) and Suzuki Rinshō's 1778 *Gunchō gaei*, an anthology of sketches by Hanabusa Icchō (viewable at https://kotenseki.nijl.ac.jp/biblio/200021583/).

The *manga* in *Gunchō gaei* is used only as part of the *daisen* title strip attached to the cover and actually uses a slightly different character for *man* (謾 instead of 漫, perhaps because one of the meanings of 謾, too, is "loose"). The book's foreword (which does not mention the word *manga* or *mankaku*) is dated 1769, but the book itself was published in 1778.

Though the *mankaku* in *Mankaku zuihitsu* is written with virtually the same characters as *manga* (漫畫, using an older form of 画 for the *ga/guwa/kaku* part), the word is actually the name of a bird to whose insatiable behavior the author Suzuki Kankei compares his love of books. *Zuihitsu* means "essays," and the book contains no artwork, so it is uncertain whether there is a connection to the word *manga* as it relates to visual art. Kankei's use of the word *manga* is based on an observation about two species of birds, an albatross (信天縁) and a spoonbill (漫畫), that is found in classic Chinese literature, such as in the collections of writings by Chao Yuezhi (1059–1129; in *Songshan wen ji*) and Hong Mai (1123–1202; in *Rong zhai sui bi*). The albatross motionlessly waits for fish to pass by, whereas the spoonbill actively hunts for them. Chao Yuezhi explains the etymology of the latter's name (漫畫) with the fact that the bird "loosely" (漫) "paints" (畫) upon the water with its beak while searching for fish. Unfortunately, there is no evidence of any connection between Suzuki Kankei's mention of the bird's name (without the accompanying etymology) and Kyōden's use of the word meaning "to sketch."

4. Imaizumi, *Ippyō zatsuwa*, 5 (for 1885). Miyamoto Hirohito, in "Ponchi to manga" (109), writes that Imaizumi's descendant Imaizumi Tarō claimed that Ippyō went to San Francisco in 1887, while a cartoon drawn by Ippyō published in the May 11, 1891, *Jiji Shinpō* depicts someone likely supposed to be the author himself going overseas in 1888. Miyamoto considers Ippyō's own written claim of having visited the United States in 1885 to be most credible (an assessment with which I agree), though Shimizu Isao writes in *Hokusai manga* (72) and *Yonkoma manga* (25) that Imaizumi had been abroad for a period of three years, implying that he considers Imaizumi Tarō's claim more credible than Ippyō's.

5. That the cartoon was in fact originally read from left to right is evident from the fact that the weight lifter exits the stage to the right, since multipanel cartoons generally depict movement in the same direction as their reading order.

6. On February 6, 1890, the newspaper had announced a *gūi* (allegorical) *manga* that was printed in the February 11 issue. Shimizu Isao in *Yonkoma manga* (25) and *Hokusai manga* (72–73) refers to this *gūi manga* as the first use of the term in the meaning of caricature and cartooning, but the *gūi manga* seems to be little more than a realistic-looking sketch of a ship in a storm. Since it was announced as an allegorical work, it is possible that the manga contains hidden symbolism, but it lacks obvious elements of exaggeration or parody. It also lacks a narrative

unfolding over multiple panels, which means that it being identified as *manga* cannot be considered a use of the word as denoting narrative cartooning or comics.

7. Imaizumi, *Ippyō zatsuwa*, 1–3.

8. Shimizu, in *Nenpyō nihon mangashi* (62), claims that the word *Ponchi* originally appeared in katakana in the *Japan Punch* itself but does not specify where and I have been unable to corroborate this claim.

9. For images of *Japan Punch* cartoons and entire issues, see Princeton University's Firestone Library's Graphic Arts Collection (https://graphicarts.princeton .edu/2014/10/16/the-japan-punch/) and the Kawasaki City Museum's website (https://kawasaki.iri-project.org/content/?doi=0447544/01800000HJ).

The majority of *Japan Punch* cartoons featured captions underneath the images, though a few also included individual captions within the drawings, enclosed in balloon shapes emerging from characters' mouths. Although such balloons look similar to contemporary speech balloons, they do not yet represent actual sound synchronous with the image and function rather as visual shorthand for assigning captions to their authors. (This distinction is further explained in chapter 2.) Note how none of the balloons in the *Japan Punch* are used to depict a conversation between two characters reacting to each other's utterances. There is no connection between *Japan Punch* cartoons and the audiovisual narrative manga like "Easygoing Daddy" that start appearing after the introduction of *Bringing Up Father* to Japan.

10. The word *shinbun* is pronounced *shimbun* (the *n* becomes an *m* sound) in Japanese, which is why some newspapers spell the English transliterations of their names that way. Because *shinbun* is the standard Romanization, I use it for consistency even if a newspaper itself favors a different spelling (regardless of its transliteration, the word is the same in Japanese). In part because of printed title-case transliterations featured by many newspapers at the time, however, title case (rather than sentence case) is used for the titles of periodicals in this book.

11. Suyama, *Nihon manga 100nen*, 18.

12. McCarthy, *Brief History of Manga*, 8.

13. Schodt, *Manga! Manga!*, 40. Schodt also mentions that "each year a ceremony is held at [Wirgman's] grave in Yokohama." This comment about the annual graveside ceremony is frequently repeated in other English-language texts on manga and a good indicator that a text is based on Schodt's work. The ceremony was held at least until the 2010s, but it should not be construed as evidence of particular posthumous fame enjoyed by Wirgman in the Japanese national consciousness. The vast majority of Japanese people, even avid manga readers, have never heard of him. None of the roughly three hundred students who attended a course I taught on manga/comics at Josai International University from 2014 to 2016 had, for example. The small graveside ceremony was organized by the Yokohama

Bungei Konwakai (Friends of the Arts Yokohama), whose website is now defunct, so it is unclear whether the group and the ceremony still exist.

14. With the 1905 founding of Kitazawa Rakuten's magazine *Tokyo Puck*, the word *Pakku* (Puck) also briefly became a synonym for *Ponchi-e*, but was never as widely used as *Ponchi-e* or *manga*.

15. Ironically, in 1911, Okamoto coauthored a book featuring "serious" sketches (of persons or scenery) called *Manga to yakubun* (Manga and translations—the book featured translations of some of Baudelaire's poems), using *manga* in its original meaning of "essayistic sketches" instead of "caricature" or "cartooning."

16. In the public domain and accessible in full in the digital collection of the National Diet Library at https://dl.ndl.go.jp/info:ndljp/pid/1225618.

17. Discovered by Takeuchi Osamu. See Takeuchi, *Kodomo manga no kyojin-tachi*, 32–33.

18. Sasaki, *Mangashi no kisomondai*, 74. *Max und Moritz* was published in two volumes as *Wampaku Monogatari* by the Rōmaji-kai (roughly, "Alphabet circle"), with all Japanese text written in the Latin alphabet. Both volumes can be viewed in the digital collection of the National Diet Library at https://dl.ndl.go.jp/info: ndljp/pid/899252 and https://dl.ndl.go.jp/info:ndljp/pid/877445, respectively.

19. Sasaki, *Mangashi no kisomondai*, 75; Okamoto, *Ippei zenshū*, 255; and Oka-moto, conversation in *Tōyō*, 29–51.

CHAPTER 1 — "POPULAR IN SOCIETY AT LARGE"

1. Consider, for example, the entirety of Helen McCarthy's depiction of these years in her videotaped presentation on the history of manga: "And the Japanese comics industry roared through the twenties and thirties." McCarthy, "History of Manga."

2. Discovered by Niimi Nue. Niimi has also found material based on *Buster Brown*, *The Katzenjammer Kids*, and Winsor McCay's *Little Nemo* in the October 1905, December 1905, and January 1906 issues (respectively) of the children's magazine *Otogi-Etoki Kodomo*.

3. The first occurrence of a Mr. Jack–like character is in the March 20, 1898, mul-tipanel cartoon "The Flirtation That Failed, or—How Dare You, You Sassy Thing!" Swinnerton continued drawing similar occasional multipanel cartoons featuring tigers dealing with philandering and jealousy before eventually dedicating a strip entirely to the subject.

4. That the translation was copied by hand is apparent from the reordering of the panels according to the traditional Japanese reading direction (top right to bottom left), with the panels separated by lines and no gutters between them. The panel border lines are of the same boldness and quality as the strip's outside border and

several intradiegetic lines, indicating that the translation was drawn anew rather than created by cutting up and rearranging the existing panels, since this would be unlikely to result in such neat panel borders. In the second panel, Kitazawa appears to have forgotten to copy the tiger stripes on Mr. Jack's head, which were likely present in the original. The reason the panels had to be rearranged was that at the time, Japanese manga, like Japanese itself, were read in columns from top to bottom, proceeding right to left (see, for example, the weight lifter cartoon published by the *Jiji Shinpō* in 1890, fig. P.1). Though most American translations of Japanese comics today keep the panels in their original order for authenticity's sake, it is at first quite jarring to read an English-language comic going against the reading direction of the written language (left to right), and Kitazawa probably thought that an inverted reading order would be similarly confusing for Japanese readers.

It is also possible that Kitazawa had another artist copy *Mr. Jack*, but as the magazine's editor, he was almost certainly involved in the decision to copy it and the person to approve the finished copy and translation.

5. A statistical analysis of Kitawaza's *Chame* manga by manga scholar Jo En, examining the presence of speech balloons (more accurately, dialogue inserted into the image, whether as a "sound image" representing actual sound or not) and external narrative text (*setsumeibun*) in them, found that only 5.1 percent exclusively used speech balloons, 2.6 percent used both, 7.7 percent neither, and 84.6 percent exclusively used external narrative text. Jo, *Nihon ni okeru*, 278.

6. Reprinted (though dated inaccurately) in Jo, 34. Jo En discovered the resemblance between the two stories.

7. It is debatable whether Little Sho's "speech balloons" truly function like post-phonograph transdiegetic speech balloons, which are "sound images" essentially representing recorded sound that is synchronous with the image (see chapter 2), since *Shō-chan no bōken*'s balloons usually read like descriptive captions that have been inserted into the image. For example, the first episode's balloons read, "I'll go to that grove over there" (Sho); "Oh, the squirrel is crying. I'll help it" (Sho); "To thank you, I will show you an interesting place" (squirrel); "This is the entrance" (squirrel).

From January 28 to (at least) March 10, 1923, the *Asahi Graph* also irregularly published a six-panel manga about the hijinks of a bird, a dog, and a monkey. These animals were not drawn in an anthropomorphic style but could nonetheless speak, make music, and even drive cars. A boy in traditional Japanese attire and hairdo named Momo-san (Peach) and resembling the early Sho-chan was occasionally featured as well. The manga could well be considered an audiovisual comic strip, given that it does not use external narration and features transdiegetic content—not only speech balloons but also occasional music notes or motion lines. Said speech balloons are similar to *Shō-chan no bōken*'s, which in combination with the style the human boy is drawn in, and the fact that this manga in the issues it appeared in was published instead of *Shō-chan no bōken*, strongly suggests that its creator may have been the latter's illustrator, Kabashima Katsuichi. While this strip, like similar earlier experiments by Kitazawa Rakuten or the single *Mr. Jack* translation, constitutes an interesting artifact regardless of the identity of its author, it does not appear to have exerted influence on the trajectory of Japanese graphic narrative.

8. Suzuki, *Bunshirō bunshū*, 190.

9. Suzuki, 190. In "Sono koro no omoide," Suzuki Bunshirō writes that Oda was involved from the beginning. Takeuchi Osamu points out, based on a statement by Kabashima, that Suzuki may have exaggerated his own role and that Oda may have even had the original idea for *Shō-chan no bōken*. Takeuchi, *Kodomo manga no kyojin-tachi*, 70–72.

10. Suzuki, "Sono koro no omoide"; Ōtsuka, *Mikkī no shoshiki*, 89–90. The January 7, 1925, issue of the *Ōsaka Asahi Shinbun* on page 2 even featured an article about a Sho-chan-themed New Year's gathering, with reportedly 237 children attending. An accompanying photograph shows most of them wearing Sho-chan hats.

11. Jo, *Nihon ni okeru*, 290.

12. Takeuchi, *Kodomo manga no kyojin-tachi*, 74. In the same text, Takeuchi hyperbolically calls *Shō-chan* the polar opposite of Miyao Shigeo's *Manga Tarō* (a Busch/Okamoto-style picture story), in an apparent contradiction to this previous labeling of it as an intermediary (76). Takeuchi elsewhere also refers to *Shō-chan no bōken* as a picture story (*e-monogatari*; 63).

13. Sakamoto Ichirō, quoted in Jo, *Nihon ni okeru*, 290.

14. Other examples include the June 17, 1924, and January 10, 1925, issues of *Shō-chan* in the *Ōsaka Asahi Shinbun*.

15. See, for example, Miriam Silverberg's *Erotic Grotesque Nonsense* regarding the moral panic about the "modern girl" in Japan at the time.

16. Suzuki, "Sono koro no omoide," 44.

17. The dead included several thousand Korean and other immigrants who were massacred by police and vigilantes espousing conspiracy theories that foreigners and socialists were to blame for the fires. (The more things change, the more they stay the same.) See Gordon, *Modern History of Japan*, 154.

18. The Asahi database Kikuzo II lists *Bringing Up Father* for the subsequent issue as well, but this appears to be a mistake.

The Sunday edition also featured a single *Bringing Up Father* topper panel until January 20, 1926, and afterward, a non–*Bringing Up Father* topper strip drawn by McManus until December 22, 1926. It used the hiragana syllabary (instead of only katakana, like the weekday edition) for everything not written with *kanji*, using katakana only for foreign names and loan words, like most Japanese writing today. It also used hiragana to write the *Oyaji* in *Oyaji kyōiku* starting on November 28, 1923, and added the original English title as well. However, seven years later, on August 20, 1930, it suddenly changed the Japanese title and header text back to a right-to-left reading order (though the dialogue text inside the panels remained unchanged). On April 6, 1927, *Oyaji kyōiku* ceased using panel numbers, indicating that by this time at the latest, the Japanese audience had become sufficiently accustomed to the American reading order.

19. The second episode of *Bringing Up Father*'s translation flipped its title (*Oyaji kyōiku*) from conventional Japanese right-to-left to a left-to-right reading order, and its third episode changed the reading direction for dialogue to top to bottom, left to right, largely eliminating the conflict (though technically still at odds with the panel order of left to right, *then* top to bottom). Writing Japanese top to bottom, left to right was and still is extremely unusual. With more advanced editing technology it would have been easier to simply mirror and rearrange the panels (so that they would be ordered and read top to bottom, *right to left*), but at the time, this would have made the copying and editing process much more difficult, which explains why the *Asahi Graph* preferred switching the reading order instead. When the strip's panel arrangement changed from a two-by-two square to a four-by-one column on May 12, 1923, the dialogue reading direction reverted to the traditional Japanese order (top to bottom, right to left), which, due to the new panel arrangement, no longer caused a conflict between different reading orders for panels and text, even though it meant that the balloon order and text direction conflicted anew. Reading Japanese top to bottom and left to right probably had proved too odd for the paper's readers.

Beginning with the second episode, the translation also featured copyright information ("by Int'l Feature Service, Inc."), including the year, which in combination with the handwritten month/day date reveals the date of original publication. Based on these original dates of publication, it is evident that the translated *Bringing Up Father* episodes were often published out of order, sometimes marginally so (for example, the May 14 and 15, 1923, *Asahi Graph* issues featured originals from March 23 and 22, 1923, respectively) and sometimes wildly (such as the episode published on May 30, 1923, whose original dates from August 25, 1922).

20. The translation had used left-to-right writing before when rendering animal sounds on April 17, 19, and 26, 1923.

21. Yanaike, *Yokogaki tōjō*, 100.

22. Yanaike, 117–130.

23. Yanaike, 130–141.

24. Comics scholar Ono Kōsei speculates that the prevalence of publications labeling their translations *honshi/honsha tokuyaku*—"contracted exclusively by

this magazine/newspaper/company"—means that the label's absence indicates a lack of authorization on the part of the syndicate owning the rights to the respective strip, and hence copyright infringement and piracy. Ono, *Amerikan komikkusu taizen*, 237. Whether or not this is true, the ubiquity of the label hints at the popularity of the comic strips so advertised; if the strips had not been considered a factor that might influence readers' decision to purchase a given publication, there would have been no need to advertise them as exclusive.

25. Letters to the editor from readers with Japanese names about American comic strips featured in the *Japan Times* suggest that a considerable number of Japanese individuals were following the English-language comic strips published in it.

26. "Famous Creator of Jiggs and Maggie Admits That He Does Not Like Corned Beef and Cabbage," *Japan Times*, February 20, 1928 (emphasis added).

27. One of these ads depicts protagonist Jiggs ogling a young woman at the beach with his wife, Maggie, approaching angrily from behind him, umbrella clenched in her hand, reminiscent of the *Mr. Jack* episode published in the *Tōkyō Puck* sixteen years prior (fig. 1.1), though most certainly coincidentally.

Advertisements for both volumes together also appeared in the *Tōkyō Asahi Shinbun* on September 14 and 23, 1926.

28. Suzuki, "Sono koro no omoide," 44.

29. Suzuki, 44.

30. McManus, *Bringing Up Father*, i. The Japanese text is an unrelated phrase McManus must have copied from somewhere; the part preceding "BRINGING UP FATHER" has been rotated by 180 degrees, perhaps as a joke.

31. Some of the *Bringing Up Father* ads merely show images of its protagonists without any speech balloons: ads for Tomi Port and Tadao wines; one each for Barber Cream shaving cream, Velvet Soap, and Tokkapin; and one of several for Zigus stoves (*Zigus* is written ジグス in Japanese katakana, the same as *Jiggs*). Other ads feature text purportedly uttered or thought by Jiggs, though not depicted transdiegetically through a speech balloon or similar tool: one Tadao ad; two for Libby Corned Beef, one of which is also the only ad to dress Jiggs in traditional Japanese attire; and one for Velvet Soap. Still others do feature utterances in speech balloons (some by Maggie as well): two (technically distinct albeit very similar except for an included picture of the product) ads for what seems to be a bicycle gear shift; one Tadao ad (with Jiggs himself silent but other characters toasting); one for Daikoku wine; one for Zenchisui athlete's foot medication; one for Acello thermometers; one for Kuzuhara frozen fish (showing Jiggs telling Maggie to serve him the advertised fish instead of his usual beloved corned beef); and two for Zigus stoves, as well as another two for stoves by different companies.

The drawing quality seen in the ads diverges widely, with some images of Jiggs that do not look remarkably different from those drawn by McManus himself and others in which he is barely recognizable, such as the Bikatsu ad strips. In the Bikatsu ads, we can be certain that we are looking at Jiggs primarily because of the strips' title featuring his name and because of Maggie's presence. Among the advertisements discussed here, I have included only those that can be said with reasonable certainty to depict Jiggs and not merely an accidentally similar character. There are a few other ads found in newspapers between 1923 and 1941, such as one for biscuits ("calcuits") featuring a stocky white man dressed in a manner similar to that of Jiggs, that could potentially be based on *Bringing Up Father*. But the Jiggs-like characters in these ads do not exhibit some of McManus's figures' trademark elements like pupil-less button eyes, making it doubtful whether they are based on his comic strip.

32. I have not been able to find *Bringing Up Father* episodes mentioning *gemai* or *genmai*, though.

33. These are (1) an ad for Tomi Port wine showing Jiggs and Maggie together with the respective protagonists from *Nonki na tōsan*, *Shō-chan no bōken*, and Nagasaki Batten's *Hitorimusume no Hineko-san* (e.g., in the *Miyako Shinbun* on September 27, 1924); (2) one for Misono Oshiroi face powder featuring Jiggs, Kuma-san from Maekawa Senpan's *Awatemono no Kuma-san*, and Oscar Jacobsson's Adamson (e.g., in the *Yamato Shinbun* on March 13, 14, 16, and 29, 1932); and (3) one featuring Jiggs and the Easygoing Daddy for what appears to be a book aimed at radio enthusiasts, published by Seibundō (e.g., in the *Hōchi Shinbun* on March 1, 1925).

34. One of these is an advertisement for Kuzuhara frozen fish titled "Magī no daidokoro keizai" (Maggie's kitchen economy), which is the only *Bringing Up Father*–based advertisement found in a magazine (*Fujokai*, December 1924) rather than a newspaper.

Another two newspaper advertisement four-panel comic strips form a two-part story called "The Invention" ("Part 1" and "Part 2"), and two more multipanel ads appeared under the title *Nihon oyaji kyōiku* ("Japanese Bringing Up Father"). The first is a four-panel strip that follows the original strip's American reading order and uses "The Insurance" ("Hoken no maki") as its episode title. Unsurprisingly, it appears to be an advertisement for insurance, although it does not specify a particular kind. Perhaps the strip was intended to make readers more susceptible to a separate advertisement for a particular brand or kind of insurance. The second *Nihon oyaji kyōiku* strip differs from the other ad strips in that it features a total of ten panels. In contrast to the first *Nihon oyaji kyōiku* ad, this one is clearly labeled "Yachiyo Seimei" (Yachiyo life), an insurance company that existed from 1913 to 1930.

35. Taking into account that I discovered all these advertisements more or less accidentally, it is likely that the ones mentioned here do not constitute an exhaustive list.

36. The article is found on the third page (emphasis added).

37. The adaptation of comic strips into other media during the prewar period was not a strictly Japanese phenomenon. American comic strips were turned into musicals and other forms of entertainment in their country of origin as well.

38. In Japanese "wagakuni ni oite saemo yosōgai no ninki wo yonde iru." *Manga no Kuni,* August 1937, 3.

39. Suzuki, *Bunshirō bunshū,* 190–191.

40. Suzuki, "Sono koro no omoide," 44. Because of this practice, the *Asahi Graph* nearly ran out of daily issues to publish, and Suzuki had several collected book volumes of *Bringing Up Father* shipped to him in order to provide him with enough material.

41. "Japanese Cartoons—Considerable Progress Made in Work of Artists during Past Ten Years," *Japan Times,* October 17, 1932.

CHAPTER 2 — "LISTEN VUNCE!"

1. Smolderen, "Of Labels, Loops, and Bubbles," 110.

2. Bishop, "Early Political Caricature in America," 230.

3. For example, "Speech balloons had been used occasionally throughout cartoon history—rather *awkwardly* in Colonial-era prints and Currier and Ives lithographs, for instance, and even in illuminated religious manuscripts of the Middle Ages." Marschall, *America's Great Comic-Strip Artists,* 60 (emphasis added).

4. "For the 20th-century reader, speech balloons are simple graphic devices through which pictorial characters speak, and it is tempting to attribute any obscurity in more ancient examples to the clumsiness or naivety of artists from another era. [...] [But] modern speech balloons—and the way we interpret them as part of an audiovisual scene played on paper—could not have existed before the technological changes of the 1890s." Smolderen, "Of Labels, Loops, and Bubbles," 90.

5. There is a James Gillray print titled "The Table's Turn'd," which consists of two panels labeled "Billy in the Devil's claws" and "Billy sending the Devil packing" and, at first glance, looks like a brief conversation extending over two panels, but the two panels are allegories of two different historical events (the landing of French troops in Wales on February 22, 1797, and the Battle of Cape St. Vincent on February 14, 1797)—in opposite chronological order at that—and thus cannot be interpreted as a single, intradiegetic conversation between Billy and the Devil.

6. Though some modern translations portray certain text in *kibyōshi* as direct speech or sound effects to make them look closer to modern comics/manga, the

original *kibyōshi* stories themselves do not distinguish between different types of text and function quite differently from audiovisual comics. See Smith, "Who Said That?"

7. A common example in movie comedies is the revelation that music assumed to be extradiegetic is revealed as intradiegetic.

8. For more on semiotics and signs, see Ferdinand de Saussure's *Course in General Linguistics*.

9. Given that *diegesis* is a Greek word, the terminology should probably be *endo*diegetic, *ecto*diegetic, and *dia*diegetic, but the philologically lackluster Greco-Roman amalgams *intra-* and *extradiegetic* are already well-established.

Randy Duncan employs a somewhat similar categorization using different terminology in "Image Functions—Shape and Color as Hermeneutic Images in *Asterios Polyp*." Craig Fischer, too, has written on "diegetic, non-diegetic, and quasi-diegetic elements" in comics in a blog post titled "Logos and the Story World of Jack Staff" from February 11, 2011, which unfortunately is no longer accessible.

10. It is uncertain to what extent the Western pre-Enlightenment inability to depict motion due to the way vision was understood applies to Japan. After all, we see something resembling motion lines/blurs in one copy of the *chōjūgiga* (drawn behind a pole-vaulting monkey) and other Japanese picture scrolls, as pointed out by Tokyo National Museum curator of Japanese painting Matsushima Masato in "Chōjūgiga?," 271. It hence appears possible that medieval Japanese thought and conception of vision permitted the representation of motion, unlike in Renaissance Europe. Nevertheless, as Matsushima adds, there is no way of connecting the motion lines occasionally found in picture scrolls to those in present-day, "Western-derived" manga, and there does not appear to be a common lineage between the two. Despite such uses of motion lines in Japanese art centuries ago, manga remained largely free of them until 1923.

11. I suspect that pain stars developed around 1892–1893 due to a sequence of three cartoons in the influential American humor magazine *Life*, on June 23, 1892; July 6, 1893; and November 30, 1893. In all three of these cartoons, someone is hit in the face and the pain felt is rendered through a transdiegetic pain/impact image. The first cartoon uses radiating straight lines for its pain image, perhaps based on the way explosions were commonly depicted at the time. The second adds a number of small *X*'s to lines, and the third uses stars and lines. Even if *Life* was not the place where pain images were used first, the fact that the two cartoons in June 1892 and July 1893 did not yet use stars, which only a few years later became standard across different publications, makes it unlikely that pain stars were used much earlier than 1893.

The appearance of both the phrase *to see stars* (in response to a blow to the head) and pain stars are likely the result of the transformation that the knowledge of vision underwent in the nineteenth century, the discovery of "the corporal sub-jectivity of the observer" described by Jonathan Crary and spotted by him first in Goethe's 1810 *Theory of Colours*. Crary, "Techniques of the Observer," 3–4. Crary cites Johannes Müller's work on the physiology of the senses as having laid much of the groundwork for the widespread acceptance of this discovery. Crary, *Techniques of the Observer*, 88–96. In a chapter subtitled "Physical Conditions Necessary for the Production of Luminous Images" (according to Crary, "a phrase that would have been unimaginable before the nineteenth century") in his *Handbuch der Physiologie des Menschen*, first published in 1833, Müller lists as one of his five causes of luminous images "mechanical influences; as concussion or blow." Crary, 90.

Knowledge of the ability to produce "luminous images" through mechanical means preexisted the nineteenth century (Crary cites Thomas Hobbes's *Leviathan*: "And as pressing, rubbing, or striking the eye, makes us fancy a light" [93]), but Crary emphasizes that while in earlier times experiences like these had been considered deceptive illusions, "in the early nineteenth century, particularly with Goethe, such experiences attain the status of optical 'truth.' They are no longer deceptions that obscure 'true' perceptions; rather they begin to constitute an irreducible component of human vision" (97). The realization that physical impact on the human body could manifest itself in one's vision (specifically, a "concussion or blow" causing one to see bright lights) thus appears possible to have come about as part of the same rethinking of vision described by Crary, which generated knowledge of the after-image and made possible the creation of motion lines and blurs. This connection provides a plausible explanation for why we see these at first glance dissimilar forms of transdiegetic content emerge together during the nineteenth century.

12. This was true in Edo-period Japan as well, as discussed by Timon Screech in *Lens within the Heart*.

13. Kunzle, *Nineteenth Century*, 349.

14. Phenakistoscope: a disc with slightly differing images spun around a verti-cally attached handle. Zoetrope: a spinning loop with slits through which images painted on the loop's inside could be viewed. Praxinoscope: another spinning loop but with images viewed via a set of mirrors placed in the middle. Zoöpraxiscope: a device projecting images from a spinning glass disc. Kinetoscope: a device similar to the zoöpraxiscope but using a film strip instead of a disc.

15. Kunzle, *Nineteenth Century*, 350.

16. Rather than solicit original content, American newspapers at first (during the early 1890s) primarily reprinted pantomime and other multipanel and single-panel cartoons from humor magazines such as *Life*, *Harper's Bazar*, and the Ger-man *Fliegende Blätter*.

17. Maresca and Ghielmetti, *Society Is Nix*, 8 (emphasis added).

18. Interestingly, there are Japanese "Punch books" (*Ponchi-bon*) from the late 1890s that combine the multipanel cartoon with *kibyōshi*-style narrative and dialogue text, but they did not have a lasting influence on Japanese graphic narrative.

19. Sterne, *Audible Past*, 2.

20. Sterne, 60.

21. One could also argue that Wilhelm Busch's use of music notes in one of the panels of his 1865 multipanel cartoon "Der Virtuos" (The virtuoso), which shows the titular virtuoso playing the piano in a variety of styles, constitutes a sound image. Since the notes appear only in the "Finale furioso" and some of them are shown falling to the floor, however, it is possible that Busch merely intended them as a visual joke implying that the pianist is playing so furiously that notes are literally flying off his sheet music (this would also explain the presence of a treble clef). On the other hand, du Maurier's sound images may have been partly inspired by Busch's music notes, considering that du Maurier's sound images look like an amalgam of phonautograms and some of the notes drawn by Busch. Even the idea for du Maurier's cartoon may have been derived from Busch's 1867 "Die feindlichen Nachbarn" (The hostile neighbors), a story about a painter enacting revenge upon her cellist neighbor for disturbing her work. Busch's story is narrated, however, and does not feature a single sound image, suggesting that Busch indeed did not intend for the music notes in the earlier "Der Virtuos" to function as one.

22. See, for example, Pisko, *Die neueren Apparate der Akustik*, 91.

23. One such example is a demonstration uploaded by the Henry Ford Museum to YouTube on July 25, 2018: "1903 Edison Phonograph Recording Demo," https://www.youtube.com/watch?v=wRTgloqx6wE.

24. See Doak, *Phonograph*, 11.

25. On April 17, 1898, the *New York Journal*'s cartoon supplement itself featured a full-page advertisement for the gramophone (the trademark name of a type of phonograph developed by Emile Berliner that used flat discs instead of cylinders as its recording medium—i.e., what we now call a "record player").

26. Even Jimmy Swinnerton—who was drawing individual anthropomorphic tigers for the *New York Journal* as early as October 29, 1897, and cartoons (usually featuring tigers) for its Sunday cartoon supplement from February 20, 1898, on—counts among the adherents of this theory. In an interview from the July 1934 *Editor & Publisher*, quoted in M. C. Gaines's "Narrative Illustration" (and by Smolderen in *The Origins of Comics*), Swinnerton claims, "It was not the fashion to have balloons showing what the characters were saying, as that was supposed to have been buried with the English Cruikshank, but along came the comic supplements, and with Dick Outcault's 'Yellow Kid,' the balloons came back and literally filled the comic sky" (Smolderen, 140–141). As discussed later in this chapter, this is not quite accurate.

While on the subject of Swinnerton, I feel compelled to correct a few pervasive misconceptions regarding his early work. The earliest drawings by Swinnerton for the *San Francisco Examiner* I have found date from April 11, 1893. Both feature bears, though not in the style Swinnerton became famous for. The first is part of a Noah's Ark joke; the second apparently about a real bear that was shot. Swinnerton drew other single-panel cartoons featuring children, though none of these feature the word *tyke* or *tykes*, as claimed in multiple texts. The claim that the *Examiner* included a Swinnerton "banner" reading "Little Bears and Tykes" as early as June 1, 1892 (predating the earliest Swinnerton cartoons I have found in the *Examiner* by almost a year), or that there was an even *earlier* series of cartoons by Swinnerton called *The Little Bears* is particularly confounding. *Examiner* artists often drew little "cartoon initials" featuring a letter that was substituted for the first one in a regular newspaper article or column, similar to initials in a decorated manuscript. For the October 9, 1893, issue a different artist (signature illegible, but beginning "Fo") had drawn such a cartoon initial featuring a bear (with a ladder and hammer, and a wooden makeshift letter *Y* above it on the wall). Swinnerton then drew a bear initial for the October 14 *Examiner*, and these bears became a regular, almost daily feature from that day on (though never referred to as "Little Bears" at least until June 1894). For more on the Little Bears, see Eddie Campbell, *The Goat Getters*, 26–31. The tigers that Swinnerton later drew for the *New York Journal* were called "Little Tigers" only twice (and once "A Little Tiger") over the period I have surveyed. When they were referred to as "Tigers" at all it was more commonly as "The Journal's Tigers" (including during their first appearance on February 20, 1898). Swinnerton started regularly drawing audiovisual comic strips in 1900, following Rudolph Dirks and Frederick Burr Opper.

27. Yasar, *Electrified Voices*, 5.

28. First, a series of nine six-panel (or in one instance, seven-panel) cartoons following the October 25, 1896, five-panel phonograph one, began one month later: "The Yellow Kid Indulges in a Cockfight—a Waterloo" on November 29; "A Three Cornered Fight in McFadden's Flats" (seven panels) on December 6; "A Dark Secret; or How the Yellow Kid Took a Picture" on December 13; "The Yellow Kid's Great Fight" (in which the Kid infamously and with the assistance of his goat beats up a Black kid while the accompanying text by Joe Kerr sports multiple racist epithets) on December 20; "The Yellow Kid Wrestles with the Tobacco Habit" on December 27; "How the Yellow Kid Planted a Seed and the Result" on January 3, 1897; "The Yellow Kid Goes Hunting Becomes [*sic*] a Dead Game Sport" on January 24; "The Yellow Kid Studies Music and Tries It on the Dog" on February 7; and "The Yellow Kid's New Phonograph Clock" on February 14, 1897. A ten-panel cartoon titled "A Few Things the Versatile Yellow Kid Might Do fer a Living" appeared

on November 22, but the ten panels simply depict the Yellow Kid in different pro-
fessions and do not form a narrative sequence.

After a break of three months, the first of seven additional multipanel cartoons
spaced out over eight months followed: "The Yellow Kid Makes a Century Record"
(four panels) on May 23; "The Yellow Kid Takes a Hand at Golf" (six panels) on
October 24; "The Yellow Kid Loses Some of His Yellow" (six panels) on October 31; "How the Goat Got 'Kilt Entirely!'" (four panels) on November 14; "The
Ryan's Arcade Gang Go Sleighing" (two panels) on December 12; "The Yellow Kid's
Revenge; or, How the Painter's Son Got Fresh" (two panels) on January 9, 1898;
and "The Yellow Kid Experiments with the Wonderful Hair Tonic" (four panels)
on January 23, the last Yellow Kid cartoon signed by Outcault apart from another
single-panel one on May 1, 1898, in which the Kid makes a cameo as an old man.

Another Yellow Kid cartoon ("Yellow Kids of All Nations") appeared on February 6, but since it is unsigned, it is likely that it was drawn by a different artist.

29. On January 3 and 10, March 21, and September 26. There are some uses in
single-panel cartoons, on April 4, July 11, and September 12.

30. Smolderen, "Of Labels, Loops, and Bubbles," 91. Murrell's and Bishop's texts
are freely accessible at www.archive.org.

31. I am emphasizing the sonic quality of the cartoon here to stress how unusual it
was at the time. The cartoon is also remarkable for its use of stand-alone exclamation points to represent sound (or emotion) that cannot be transcribed into words,
a transdiegetic element seen as early as 1888 in *Life* but still uncommon at the time.

32. Often this link is supported with an image of Dirks's March 27, 1898, Yellow
Kid parody featuring the Katzenjammer Kids (and a speech balloon, albeit for a
dog), implying that the *Katzenjammer Kids* simply took over where the *Yellow Kid*
left off. Dirks also drew the Kid in a February 20, 1898, cartoon.

33. The reason Dirks eventually switched from speech lines to speech balloons
was likely that by neatly enclosing all the words belonging to one character, the latter made it easier to delineate different characters' utterances from each other—a
necessity with increasing verbal content per panel.

34. Brian Walker (son of cartoonist Mort Walker), too, points out that Rudolph
Dirks "pioneered the use of many comic devices that eventually became part of the
art form's visual language. Parallel lines and dust clouds to indicate speed, dotted
lines to represent eye contact, and sweat beads to suggest fear or nervousness were
among the many forms of graphic communication that appeared regularly in the
panels of The Katzenjammer Kids." Walker, *Comics*, 36.

35. This *Katzenjammer Kids* episode also features a creative use of transdiegetic
tears, which first flow downward to express sadness, before suddenly changing
direction upward in the following panel to express surprise instead.

36. The Edison Toy Phonograph Company produced talking dolls for the first time in early 1890, based on an idea presented to Edison in 1887 by inventors William Jacques and Lowell Briggs, though the dolls proved too unreliable and the company ceased operations in October 1890. Morton, *Sound Recording*, 18–19. An image of such a doll can be found in Umeda, *Chikuonki no rekishi*, 4.

37. Other cartoons in the *New York Journal* tied to sound-recording technology, parrots (the phonograph's stand-in), or the act of misattributing the source of sound include a December 4, 1898, cartoon about phonographs; a six-panel cartoon titled "The Story That Wasn't Printed—and the Reason for It" on January 1, 1899, in which an editor demands "more copy" through an intercom; a January 29, 1899, Jimmy Swinnerton cartoon featuring his tiger characters and titled "The Foxy Lover and the Hired Band," in which one of the tigers pretends to serenade a tigress while the music is actually being produced by the hired band; "The Parrot Learned Not Wisely but Too Well," a February 26, 1899, five-panel cartoon about a parrot repeating swear words, likewise by Swinnerton; and a September 10, 1899, cartoon about gramophones (phonographs) by Fred Opper. All these examples use sound *lines* and no balloon shapes.

38. Though Outcault had stopped working for the *New York Journal* in early 1898, Dirks had used a word balloon similar to Outcault's in a single-panel cartoon reminiscent of Outcault's mass scenes of children, called "Little Willie's Dream after His Mamma Had Told Him What Happens to Little Boys Who Are Kind to Animals," on August 14, 1898. Jimmy Swinnerton, too, had started occasionally using such word balloons in similar mass scenes starring his tiger characters as early as March 12, 1899, so it is obvious where Dirks would have gotten the idea of using word balloons in cartoons. Dirks himself sporadically drew single-panel animal cartoons for the *New York Journal* in which he sometimes used word balloons, which retained their primary characteristic as "labels," such as in an April 30, 1899, cartoon called "The Rag-Time Craze in the Jungle," which shows animals making music and dancing without any sound images except a single word balloon attached to an elephant that reads "My Annelizer," presumably a reference to a popular song at the time.

39. The joke appears to have been popular in the late 1890s; Horace Taylor's cartoon cover for the September 12, 1897, American Humorist (the name of the *New York Journal*'s cartoon supplement at the time), "This Was Jubilee Year for the Mosquitoes, and They Ought to Celebrate," too, shows a mosquito asking, "When is a door not a door?"

40. This is not entirely dissimilar to how some films, like Charlie Chaplin's 1936 *Modern Times*, still used intertitles instead of recorded dialogue for many scenes even after *The Jazz Singer* had established the use of recorded dialogue in 1927.

41. Gottlieb, "Untertitel," 196. For more on the connection between audiovisual comics and the cinema, see also Gardner, *Projections*, 1–28.

42. Walker, *Comics*, 12 (emphasis added). Walker wrongly attributes the spread of speech balloons to the Yellow Kid, but this does not render invalid his claim about their nature.

43. Yomota, *Nihon eiga 110nen*, 44.

44. Yasar, *Electrified Voices*, 90–91.

45. Gordon, *Modern History of Japan*, 155.

46. Umeda, *Chikuonki no rekishi*, 121.

47. Kurata, *Nihon rekōdo bunkashi*, 36.

48. Katō, *Chikuonki no jidai*, 123.

CHAPTER 3 — WHEN KRAZY KAT SPOKE JAPANESE

1. Jo, *Nihon ni okeru*, 315–349. Jo lists a handful of graphic narratives begun before 1923 whose first and last issues are more than three years apart, but these do not appear to have been regularly published and some of the information—for example, for the manga *Nū-bō no sekai*—is inaccurate.

2. In *Nihon manga 100nen*, Suyama Keiichi writes of the lengths of publication of *Nonki na tōsan* and *Shō-chan no bōken*—three years and two and a half, respectively—as evidence of their "overwhelming popularity" (110). Though Suyama briefly mentions *Bringing Up Father*, he does not mention *Little Jimmy*, *Happy Hooligan*, *And Her Name Was Maud*, *Adamson*, or *Felix the Cat*, all of which ran for at least two and a half years.

3. *Amerika manga*, using a different word for the United States than *Oyaji kyōiku*, which used the more formal *beikoku*.

4. *Little Jimmy* also, on October 11, 1924, used only Chinese characters to represent dialogue spoken in Chinese, a device common in Japanese comics today, though it is unlikely that the *Little Jimmy* episode was responsible for this development.

5. The name was corrected to "Bīrī Debekku" on December 9. On May 29, 1925, the title inexplicably changed the order of its protagonists to *Aiba to Gūtaro-kun* for the remainder of its run.

6. Shishido, *Amerika no yokoppara*, 3–7.

7. *Patty* ended after the *Japan Times* published three decidedly negative reader responses to it. When *Patty* had briefly replaced *Bringing Up Father* before on June 19, 1929, the newspaper had explained that this was due to *Bringing Up Father*'s "hardly being a fair representation of American life today." One of the reader responses to *Patty* asked for Jiggs to return, however, and he did. This episode implies that newspapers took readers' letters into account when deciding which comic strips to print, though the reasoning for replacing *Bringing Up Father* appears arbitrary.

8. *Polly and Her Pals* was historic in a second aspect: it strikingly differed from other manga at the time in that it was the first comic strip in Japanese history to have type-lettered sound images (speech balloons), which would later become the standard method of lettering in the Japanese comics industry, though *Polly and Her Pals'* type-lettering was more an interesting artifact rather than the origin of this development. Type-lettering of comic strips was significantly more difficult than lettering by hand at the time, which explains the rarity of the former at the time. *Little Jimmy's* translation also employed type-lettering during a single episode on April, 20, 1923, but quickly switched back to hand-lettering.

9. Prior announcements of the ad space in both newspapers instruct potential clients to contact this agency (Hōkoku Tsūshinsha), and both ad spaces were announced in late October (October 26 and 28 for *Little Jimmy*, October 29, 30, and 31 for *Tillie the Toiler*; the reported cost was 32 yen per advertisement), with ads in both starting on November 1, 1924.

10. Indeed, Fisher today is remembered in comics history as the father of the daily strip, although he was not the first artist to attempt a daily strip; this honor belongs to Clare Briggs and his 1903 *A. Piker Clerk*, which preceded *Mutt and Jeff* by four years and whose basic plot of a horse racing enthusiast betting on races Fisher likely copied for *A. Mutt*, *Mutt and Jeff's* original title prior to the introduction of Jeff. Fisher became the one to popularize the daily format and see it taken up by other strips, however.

11. Harold Knerr started drawing *The Katzenjammer Kids* for Hearst after Dirks was dismissed due to an unapproved vacation, reportedly. Dirks continued drawing his strip under the (eventual) title *The Captain and the Kids*.

12. The temporal proximity between the translated episode and the institution of the award reveals (despite the absence of a dated signature or copyright information specifying the year or original appearance) that the translation of *Mutt and Jeff* was published with less delay than other translated strips.

13. As *Zigus to Magī* (Jiggs and Maggie) during the period from February 15, 1924, to April 22, 1925, with an absence of *Mutt and Jeff* from January 21 to April 2, 1925, and of Jiggs and Maggie from January 12 to April 13, 1925.

14. *Mutt and Jeff* did not appear from February 1 to 5 or on February 11, so Tanaka is likely referring to one of these days. February 4 is the only issue that also did not feature *Shō-chan no bōken*, which makes it the most likely one, given Tanaka's claim that the issue did not feature a single manga.

15. The March 1926 *Popular Mechanics* article "How Cartoons Are Syndicated" also claims that an anonymous paper temporarily ceased printing *Orphan Annie* to test readers' reactions to its disappearance (456).

16. Two stand-alone advertisements with Mutt and Jeff can also be found in the *Ōsaka Asahi Shinbun*. The first is a one-panel cartoon for a potion by beverage maker

Akadama, showing Jeff recommending the product to Mutt and drawn quite similar to Fisher's style. The other is a six-panel graphic narrative–style ad for fountain pens, stretching from the bottom right of the page to its left. This ad preserved the American left-to-right reading order for dialogue text despite the panels' arrangement from right to left, showing how much this reading order had come to be identified with American comics. It also featured external narrative text explaining the advertisement's plot, however. The characters only bear a superficial resemblance to Fisher's but refer to each other as Mutt and Jeff.

17. These products range from the pharmaceutical Seirogan, which can still be purchased today, to the beverage Rakupisu, which sounds like a parody of the ever-popular Calpis (Karupisu), but based on the survival of a prewar Rakupisu store sign offered on a Japanese auction site, it appears to have been a genuine product.

18. There also is at least one instance of *Happy Hooligan* filling only the bottom half of the page again (on February 2, 1927), but this appears to have been a rare exception.

19. Between August 1925 and January 1927, *Happy Hooligan* was temporarily "replaced" by Opper's *Mr. Dough and Mr. Dubb*. Because *Mr. Dough and Mr. Dubb* is set in the same universe as *Happy Hooligan* and even features Happy as a character, the strip was less a replacement than a continuation of *Happy Hooligan* under a different title, though. On February 6, 1927, the strip again bore Happy Hooligan's name and remained *Happy Hooligan* (*Happī Furigan*) until its final episode on January 26, 1930. From February to May 1926, Opper's *Our Antediluvian Ancestors*, a strip about prehistoric life, served as the topper strip for *Mr. Dough and Mr. Dubb*. It was followed by a single cartoon, translated as *rakutenka* (optimist), the next week, before being replaced more permanently on June 6 by Opper's strip about a stubborn mule named Maud (*And Her Name Was Maud*). Maud's adventures continued to accompany *Mr. Dough and Mr. Dubb* and *Happy Hooligan* until the strips' final (January 26, 1930) episode, on which day it was even featured as a separate strip instead of as only a topper to *Happy Hooligan*.

20. Takeuchi, *Kodomo manga no kyojin-tachi*, 123.

21. The original strip is included in Bill Blackbeard's *Smithsonian Collection of Newspaper Comics*, 115.

22. There is one surviving source describing the copying process in the 1900s, however. Kawabata Ryūshi—who was the artist of, among other works, cartoons for the satire magazines *Tokyo Puck* and *Tōkyō Hāpī*—in his autobiography *Waga ga-seikatsu* (My painterly life) writes about the process that the *Miyako Shinbun* was using around the year 1906, "in particular, for copying manga published in foreign magazines." It employed a "chalk board" (*chōku-ita*) covered in chalk that had been mixed with glue. The copying artist would trace the foreign cartoon

onto the hardened chalk, carving grooves into it in the process. Afterward, lead was poured into the grooves in order to produce a printing plate. Kawabata, *Waga ga-seikatsu*, 30–31. The 1908 *Mr. Jack* translation in *Tokyo Puck* may well have been created using this process. Given that the *Happy Hooligan* translation appeared roughly two decades after the time that Kawabata is writing about, copying techniques would have changed by then, however, and utilized photoengraving.

23. "How Cartoons Are Syndicated," *Popular Mechanics*, March 1926, 454–455.

24. For images other than line art, such as photographs, a half-tone process using punctured screens that creates a new image consisting of dots is used instead.

25. "Japanese Cartoons—Considerable Progress Made in Work of Artists during Past Ten Years," *Japan Times*, October 17, 1932.

26. The May issue featured a *Felix* story titled (in the table of contents only) "Kyūpitto no ya" (Cupid's arrow) by "P. Suriban" of four pages or twenty-four panels, while the June issue included only a single double-page spread of a twelve-panel *Felix* story, with no title or name of author provided.

27. Okamoto's disavowal of familiarity with foreign graphic narratives is surprising given both his adaptations of works by Wilhelm Busch and September 3, 4, and 5, 1922, articles he wrote on American newspaper comics for the *Tōkyō Asahi Shinbun*. The *Asahi Shinbun* articles discussed newspaper comic strips aimed at adults (*Bringing Up Father* and *Mutt and Jeff*), though, and perhaps Okamoto meant that he was unfamiliar not with foreign manga in general but with those aimed at *children*. See Takeuchi, *Kodomo manga no kyojin-tachi*, 32–33; Okamoto, *Ippei zenshū*, 255; Okamoto, conversation in *Tōyō*; and Sasaki, *Mangashi no kisomondai*, 75, for Okamoto Ippei's embrace of Wilhelm Busch.

28. Suzuki, *Bunshirō bunshū*, 190. Okamoto and Oda nonetheless did not include Payne's name with his work.

29. In addition to *Kingu* (March to June 1927), the *Jidō manga-shū* (1927), and the *Asahi Graph* (September 1928 to October 1940), *Adamson* was also published in volume 6 of the 10-volume series *Gendai manga taikan* (Modern manga survey), titled *Tōzai manga-shū* (Collection of Eastern and Western manga; 1928); the comics monthly *Manga Man* (August 1929 to January 1931); and the children's magazine *Yōnen Kurabu* (June and November 1936).

30. Minejima, *Kondō Hidezō no sekai*, 86.

31. Much misinformation exists concerning early comics copyright and lawsuits. For clarification, see Mark D. Winchester's "Litigation and Early Comic Strips."

32. Despite an extensive search for them, I have not been able to find the May advertisements Matsui is writing of, though there is an ad for *Manga Man* in the July 6, 1929, *Tōkyō Asahi Shinbun*. At that point in time, the magazine's name had been finalized, including the *gekkan* (monthly) part, so the decision

to publish monthly rather than weekly may have been made between May and early July 1929.

33. *Manga Man*, August 1929, 30. It is unclear what exact position Matsui held at the magazine. The first issue's mission statement was written by him and in a New Year's greeting in the January 1931 issue, his name is the only one listed before Kubo's. Later editor's notes are usually signed "K," implying that they were written by either Matsui (Komazō) or Kubo. Kubo is the only *Manga Man* staff referred to in accounts by artists working for the magazine.

34. Specifically, Knerr's *Dinglehoofer und His Dog* (August 1929 to January 1930), Jimmy Murphy's *It's Papa Who Pays!* (December 1929), Russ Westover's *Tillie the Toiler* (December 1929 to January 1930, using the same title—*Oshare no Chirī*—that the *Chūgai Shōgyō Shinpō* had used) and *The Van Swaggers* (January 1930), George E. Studdy's *Bonzo* (August 1929 to March 1930), and Oscar Jacobsson's *Adamson* (August 1929 to January 1931).

35. See also Inui Shin'ichirō, *"Shinseinen" no koro*, 171, about the cost of color-printing at that time.

36. See also Suyama, *Nihon manga 100nen*, 142.

37. Tōkyōdō, *Shuppan nenkan*, 501.

38. Suyama (*Nihon manga 100nen*, 142) and others claim that *Manga Man* ended in June 1931, but no public records of a June 1931 issue survive.

39. Inui, *"Shinseinen" no koro*, 21.

40. Mizutani, "Amerika manga ni tsuite," 56.

41. Mizutani, 56; Inui, *"Shinseinen" no koro*, 54–55.

42. Mizutani, "Amerika manga ni tsuite," 56. From his examples, it is apparent that Mizutani is mostly talking about single-panel cartoons when he says "manga" (calling comic strips [*tsuzuki manga*] and animation a different topic), though his comments apply to both.

43. Inui, *"Shinseinen" no koro*, 8–12.

44. Inui, 13–18.

45. Inui, 55.

46. A major difference between the *Shinseinen* translations and the majority of translated American strips previously published in Japan is that the comic strips in *Shinseinen* rarely preserved the original reading direction for panels or text. In most cases, *Shinseinen* rearranged the panels to read either right to left or top to bottom while changing text to right to left (the traditional Japanese horizontal reading order). Panels for the most part were not mirrored, which occasionally led to awkward discrepancies when each individual panel was clearly intended to be read left to right but the sequence of panels and the text within them had to be read in the opposite direction. There does not seem to have been a consistent

translation policy at *Shinseinen*: though most translations were hand-lettered, the *Mickey Mouse* translation in September 1932 featured printed dialogue, which was furthermore arranged mostly top to bottom instead of the usual way (right to left). Some translations and panels replaced intradiegetic and onomatopoetic transdiegetic English writing, others did not. And though the panel order was rearranged for most strips, some, like said *Mickey Mouse* translation or the eight pages of *Pete the Tramp* in February 1931 (but not the *Pete the Tramp* translation in April 1936), were kept in their original panel order. Finally, at least one example of mirroring ("panel flipping") exists as well. In the March 1931 issue, a multipanel cartoon, probably by Milt Gross, had been mirrored, as is evident from a speech balloon left untranslated that reads "WHEW!" backward. This may be the first instance of panel flipping in the history of comics translation, a phenomenon that has received academic attention mostly with regards to occurrences of it during the first period of serious comics translation from Japanese into European languages roughly half a century later.

47. These, too, were billed as exclusives and credited to "Dick Heumor" [*sic*] (in uncommon fashion in the Roman alphabet) and Columbia. They also credited Minagawa Akira as an editor. Minagawa drew the comic strip *Taa-bō no bōkenryokō* (Taa's adventure travels) for *Shufu no Tomo* at the same time, and the speech balloons for that strip match the ones used in both the *Mickey Mouse* and *Scrappy* strips, indicating that these were copied from still images and equipped with speech balloons by said Minagawa Akira.

48. *Manga no Kuni*, July 1937, 8.

CHAPTER 4 — FROM ASŌ YUTAKA TO TEZUKA OSAMU

1. See Waugh, *Comics*, 6; and Smolderen, *Naissances de la bande dessinée*, 90.

2. Suzuki, *Bunshirō bunshū*, 189; Suzuki, "Sono koro no omoide," 44.

3. This is true except for a single episode on April 8, 1923, which was written in the audiovisual comic strip format, featuring speech balloons and question-mark emanata (transdiegetic devices showing emotion). *Bringing Up Father* had introduced emanata with its first episode a week earlier and featured a question mark emanatum on April 7; Asō may have copied this device from there.

4. Jo En claims that Asō's protagonist was also inspired by Paw from *Polly and Her Pals*. Jo, *Nihon ni okeru*, 81. *Nontō* predates the first issue of *Polly* in translation (July 1, 1923), though it is possible that Asō consulted the original strip (and potentially others) in American newspaper copies available in Tokyo.

5. Although the majority of translated American comics after *Bringing Up Father* followed this example and preserved their original reading order, recall that the

1908 *Tokyo Puck*'s translation of *Mr. Jack* had rearranged its panels to accommodate the Japanese top-bottom right-left reading order.

6. Shimizu, *Manga tanjō*, 180.

7. One final six-panel issue appeared on December 2.

8. Suyama, *Nihon manga 100nen*, 106.

9. With the rise of Japanese fascism Asō's work appears to have largely disappeared from publication, although he wrote militaristic progovernment strips in 1939 in *Hi no De* and the *Hōchi Shinbun* (bringing back the *Nontō* family).

10. As is obvious from this list, women's magazines played a significant role in popularizing audiovisual comics among the Japanese population.

11. Drawn by "田邊勝," likely read "Tanabe Masaru," or perhaps "Tabe Shō." The name of the protagonist, Fumi-chan (文ちゃん), could also be read as "Bun-chan."

12. The earliest such known use in Japan occurred in *Bringing Up Father* in the February 1926 *Zen-Kansai Fujin Rengōkai*. Given that *Osora to Butaroku* does not use heart shapes to signify love, that usage was likely introduced by American comics.

13. Other strips also used the same conflicting mix of reading orders, such as the weekly *Sunday Mainichi*'s *Rajio manga* by Ōyama Kazuhiko on November 1, 1925.

14. The last Japanese strip using the American reading order that I have found appeared in January 1936 in *Hi no De*.

15. Takeuchi, *Kodomo manga no kyojin-tachi*, 13.

16. Considering that *Nonki na tōsan* was the first Japanese comic with left-to-right writing, it is ironic that the exception to this is Asō Yutaka's contribution, though it too switches to the American direction in the following month's issue in September.

17. From the second issue onward, *Hanashita Nobio-kun* featured white balloons, though now without an outline, and writing top to bottom, right to left while keeping the American reading order for panels (left to right, top to bottom).

18. Asō's strip in the first issue and Miyao's in the second apparently being the exceptions to the rule.

19. Takeuchi, *Kodomo manga no kyojin-tachi*, 61. Miyao published another comic strip in *Fujokai* from January to June 1938: *Kobuta no Ton-chan* (Ton the little pig). The appearance of animal characters as protagonists, too, is most likely the result of American comic strip translations, as they were unheard of prior to the publication of *Felix the Cat* in *Hachisuzume* and the *Jiji Shinpō*.

20. Yokoyama, *Waga yūgiteki jinsei*, 44.

21. Yokoyama, 187.

22. Instead of the standard Japanese word for "Western," Yokoyama uses *batakusai*—literally "smelling of butter," an old-fashioned expression for "European/American." Yokoyama, 44.

23. Sugiura, *Issun saki ha hikari*, 208.

24. Yokoyama, *Waga yūgiteki jinsei*, 189–190.

25. Minejima, *Kondō Hidezō no sekai*, 86. Minejima speculates that Kondō was likely influenced by American comics this way.

26. Yokoyama, *Waga yūgiteki jinsei*, 190.

27. Kōmori, "Manga purodakushon-ron (1)," 65–66.

28. Inui, *"Shinseinen" no koro*, 57–59. Inui remembers that Yokoyama had even drawn the cover, though this claim may be incorrect.

29. Surprisingly, Yokoyama does not mention this fact in his autobiography, despite mentioning his move to said address (it was his uncle's). It was possible to deduce Yokoyama's address as well as the month in which *Manga Man* began using it by combining the information in Yokoyama's and Inui's autobiographies with the editorial information from *Manga Man* issues.

30. See Kure, *Gendai manga no zentaizō*, 120–122.

31. Takeuchi, *Kodomo manga no kyojin-tachi*, 115.

32. Okamoto, *Manga kōza*, 1:109.

33. See Takeuchi, *Kodomo manga no kyojin-tachi*, 113–119; and Kure, *Gendai manga no zentaizō*, 122.

34. Ōtsuka, *Mikkī no shoshiki*, 214.

35. Shishido, *Amerika no yokoppara*, 3–7.

36. This is true even when including "hybrid" works that adopted some trans-diegetic content but still relied on extradiegetic narration in the latter category.

37. *Jochū-san no yōkō* mixes English and Japanese speech balloons and in this regard bears a fascinating resemblance to the comic *Yonin no shosei* (The four immigrants) published by Henry Kiyama in San Francisco in 1931 (but written earlier).

38. See Shimizu, *Yonkoma manga*, 65, for an example of this claim.

39. Examples of such Japanese strips featuring these American characters can be found, for example, in *Hi no De* in March 1936 and *Kodomo Manga* in August and October 1936 and April 1937.

40. For example, on November 28, 1923, in the *Tōkyō Asahi Shinbun* and in February 1926 and January 1928 in *Zen-Kansai Fujin Rengōkai*.

41. For example, in August 1926 in *Zen-Kansai Fujin Rengōkai*.

42. During a story line in May 1926 in the *Kokumin Shinbun*.

43. Jo, *Nihon ni okeru*, 258–259.

44. Takeuchi, *Kodomo manga no kyojin-tachi*, 144.

45. Takeuchi, 105, 254.

46. The first is obvious from the number of advertisements featuring Norakuro, as well as blatant imitations of him, while the second is evidenced by the number of comic strips Tagawa was asked to draw for various publications.

47. See also Takeuchi, *Kodomo manga no kyojin-tachi*, 91, 112.

48. Tagawa Suihō, *Tagawa Suihō shinsaku rakugo-shū*, 202–203.

49. Shimizu Isao speculates specifically that the idea for *Norakuro* came from *Shōnen Kurabu* editor in chief Katō Ken'ichi, who, inspired by *Felix the Cat*, proposed a comic strip about a dog playing soldier. Shimizu, *Manga no rekishi*, 136.

50. Takeuchi, *Kodomo manga no kyojin-tachi*, 20, 116.

51. According to manga historian Ono Kōsei in a (Japanese) History Channel special on Felix the Cat called *Firikkusu za kyatto no shinjitsu* (The truth about Felix the Cat), uploaded as "Kuroneko Firikkusu ha kōshite umareta (*Firikkusu za kyatto no shinjitsu*)" by user Isigami to YouTube on May 11, 2018, https://www .youtube.com/watch?v=2YkM5xon5_c.

52. Other examples are the first *Norakuro* episode in January 1931 and the November 1930 issue of his strip *Yukai na renchū* (A delightful bunch) in *Kingu*.

53. Tagawa Suihō, interview by Katō Hidetoshi and Kawai Hidekazu, *Shokun!*, April 1979, 226.

54. Kawasaki City Museum, *Norakuro de arimasu!*, 43 (breadth of output), 89–90 (order to cease drawing *Norakuro*). Tagawa's influence was, of course, in part due to his willingness to accommodate the fascist regime as necessary, which allowed him to remain widely published while other *mangaka* faced repercussions for their opposition, such as Tagawa's former MAVO colleague Yanase Masamu, who was arrested and tortured as a thought criminal in 1932.

55. For more on Tagawa's tutoring of Hasegawa and other students of his, see Takamizawa, *Norakuro hitoribocchi*, 133–149.

56. *Maa-chan no nikkichō*'s title was written left to right, as had become standard.

57. Ban and Tezuka Production, *Tezuka Osamu monogatari*, 31.

58. Tezuka, *Tezuka Osamu manga no ōgi*, 63. In the interview, Tezuka recalls that he read *Bringing Up Father* in the *Asahi Shinbun* copies that his father began saving in 1928 or 1929, although *Bringing Up Father* ceased to be printed in the *Asahi Shinbun* in 1925, so Tezuka appears to be either misremembering the dates or confusing the *Asahi Shinbun* and the *Asahi Graph*.

59. Tezuka, *Rosutowārudo metoroporisu*, 238–239.

60. Ban and Tezuka Production, *Tezuka Osamu monogatari*, 252; Tezuka, *Tezuka Osamu taidanshū 3*, 90.

61. I learned about the existence of this booklet from Adam Buttrick. Images of an auction catalog (*Mandarake ZENBU*, vol. 46) featuring the booklet (valued at 750,000 yen) are accessible at the *Mandarake* mail-order website, https://order .mandarake.co.jp/order/detailPage/item?itemCode=1025011779.

62. Tezuka, *Tezuka Osamu taidanshū 2*, 125–126.

63. See Sasaki, *Mangashi no kisomondai*, 6–7.

64. Ryan Holmberg has also articulated a credible theory that Tezuka was inspired by a copy of *Walt Disney's Mickey Mouse "Outwits the Phantom Blot."* See Holmberg, "Heirs of Gottfredson."

65. Fumio, *Tezuka Osamu no "Shintakarajima,"* 151–165.

66. As described earlier in this chapter, the big eyes that are now seen as a hallmark of manga are actually a leftover from prewar American comic strips and animation that fell out of favor in the United States but survived in Japan due to the popularity of Tezuka's work.

67. Takeuchi credits Tagawa with having established the "comic strip form using speech balloons" in Japan. Takeuchi, *Kodomo manga no kyojin-tachi*, 112.

68. Jo, *Nihon ni okeru*, 264–270.

69. The series also featured a supplement, which consisted of a comic strip drawn by Miyao.

70. Yomota, *Nihon eiga 110nen*, 45.

71. Mizutani, "Amerika manga ni tsuite," 56.

72. Mizutani, 56; Inui, *"Shinseinen" no koro*, 54–55.

73. See an editorial in *Manga no Kuni*, August 1937, 8–10; Jo, *Nihon ni okeru*, 110; Yokoyama, *Waga yūgiteki jinsei*, 187; and Takeuchi, *Kodomo manga no kyojin-tachi*, 23.

74. Okamoto, *Jidō manga-shū*, 2.

75. Harootunian, *Overcome by Modernity*, xi.

76. Of course, bolstering a nation's comics industry would, ceteris paribus, unlikely make the difference between becoming a "rising" or "fallen" power. Any such active struggle to attain an outward appearance (here: a vibrant comics culture) that should be the natural consequence of a separate underlying cause (here: national prosperity) must strike one as irrational, given that attainment of said appearance by other means would not mean the attainment of its desired cause. Yet there is a historical model for such behavior in Max Weber's depiction of certain strands of Protestantism as striving to attain economic success because such success is seen as indicative of divine predestination. Much as such economic success, brought about by the "Protestant ethic," would not alter the existence or absence of divine blessing, a vibrant comics culture brought about by the efforts of newspaper editors would not switch Japan's trajectory from that of a fallen nation to that of a rising one, but in neither case did the irrationality of the effort prevent it.

77. The sexual arousal nosebleed is particularly fascinating as a kind of "post-transdiegetic" sign, in that it uses a visual signifier to depict a nonvisual phenomenon (mental arousal) but can also be read as such by intradiegetic characters, not just by extradiegetic readers.

78. Anyone whose national pride may have been buoyed or injured by this history would do well to read Arthur Schopenhauer's position on such pride.

EPILOGUE

1. Hosokibara, *Nihon mangashi*, 2 (preface; page numbering begins from 1 anew after the preface).

2. Hosokibara, 2–3 (preface).

3. Hosokibara, 2.

4. "Manga to ha uchūkan no manbutsu ni tsukite, sono genjō narabi ni sōgokan no kōshō suru jissō wo kaibōeiteki shi, sono kekka no bi wo hyōgen suru kaiga wo iu." Hosokibara, 2.

5. Hosokibara, 3.

6. Hosokibara, 4–5 (preface).

7. These stark differences are likely one reason Hosokibara cautions that manga lacks a coherent lineage.

8. Hosokibara, 8–9; Ōtsuka, *Mikkī no shoshiki*, 17.

9. "The Ancient Roots of Manga: The Choju Giga Scrolls," Consulate-General of Japan in New York, July 2008, https://www.ny.us.emb-japan.go.jp/en/c/2008/japaninfo0807.html.

10. Ōtsuka, *Mikkī no shoshiki*, 18. See also Ishiko, *Sengo mangashi nōto*, 13; Shimizu, *Nihon manga no jiten*, 140; and Kawasaki City Museum, *Nihon no manga 300nen*, 166.

11. Matsumoto and Hidaka, *Manga daihakubutsukan*, 374 (emphasis added).

12. Ōtsuka Eiji points this out by asking rhetorically whether Tagawa Suihō's Norakuro, the first major modern anthropomorphic manga protagonist created by a Japanese author (in late 1930), resembles more closely a character from the *chōjūgiga* or Mickey Mouse (the answer being the latter). Ōtsuka, *Mikkī no shoshiki*, 12–13. Tagawa was inspired by Felix the Cat, not Mickey, however.

13. Shimizu, *Yonkoma manga*, i; Koyama-Richard, *One Thousand Years of Manga*, 58.

14. Matsushima, "Chōjūgiga?," 271.

15. For example, manga historian Ishiko Jun, recognizing that the *chōjūgiga* "is called the originator [*ganso*] of Japanese manga," writes that the tradition of caricature of which it was a part "for some reason came to an end." Ishiko explains that the reason likely was the political persecution of satirists. Ishiko, *Nihon mangashi*, 19, 22. Miyamoto Hirohito similarly finds that "the [form of] expression referred to by the name 'manga' was only developed from the latter half of the Meiji period onward." Miyamoto points out that both the word *manga* in its current meaning and the historical view that sees the works to which it refers as descendants of

the *chōjūgiga* came about only around the end of the Meiji (1868–1912) and the beginning of the Taishō period (1912–1926), several centuries after the *chōjūgiga*. Miyamoto, "Manga no kigen," 292.

16. Kern, "Manga versus *Kibyōshi*," 237. Ironically, on a Japanese TV show celebrating "traditional Japanese culture" (*Wafū sōhonke*, March 9, 2017), Kern has also referred to *kibyōshi* as "the roots of modern manga." Given the incentives involved in each case, the assessment in his book is likely the more reliable one.

17. Matsushima, "Chōjūgiga?," 269. Matsushima rather fears that looking at the *chōjūgiga* as a manga may limit one's appreciation of it.

18. Kure, *Gendai manga no zentaizō*, 118.

19. Kern, "Manga versus *Kibyōshi*," 237.

20. Annie Manion describes a similar phenomenon with regards to animated films in her dissertation "Animation before the War," 19–20. Matsushima Masato suspects that securing for manga some of the prestige of "high" art may also have been Hosokibara Seiki's motivation. Matsushima, "Chōjūgiga?," 270.

21. One may wonder why a bank would be so supportive of exhibitions on picture scrolls and comics, but the primary purpose of such sponsorship of museums and exhibitions is simply to allow visitors to associate the sponsor with high culture rather than high crime.

22. "GIGA MANGA: From Edo Giga to Modern Manga," Sumida Hokusai Museum, accessed May 15, 2021, https://hokusai-museum.jp/modules/Exhibition/exhibitions/view/1140.

23. Takemura Makoto, "'GIGA MANGA: Edo giga kara kindai manga he'—jidai koeta hyōgen tadoru," *Mainichi Shinbun*, November 21, 2020, https://mainichi.jp/articles/20201121/ddm/010/040/011000c.

Labeling largely unconnected earlier art as the *genryū* (source, origin) or *genten* (starting point) of contemporary manga forms a pattern in Shimizu's work. In his 2007 *Nenpyō nihon mangashi* (Chronological Japanese manga history), Shimizu claims that "the source [*genryū*] of narrative manga was hand-drawn works [*nikuhitsuga*] like the *chōjūgiga* or the *hōhigassen* ['fart battle'] picture scroll" (131). In the 2009 *Yonkoma manga* (Four-panel manga), on the other hand, Shimizu writes that Okamoto Ippei "pioneered story manga called 'manga novels' [*manga shōsetsu*]. The origin [*genryū*] of contemporary comics [*komikku*] begins here" (42). In his 2014 book *Hokusai manga*, Shimizu appears to revise the claims made in *Yonkoma manga* by saying that it was actually *Hokusai*'s works that "became the origin [*genryū*] of contemporary characters" and that Hokusai manga are "the starting point [*genten*] of contemporary Japanese manga" (12).

24. Ōtsuka, *Mikkī no shoshiki*, 7–8.

25. Matsumoto and Hidaka, *Manga daihakubutsukan*, preface.

26. Suyama, *Nihon manga 100nen*, 1.

27. Kawasaki City Museum, *Nihon no manga 300nen*, 3. While "rest of the world" sounds more natural in English, I have kept the original quotation's literal meaning. The tendency to think of Japan and the (rest of the) world as a dichotomy can also be glimpsed in Ishiko Junzō's *Sengo mangashi nōto* when Ishiko writes, "The following saying exists *in foreign countries* [*gaikoku ni*]" (8; emphasis added).

28. Ishiko, *Sengo mangashi nōto*, 6.

29. Shimizu, *Nenpyō nihon mangashi*, 22. Considering that the first scroll of the *chōjūgiga* was created in the twelfth century, "a thousand years" is rounding it up a bit.

30. Shimizu, *Nihon manga no jiten*, 17.

Shimizu not only appears to be as invested in affirming the particular excellence of Japanese works as other proponents of the *chōjūgiga* origin theory but elsewhere even offers strategic advice to Japanese publishers to ensure the continued preeminent status of Japanese manga. After asserting that "at present, probably no other country has given birth to so many four-panel manga," he cautions that "to sustain this development, a fertile ground must be produced that gives birth to high-quality four-panel manga that will be published in translation abroad as well." Shimizu, *Yonkoma manga*, 178.

31. Gravett, *Manga*, 18.

32. Ministry of Education (Japan), *Chūgakkō*, 98 (emphasis added). *Chōjūjinbutsugiga* is another term for the *chōjūgiga*. While the first, most famous scroll (the one primarily cited as an ancestral manga) contains no humans (*jinbutsu*), other scrolls do.

33. According to the Ministry of Culture and Education's definition, photorealism and naturalism might be the only schools of art that would not qualify as manga, and the addition of "and so on" at the end does not exactly improve its precision. Ironically, the definition technically excludes realistically drawn Japanese comics and photo comics—works without simplification, symbolism, or exaggeration—from the category of manga.

34. See Okakura, *Book of Tea*.

35. Many best-selling manga may indeed be low-brow "trash" (not to speak of pervasive sexism and such—did you know women scream differently from men? *Kyaaa!*), but the same is true for films and novels. Yet the latter are much more readily equated with critically acclaimed high-brow works (even if not representative of each medium in terms of market share) than manga or comics, indicative of each medium's status within academia and the culture industry.

BIBLIOGRAPHY

Bahan, ed. *4 koma manga no sōshisha—Asō Yutaka*. Oita, Japan: Kyokutō Insatsushikō, 1992.

Ban Toshio and Tezuka Production. *Tezuka Osamu monogatari—osamushi tōjō 1928–1959*. Tokyo: Asahi Shinbunsha, 1994.

Bishop, Joseph Bucklin. "Early Political Caricature in America." *Century Magazine*, June 1892, 219–231. https://archive.org/details/earlypoliticalcaoobish/mode/2up.

Blackbeard, Bill. *R. F. Outcault's "The Yellow Kid": A Centennial Celebration of the Kid Who Started the Comics*. Northampton, Mass.: Kitchen Sink Press, 1995.

———, ed. *The Smithsonian Collection of Newspaper Comics*. Washington, D.C.: Smithsonian Institution Press, 1978.

Campbell, Eddie. *The Goat Getters*. San Diego: Idea and Design Works, 2018.

Crary, Jonathan. "Techniques of the Observer." *October*, no. 45 (Summer 1988): 3–35.

———. *Techniques of the Observer: On Vision and Modernity in the Nineteenth Century*. Cambridge, Mass.: MIT Press, 1990.

Doak, Robin S. *The Phonograph*. Milwaukee: World Almanac Library, 2006.

Duncan, Randy. "Image Functions—Shape and Color as Hermeneutic Images in *Asterios Polyp*." In *Critical Approaches to Comics: Theories and Methods*, edited by Matthew J. Smith and Randy Duncan, 43–54. New York: Routledge, 2011.

Eighth Graphic Arts Production Yearbook. New York: Colton Press, 1948.

Exner, Eike. "A Brief History of the Translation of American Comic Strips in Pre–World War II Japan and the Origins of Contemporary Narrative Manga." *International Journal of Comic Art* 18, no. 2 (Fall/Winter 2016): 156–174.

———. "'Bringing Up Manga': How Editors in the 1920s and 1930s Helped Create Contemporary Japanese Comics." In *The Comics World*, edited by Benjamin Woo and Jeremy Stoll, 51–71. Jackson: University Press of Mississippi, 2021.

———. "The Creation of the Comic Strip as an Audiovisual Stage in the *New York Journal* 1896–1900." *ImageTexT* 10, no. 1 (2018). http://www.english.ufl.edu/ imagetext/archives/v10_1/exner/.

Gaines, M. C. "Narrative Illustration: The Story of the Comics." *Print* 3, no. 2 (Summer 1942): 25–38.

Gardner, Jared. *Projections: Comics and the History of Twenty-First-Century Story-telling*. Palo Alto, Calif.: Stanford University Press, 2012.

Genette, Gerard. *Narrative Discourse*. Ithaca, N.Y.: Cornell University Press, 1980.

Gerow, Aaron. *Visions of Japanese Modernity: Articulations of Cinema, Nation, and Spectatorship, 1895–1925*. Berkeley: University of California Press, 2010.

Gordon, Andrew. *A Modern History of Japan: From Tokugawa Times to the Present*. New York: Oxford University Press, 2003.

Gordon, Ian. *Comic Strips and Consumer Culture 1890–1945*. Washington, D.C.: Smithsonian Institution Press, 1998.

Gottlieb, Henrik. "Untertitel. Das Visualisieren filmischen Dialogs." In *Schrift und Bild im Film*, edited by Hans-Edwin Friedrich and Uli Jung, 185–214. Bielefeld, Germany: Aisthesis, 2002.

Gravett, Paul. *Manga: Sixty Years of Japanese Comics*. New York: Harper Design International, 2004.

Groensteen, Thierry. *The System of Comics*. Jackson: University Press of Mississippi, 2009.

Harootunian, Harry. *Overcome by Modernity: History, Culture, and Community in Interwar Japan*. Princeton, N.J.: Princeton University Press, 2000.

Holmberg, Ryan. "The Heirs of Gottfredson: Osamu Tezuka." In *Walt Disney's Mickey Mouse "Outwits the Phantom Blot,"* by Floyd Gottfredson, David Gerstein, and Gary Groth, 280–285. Seattle: Fantagraphics Books, 2014.

Hosokibara Seiki. *Nihon mangashi*. Tokyo: Yūzankaku, 1924.

Imaizumi, Hidetarō. *Ippyō zatsuwa*. Tokyo: Seishidō, 1901.

Inui Shin'ichirō. *"Shinseinen" no koro*. Tokyo: Hayakawa Shobō, 1991.

Ishiko Jun. *Nihon mangashi*. Tokyo: Shakaishisōsha, 1988.

Ishiko Junzo. *Sengo mangashi nōto*. Tokyo: Kinokuniya Shoten, 1975.

Jo En. *Nihon ni okeru shinbun rensai kodomo manga no senzenshi*. Tokyo: Nihon Kyōhōsha (Duan Press), 2012.

Kasza, Gregory J. *The State and the Mass Media in Japan, 1918–1945*. Berkeley: University of California Press, 1988.

Katō Hidetoshi and Kawai Hidekazu. "Kyōdō kenkyū 'taishō jidai'—4—'Norakuro' zenshi—Tagawa Suihō-shi ni kiku." In *Shokun! Nihon wo genki ni suru opinion zasshi*, 11, no. 4, 222–237. Tokyo: Bungeibunshū, 1979.

Katō Michio. *Chikuonki no jidai*. Tokyo: Chopin, 2006.

Kawabata Ryūshi. *Waga ga-seikatsu*. Tokyo: Dai Nippon Yūbenkai Kōdansha, 1951.

Kawasaki City Museum. *Nihon no manga 300nen*. Exhibition catalog. 1996.

———. *Norakuro de arimasu! Tagawa Suihō to kodomo manga no wandārando*. Exhibition catalog. 2019.

Kern, Adam L. *Manga from the Floating World: Comicbook Culture and the Kibyōshi of Edo Japan*. Cambridge, Mass.: Harvard University Asia Center, 2006.

———. "Manga versus *Kibyōshi*." In *A Comics Studies Reader*, edited by Jeet Heer and Kent Worcester, 236–243. Jackson: University Press of Mississippi, 2009.

Kōmori Ikuya. "Manga purodakushon-ron (1)." *Senshū Kokubun*, no. 85 (September 2009): 63–82.

Koyama-Richard, Brigitte. *One Thousand Years of Manga*. Paris: Flammarion, 2014.

Kunzle, David. *The Early Comic Strip: Narrative Strips and Pictures Stories in the European Broadsheet c. 1450 to 1825*. Berkeley: University of California Press, 1973.

———. *The Nineteenth Century*. Vol. 2 of *The History of the Comic Strip*. Berkeley: University of California Press, 1990.

Kurata Yoshihiro. *Nihon rekōdo bunkashi*. Tokyo: Iwanami Shoten, 2006.

Kure Tomofusa. *Gendai manga no zentaizō*. Tokyo: Futabasha, 1997.

Lefèvre, Pascal, ed. *Forging a New Medium: The Comic Strip in the Nineteenth Century*. Brussels: VUB University Press, 1998.

Library of Congress. "Inventing Entertainment: The Early Motion Pictures and Sound Recordings of the Edison Companies." Accessed January 14, 2017. https://www.loc.gov/collections/edison-company-motion-pictures-and-sound-recordings/.

Mainardi, Patricia. *Another World: Nineteenth-Century Illustrated Print Culture*. New Haven, Conn.: Yale University Press, 2017.

Manion, Annie. "Animation before the War: Nation, Identity, and Modernity in Japan from 1914–1945." PhD diss., University of Southern California, 2014.

Maresca, Peter, and Philippe Ghielmetti, eds. *Society Is Nix: Gleeful Anarchy at the Dawn of the American Comic Strip 1895–1915*. Palo Alto, Calif.: Sunday Press Books, 2013.

Marschall, Richard. *America's Great Comic-Strip Artists*. New York: Abbeville Press, 1989.

Matsumoto Reiji and Hidaka Bin. *Manga daihakubutsukan*. Tokyo: Buronzusha, 1980.

Matsushima Masato. "Chōjūgiga ga manga wo unda no ka?" In *Masterpieces of Kosan-ji Temple: The Complete Scrolls of Choju Giga, Frolicking Animals*, exhibition catalog, 269–274. Tokyo: Tokyo National Museum, 2015.

McCarthy, Helen. *A Brief History of Manga*. Lewes, U.K.: Ilex Press, 2014.

———. "A History of Manga." Presentation at D&AD Japan London PechaKucha event, May 23, 2012. https://www.youtube.com/watch?v=dTp25fdooqU.

McCloud, Scott. *Understanding Comics: The Invisible Art.* New York: HarperPerennial, 1994.

McManus, George. *Bringing Up Father—Third Series.* New York: Cupples & Leon, 1919.

Memmi, Albert. *The Colonizer and the Colonized.* Boston: Beacon Press, 1967.

Minejima Masayuki. *Kondō Hidezō no sekai.* Tokyo: Seiabō, 1984.

Ministry of Education (Japan). *Chūgakkō gakushū shidō yōryō kaisetsu—bijutsuhen.* July 2008. https://www.mext.go.jp/component/a_menu/education/micro_detail/__icsFiles/afieldfile/2011/01/05/1234912_008.pdf.

Miyamoto Hirohito. "Manga no kigen: Fujun na ryōiki toshite no seiritsu." *Sekai no bungaku,* no. 110, 292–295. Tokyo: Asahi Shinbun Shuppan, 2001.

———. "Ponchi to manga, sono shinbun to no kakawari." In *Shinbun manga no me—hito seiji shakai,* exhibition catalog, 106–109. Yokohama: Newspark, 2003.

Miyao Shigewo. *Nihon no giga.* Tokyo: Daiichi Hōki Shuppan, 1967.

Mizutani Jun. "Amerika manga ni tsuite." *Tōyō* 1, no. 6 (October 1936): 56–57.

Morgan, Harry. *Principes des littératures dessinées.* Angoulême, France: An 2, 2003.

Morton, David L. Jr. *Sound Recording—the Life Story of a Technology.* Westport, Conn.: Greenwood Press, 2004.

Muneo Matsuji. *Beikoku shinbungyō no kenkyū.* Tokyo: Ganshōdō Shoten, 1925.

Murrell, William. *A History of American Graphic Humor (1865–1938).* New York: Macmillan, 1938.

Noguchi Fumio. *Tezuka Osamu no "Shintakarajima"—sono densetsu to shinjitsu.* Tokyo: Shōgakukan, 2007.

Obushi Hajime. *Shiryō ga kataru kindai nihon kōkokushi.* Tokyo: Nihon Tosho Center, 2012.

Okakura Kakuzō. *The Book of Tea.* Rutland, Vt.: Charles E. Tuttle, 1975.

Okamoto Ippei. Conversation in *Tōyō* 1, no. 6 (October 1936): 29–51.

———. *Jidō manga-shū.* Vol. 23 of *Shōgakusei zenshū.* Tokyo: Kōbunsha, 1927.

———. *Manga kōza.* Vol. 1. Tokyo: Kensetsusha, 1934.

———. *Manga to yakubun.* Tokyo: Kōbundō, 1911.

———. *Ippei zenshū.* Tokyo: Senshinsha, 1929.

Ono Kōsei. *Amerikan komikkusu taizen.* Tokyo: Shōbunsha, 2005.

Ōshiro Noboru, ed. *OH! Manga.* Tokyo: Shōbunsha, 1982.

Ōtsuka Eiji. *Mikkī no shoshiki.* Tokyo: Kadokawa Gakugei Shuppan, 2013.

Overstreet, Robert M., ed. *The Overstreet Comic Book Price Guide.* Timonium, Md.: Gemstone, 2016.

Oyola, Osvaldo. "The International Comic Arts Forum 2016." *Middle Spaces* (blog), April 26, 2016. https://themiddlespaces.com/2016/04/26/icaf2016/.

Petersen, Robert S. "The Acoustics of Manga." In *A Comics Studies Reader,* edited by Jeet Heer and Kent Worcester, 163–172. Jackson: University Press of Mississippi, 2009.

Pisko, Franz Josef. *Die neueren Apparate der Akustik: Für Freunde der Naturwissenschaft und Tonkunst.* Vienna: C. Gerold's Sohn, 1865.

Sakamoto Ichirō. "Kodomo sutōri manga ryakushi." *Dokusho Kagaku,* no. 15 (1971): 1–16.

Sasaki Minoru. *Mangashi no kisomondai.* Tokyo: Office Heliar, 2012.

Satō Tadao. *Nihon eigashi 1, 1896–1940.* Tokyo: Iwanami Shoten, 2006.

Schodt, Frederik L. *Manga! Manga! The World of Japanese Comics.* New York: Kodansha America, 2013.

Screech, Timon. *The Lens within the Heart: The Western Scientific Gaze and Popular Imagery in Later Edo Japan.* Honolulu: University of Hawai'i Press, 2002.

Shimizu Isao. *Hokusai manga.* Tokyo: Heibonsha, 2014.

———. *Manga no rekishi.* Tokyo: Iwanami Shoten, 1991.

———. *Manga tanjō.* Tokyo: Yoshikawa Kōbun-kan, 1999.

———. *Nenpyō nihon mangashi.* Kyoto: Rinsen Shoten, 2007.

———. *Nihon manga no jiten.* Tokyo: Sanseidō, 1985.

———. *Yonkoma manga.* Tokyo: Iwanami Shoten, 2009.

Shishido Sakō. *Amerika no yokoppara.* Tokyo: Heibonsha, 1929.

Silverberg, Miriam. *Erotic Grotesque Nonsense—the Mass Culture of Japanese Modern Times.* Berkeley: University of California Press, 2007.

Smith, Christopher. "Who Said That? Textuality in Eighteenth Century *Kibyōshi.*" *Japan Forum* 29, no. 2 (2016): 279–298.

Smolderen, Thierry. *Naissances de la bande dessinée.* Brussels: Les Impressions Nouvelles, 2009.

———. "Of Labels, Loops, and Bubbles: Solving the Historical Puzzle of the Speech Balloon." *Comic Art,* no. 8 (2006): 90–112.

———. *The Origins of Comics—from William Hogarth to Winsor McCay.* Jackson: University Press of Mississippi, 2014.

Statistics Bureau of Japan. "Population by Age (Single Year) and Sex (as of October 1 of Each Year)—Total Population (from 1920 to 2000)." Statistics of Japan. Last modified January 11, 2008. https://www.e-stat.go.jp/en/stat-search/files?page=1&layout=datalist&toukei=00200524&tstat=000000090001&cycle=0&tclass1=000000090004&tclass2=000000090005&tclass3val=0.

Sterne, Jonathan. *The Audible Past: Cultural Origins of Sound Reproduction.* Durham, N.C.: Duke University Press, 2003.

Stewart, Ronald. "Manga Studies #2: Manga History: Shimizu Isao and Miyamoto Hirohito on Japan's First Modern 'Manga' Artist Kitazawa Rakuten." Comics Forum, June 4, 2014. https://comicsforum.org/2014/06/14/manga-studies-2-manga-history-shimizu-isao-and-miyamoto-hirohito-on-japans-first-modern-manga-artist-kitazawa-rakuten-by-ronald-stewart/.

Sugiura Yukio. *Issun saki ha hikari: Waga manga jinsei*. Tokyo: Tōkyō Shinbun Shuppankyoku, 1995.

Suyama Keiichi. *Manga hakubutsushi nihon-hen*. Tokyo: Banchō Shobō, 1972.

———. *Manga hakubutsushi sekai-hen*. Tokyo: Banchō Shobō, 1972.

———. *Nihon manga 100nen—seiyō Ponchi kara SF manga made*. Tokyo: Haga Shoten, 1968.

Suzuki Bunshirō. *Bunshirō bunshū*. Tokyo: Dai Nippon Yūbenkai Kōdansha, 1952.

———. "Sono koro no omoide." *Asahi Graph*, October 19, 1938, 44–45.

Tagawa Suihō. *Tagawa Suihō shinsaku rakugo-shū*. Tokyo: Kōdansha, 1976.

Takahata Isao. *Jūniseiki no animēshon*. Tokyo: Tokuma Shoten, 1999.

Takamizawa Junko. *Norakuro hitoribocchi*. Tokyo: Kojinsha, 1996.

Takeuchi Osamu. *Kodomo manga no kyojin-tachi*. Tokyo: San'ichi Shobō, 1995.

Tezuka Osamu. *Rosutowārudo metoroporisu*. Tokyo: Kōdansha, 2009.

———. *Tezuka Osamu bunko zenshū: Rosuto wārudo, metoroporisu*. Tokyo: Kōdansha, 2009.

———. *Tezuka Osamu manga no ōgi*. Tokyo: Kōdansha, 1997.

———. *Tezuka Osamu taidanshū 2*. Tokyo: Kōdansha, 1997.

———. *Tezuka Osamu taidanshū 3*. Tokyo: Kōdansha, 1997.

Tōkyōdō, eds. *Shuppan nenkan*. Tokyo: Tōkyōdō, 1930.

Turner, Gerard L'Estrange. *Nineteenth-Century Scientific Instruments*. London: Sotheby, 1983.

Uchikawa Yoshimi. "Shinbun dokusha no hensen." *Shinbun kenkyū* 120 (July 1961): 19–27.

Umeda Haruo. *Chikuonki no rekishi*. Tokyo: PARCO, 1976.

Walker, Brian. *The Comics—the Complete Collection*. New York: Abrams Comics-Arts, 2011.

Walker, Mort. *The Lexicon of Comicana*. Lincoln: iUniverse.com, 2000.

Waugh, Coulton. *The Comics*. New York: Macmillan, 1947.

Weisenfeld, Gennifer. *Imagining Disaster: Tokyo and the Visual Culture of Japan's Great Earthquake of 1923*. Berkeley: University of California Press, 2012.

———. *Mavo: Japanese Artists and the Avant-Garde, 1905–1931*. Berkeley: University of California Press, 2002.

———. "Publicity and Propaganda in 1930s Japan: Modernism as Method." *Design Issues* 25, no. 4 (2009): 13–28.

Winchester, Mark. D. "Litigation and Early Comic Strips: The Lawsuits of Outcault, Dirks, and Fisher." *Inks* 2, no. 2 (1995): 16–25.

Wright, Ernest Hunter, and Mary Heritage Wright, eds. *Richards Topical Encyclopedia*. Vol. 10. Kingsport, Tenn.: Kingsport Press, 1945.

Yamamoto Taketoshi. *Kindai nihon no shinbundokushasō*. Tokyo: Hōsei Daigaku Shuppankyoku, 1985.

Yanaike Makoto. *Yokogaki tōjō*. Tokyo: Iwanami Shoten, 2003.

Yasar, Kerim. *Electrified Voices—How the Telephone, Phonograph, and Radio Shaped Modern Japan, 1868–1945*. New York: Columbia University Press, 2018.

Yokoyama Ryūichi. *Waga yūgiteki jinsei*. Tokyo: Nihon Tosho Center, 1997.

Yomota Inuhiko. *Nihon eiga 110nen*. Tokyo: Shūeisha, 2014.

Yoshimi Shunya. *Koe no shihonshugi*. Tokyo: Kawade Shobō, 2012.

INDEX

Adamson (Jacobsson), 122–124, 225n29; influence on Tezuka, 172; in *Manga Man*, 156
Adamson—Manga dokushū shidō (Tezuka), 172, 230n61
adventure comics, 133
advertisements: for *Bringing Up Father* anthologies, 42; featuring *Bringing Up Father*, 42, 45–48, 124, 213n27, 213–214n31, 214nn33–34; featuring *Mutt and Jeff*, 110–111, 223–224n16; featuring other characters, 47, 124, 214n33; for gramophones, 218n25; horizontal writing in, 153; underneath manga, 103, 223n9; for *Manga Man*, 125; for motion pictures, 8
Akachan kakka (Asō), 146
Akira (Ōtomo), 2
American Weekly, 125
Amerika no yokoppara (Shishido), 101, 162
Anderson, Carl, 134
And Her Name Was Maud (Opper), 163, 224n19
animals, anthropomorphic, 120–122, 167–170, 183–184, 228n19. See also *Krazy Kat*; Mickey Mouse; *Norakuro*
animated films: in Denmark, 131; in Japan, 26, 119; manga adapted from, 132, 134–137
An-kō (Yokoyama), 157–158
anthropomorphism. *See* animals, anthropomorphic
A. Piker Clerk (Briggs), 223n10

Asahi Graph: *Adamson* in, 123; *Bringing Up Father* in, 33–35, 42, 50–52, 123; influence on manga, 157; *Newlyweds* in, 104; New Manga Group in, 157, 159; *Shijūsō*, 159–163; *Shō-chan no bōken* in, 30; Tezuka reading, 171–173
Asahi Kyūyū Kaihō, 143
Asahi Shinbun: *Bringing Up Father* in, 48, 51; horizontal writing in, 39; *Jinsei benkyō*, 145; mention of Mickey Mouse, 131; *Mutt and Jeff* in, 50, 105–110; *Newlyweds* in, 103; Okamoto in, 23–24, 164; *Shō-chan no bōken* in, 32, 152; Tezuka reading, 171–173
Asō Yutaka: on editor's influence, 142–144; later career of, 228n9; in *Manga Man*, 126; as mentor, 161 (see also *Shijūsō*); miscellaneous manga by, 145–146; *Nonki na tōsan* (see *Nonki na tōsan*); *Shijūsō*, 159–163
audiovisual comics: adaptations in other media, 215n37; increasing prevalence of, 7, 153–154, 157, 163–165, 174; as mechanical recordings, 55, 63–65; as mimetic entertainment, 10, 54–55, 138, 175; modern nature of, 59–60, 89–91, 128; popularity of the medium of, 109, 119, 139, 213n24; as response to sound-recording technology, 68–87, 215n4; synchronicity of sound and image, 67–68, 93
Awatemono no Kuma-san (Maekawa), 124, 214n33

243

ABOUT THE AUTHOR

EIKE EXNER is a historian of graphic narrative whose writing has been featured in the *International Journal of Comic Art*, *ImageTexT*, and *The Comics World*. His extensive archival research for this book, undertaken while teaching on comics/manga in Japan, received the 2016 John A. Lent Award in Comics Studies.